RECONCEPTUALIZING
PHYSICAL EDUCATION

THROUGH CURRICULAR & PEDAGOGICAL INNOVATIONS

JOY BUTLER · EDITOR

Table of Contents

EDITOR'S FOREWORD V
JOY BUTLER

1. **TGFU – WOULD YOU KNOW IT IF YOU SAW IT?**
   BENCHMARKS FROM THE TACIT KNOWLEDGE OF THE FOUNDERS......................1
   JOY BUTLER

2. **ENACTING CHANGE IN A SECONDARY**
   PHYSICAL EDUCATION DEPARTMENT...29
   GEORGE KANAVOS, STEVE MCGINLEY

3. **CHINESE TEENAGE MALES' EXPERIENCES**
   IN PHYSICAL ACTIVITY SETTINGS...53
   CHARMAINE LUM

4. **THE EXPERIENCES OF BOYS IN PE AS THEY ENCOUNTER**
   THE TGFU MODEL FOR THE FIRST TIME.......................................71
   PAISLEY RANKINE

5. **WHERE HAVE ALL THE KIDS GONE?**
   DECLINING ENROLLMENT IN SENIOR
   PHYSICAL EDUCATION CLASSES..89
   DAVID DUNKIN, KARA WICKSTROM

6. **WHERE HAVE ALL THE GIRLS GONE?**
   FEMALE CHOICE IN SENIOR ELECTIVE PE....................................105
   ANGELA BIGIOLLI

7. **HELPING INCREASE GIRLS PHYSICAL SELF-EFFICACY**
   THROUGH TGFU AND THE GPAI..121
   BRENT JACKSON

8. **REFLECTIONS ON PLAYER LEARNING:**
   A SELF-STUDY OF COACHING PRAXIS..143
   SIMON DYKSTRA

9. **NARRATIVE INQUIRY OF ONLINE PE:**
   WHAT IS THE EXPERIENCE OF ONLINE PE STUDENTS?..........................161
   SUSAN KIMURA

10. **RECONCEPTUALIZING AND REFRAMING PEDAGOGY, CURRICULUM**
    AND RESEARCH THROUGH COMPLEXITY THINKING..............................177
    ALAN OVENS, TIM HOPPER, JOY BUTLER

APPENDICES..193

ABOUT THE AUTHORS..201

ACKNOWLEDGEMENTS...205

Editor's Forward

The authors in this book are all practicing teachers from British Columbia, Canada and part of the second two-year Master of Education Physical Education cohort that began in July 2012 at The University of British Columbia. Many were at the same career stage – highly competent professionals ready to move up a gear by refining and expanding their ideas of teaching and learning and eager to make changes in the profession. All were drawn to the cohort for an opportunity to re-examine their practice. Using Teaching Games for Understanding (TGfU) as a catalyst for thinking about ontological and epistemological issues in physical education, teachers explored constructivist, student centered, and holistic approaches. They also examined their positions on continuums of belief from inclusion to elitism, transaction to transmission, integration to dualism, tactical understanding to skill acquisition, discovery to representation, concepts to techniques and finally between demonstration and creation of understanding rather than mastery. Many have become ambassadors for new ideas that challenge some of our entrenched education values.

The cohort was composed of 17 practicing physical educators, drawn from across British Columbia. Many of these teachers were at the same career stage, looking to make advancements in their schools and to make a difference in their teaching. All were interested in curricular and pedagogical innovations such TGfU, Sport Education, Physical Literacy, Movement Education, and Inventing Games.

Our authors' two-year journey with TGfU took them through a summer institute in 2013 (shared with drop-in professional development teachers) and nine tailored courses with research foci around physical education. The courses were offered in a variety of formats ranging from face-to-face during three times one-week intensive summer courses (EDCP530, EDCP585B, EDCP585C); face-to-face over six Saturdays for the EDUC500 course; on-line for two courses (EDCP565 and EDCP562) and hybrid format combining on-line and two Saturdays for EDCP513, hybrid of one Saturday research workshop and tutorials sessions for EDCP508B and EDCP590.

For those travelling long distance, the on-line courses were not only saved members time, but also allowed them to construct an ongoing community of practice, as they contacted each other regularly and met in fortnightly Saturday sessions, and in the summer institutes. As practicing teachers, they valued the opportunities they encountered for dialogue and group work with other professionals in their field, as they challenged and supported each other throughout the two years. This made for intellectually richness, extremely high completion rates, and a very high standard of course work and final projects.

They completed a wide range of assignments, which included end of year presentations in conference style settings, PechaKucha presentations, public speaking, curriculum development and design, creating assessment tools and engaging in critical readings of core articles and books. They made posters of research proposals and shared their writing in an online blogs. Groups taught the class, attended practical sessions and workshops, and learned to use new technologies such as PowerPoint, wikis, voiceover thread, videos, and mindmaps. Very importantly, they were exposed to many minds of the best contemporary thinkers and writers in PE.

The end products were 12 stellar research-based graduating projects and 1 MA thesis. Most, if not all, of the members of the cohort experienced paradigm shifts in their constructs of teaching, learning and knowing in Physical Education. We are proud to be able to share some of their pioneering research, which we believe will be of great interest to others in the field who are interested in constructivist, student-centred, and holistic approaches to teaching and learning in games education. We expect that the conversations and collaborations will continue well into the future, and that this emerging community of practice will provide mentoring and generate new research to move our profession forward in ways that we cannot currently imagine.

It has long been argued that research by teachers about their own classrooms and school practices functions as a powerful mechanism for professional change, as it generates new ways of thinking about practice. We believe that this cohort and cohorts to come will help generate healthy and sustainable programs of teacher research, distributed across schools, teacher groups, school-university partnerships, and regional and national forums. This may take time, but it is our ultimate hope to bridge the chasm between theory and practice and between schools and universities.

COLLECTIVE LEARNING AND TEACHER-RESEARCHERS

"Teachers who operate from an ecological complexity worldview see all educational agents – learners, teachers, administrators, curriculum, school, community and culture – as parts of a sustainable learning system." (Butler, Storey, and Robson, 2012, p. 1)

Elsewhere, I have argued that the epistemological and ontological world-view best suited to the Teaching Games for Understanding approach is Eco-logical Complexity (Butler, Storey, & Robson, 2012). This philosophical and ethical position is woven together from three strands, social constructivism, complexity, and ecological thinking, all of which see the individual learner as being nested within larger systems, such as the game, the class, the school, the community, and on into broader social structures. Currently, such systems, all of which provide learning opportunities to the individuals who comprise them, are the focus of much conversation in the educational literature. Rather than framing learning as an individual project (a belief maintained in Piag-etian theories), many, if not most, contemporary curriculum theorists would rather frame it as situated and social, as they argue that "the social construc-tionist, human cognition is…diffuse, distributed, and collective" (Davis & Sumara, 2006, p. 117).

The phrase most often quoted by contemporary educators who consider the role played by the collective in supporting the learning of its individual members is that the wisdom of crowds is greater than the total of the intel-ligence of its individual members (Surowiecki, 2004). Before the language of complexity thinking made its way into educational discourses, TGfU advo-cates were already considering the power of the group. Thorpe, Bunker, and Almond, the originators of the TGfU model, placed collectivity at its heart as they structured learning experiences through mini and small-sided games. Furthermore, they suggested that these small groups of learners might draw upon the wisdom of their collectives by engaging in debate and discussion of strategies, tactics, and effective movement patterns (Thorpe, Bunker, & Al-mond, p. 58). Such collectives "develop capacities that can exceed the possi-bilities of the same group of agents if they were made to work independently" (Davis & Sumara, 2006, p. 81).

In the same way, teachers cannot effect meaningful and sustainable change in a vacuum. All too often, curriculum initiatives offered in standalone gradu-ate courses flounder when teachers test them in the waters of their practice. The ideas offered in professional development courses must be contextualized within other interactive systems. Teachers need careful, structured support through processes of change.

The changes discussed here are fueled by a core belief in empowering student learners (Butler, 1993). Beginning teachers enter their training with a strong emphasis upon the emotional understanding of their students. How-ever, the behaviorist focus of many PETE programs, together with the stresses and self-perpetuating culture of our schools, discourages them from focusing on student affect and encourages them instead to teach for narrowly defined and definable skills. It is only later that some more experienced teachers rediscover the dream through a passion for adventure, creativity and exploration or, as Kretchmar (2005) would have it, the search for 'delight.' Through all these five stages and for all three populations (pre-service, beginning and experienced teachers as they consider TGfU), moving from the comfort zone into unfamiliar areas can be a challenge. Paradoxically, this very discomfort—the disconnect between avowed principle and actual practice, educational philosophy and teaching methodology—can be a wonderful incentive. Because TGfU is dependent upon the introduction of a clearly stated educational philosophy, whether individual or institutional, it can become a useful medium through which teachers at all stages of their careers can evaluate their current practice in order to place the learner at the centre of the learning experience. For the same reason, TGfU can also provide a lens though which PETE programs and schools can examine and then balance the various and sometimes competing demands made upon Physical Education (Butler, 2005).

The following conditions seem central to the provision of an appropriate context for change and experimentation. Several chapters in this book expand upon the following summary:

1. Healthy dialogue in the exchange of diverse ideas

2. Practices that are empathetic, communicative and participatory

3. Teachers who tolerate uncertainty and are willing to try things out

4. Links between faculty from education programs and teachers and administrators

5. Administrative support

It is from this platform, the need for teacher change, philosophical clarity, and a reconceptualized Physical Education curriculum, that the TGfU graduate cohort was launched in 2009 and the second in 2012.

There are many pedagogical advantages in a cohort design, which is rapidly becoming the preferred organizational model in educational leadership programs (Barnett et al., 2000). Barnett and his colleagues have found that students working in cohorts learn better and more, and are able to reflect more deeply and from a wider range of theoretical perspectives (Barnett et al., 2000; Hill, 1995; Norton, 1995). They are also more highly motivated, committed, and persistent in their studies (Hill, 1995) and more likely to complete programs and to develop robust professional networks and ongoing relationships with colleagues.

When PETE students compare TGfU or other innovations with the model with which they are more familiar, questions such as the following arise:

1. How much emphasis should we place on skill acquisition and how much on conceptual understanding to help learners make sense of information and experiences?

2. Should students know 'how to' before they know 'what to'?

3. Should tactics and strategies be taught before skills?

4. What is the role of the teacher in helping students acquire knowledge and construct meaning?

5. How does the learner demonstrate what they have learned?

As they considered these vital questions, the members of the cohort also considered their own place in the complex learning systems in which they are embedded. The collective processes of the cohort have enabled new insights into curriculum development, teaching and learning possibilities, and provided a strong advocacy group for making change in district and school decisions. Several members of the 2012-2014 cohort have conducted workshops in their own districts and most have linked their research with some forms of investigating key issues in physical education. These are represented in this book More Reconceptualizing PE through Teaching Games for Understanding and builds on the work of the first PE cohort and their successful publication: Reconceptualizing PE through Teaching Games for Understanding (2012).

This book continues the goals of the first:

- Provide examples of teacher-researcher research
- Exemplify theme-driven teacher research
- Expand the body of research about curricular and pedagogical innovations
- Make that body of research accessible for teachers by teachers
- Provide resources for and help in the creation of communities of practice

All intellectual work builds upon and is informed by the work of other scholars. In this case, the members of the cohort were fortunate to learn from many of the most highly regarded, contemporary international thinkers and writers in TGfU. These include our summer institute visiting scholars: Dr. James Mandigo (Brock University, ON) – TGfU and Physical Literacy;

Dr. Nancy Francis (Brock University, ON) – Movement Education; Dr. Joanna Sheppard (University of Fraser Valley, BC) – TGfU; Dr. Stephen Mitchell (Kent State, Ohio, US) – Teacher Accreditation and TGfU and the other instructors of the two year program (listed on the following page).

PROGRAM INSTRUCTORS

1 EDCP530: Dr. James Mandigo (Brock University, ON) & Dr. Joy Butler (UBC)

2 EDCP562: Dr. Alex DeCossen (UBC)

3 EDUC500: Dr. Jeanne Kentel (UBC)

4 EDCP508C: Dr. Jeanne Kentel (UBC)

5 EDCP585B: Dr. Nancy Francis (Brock University, ON) & Dr. Joanna Sheppard (UFV)

6 EDCP585C: Dr. Stephen Mitchell (Kent State, Ohio, US) & Dr. Joy Butler (UBC)

7 EDCP501: Dr. Joy Butler (UBC)

8 EDCP531: Dr. Kath Sanford (UVic) & Dr. Tim Hopper (UVic)

9 EDCP508B: Dr. Joy Butler (UBC) & Dr. Alex DeCossen (UBC)

10 EDCP590: Dr. Joy Butler (UBC) & Dr. Alex DeCossen (UBC)

In addition to the initial input of these scholars, all the chapters in this book were subject to two reviews after their completion. These served to strengthen the work and make it ready for scholarly publication. Our reviewers in the first review are listed below. The second review was based on peer reviews. Finally all chapters were screened through our copy-editor for final proofing.

REVIEWERS

Helena Baert, Ph.D,

Physical Education Department, State University of New York, UNY Cortland, NY, US

Louise Humbert, Ph.D, Associate Dean,

College of Kinesiology University of Saskatchewan, Saskatoon, Saskatchewan

Shannon Kell, Ph.D,

Physical Education and Recreation Studies, Mount Royal University, Calgary, Alberta

Jeanne Kentel, Ph.D,

Department of Curriculum and Pedagogy, Faculty of Education, University of British Columbia, Vancouver, British Columbia

Stephen Price, Ph.D,

Physical Education and Recreation Studies, Mount Royal University, Calgary, Alberta

Greg Rickwood, Ph.D,

Schulich School of Education, Nipissing Univeristy, North Bay, Ontario

Abstracts

This book includes ten chapters, including eight chapters by the cohort. The cohort chapters are book-ended by the first and last chapters written by the cohort advisor and colleagues.

Chapter One

TGFU – WOULD YOU KNOW IT IF YOU SAW IT? BENCHMARKS FROM THE TACIT KNOWLEDGE OF THE FOUNDERS

JOY BUTLER

TGfU Would you know if you saw it? Benchmarks from the tacit knowledge of the founders.

This chapter explores the tacit expert knowledge and understanding about games curriculum and pedagogy of three men, Len Almond, David Bunker, and Rod Thorpe, credited as the founders of the Teaching Games for Understanding (TGfU) model. The model emerged from teacher practice in the late 1970s and was little theorized at the time, apart from a handful of articles written by the founders. This paper attempts to retrospectively theorize and represent the founders' ideas in terms of the beliefs, intentions, and actions they believed to be fundamental to TGfU. From here, some benchmarks are proposed so that TGfU can be more easily recognized when it is being practised and researched. Data were collected through two online sequential questionnaires, informal personal telephone interviews, and emails. All data were member checked throughout the two-year study. Both of the questionnaires were completed by the three founders in the persona of their 'ideal' TGfU teacher, in the hope that this would lead to greater clarity of response. The first questionnaire, called the Teaching Perspectives Inventory (TPI), was developed by Daniel Pratt and builds a profile of teacher beliefs, intentions, and actions, which are then grouped into five perspectives and ranked by personal bias. Questions posed on SurveyGizmo formed the second questionnaire, which helped the founders reflect further about their ideal teacher's beliefs, intentions, and actions, as they became apparent in the dominant and recessive perspectives identified in the TPI profiles. The findings were grouped into the founders' beliefs and intentions about: (1) learners and learning; (2) content; and (3) teachers' role and responsibilities. The data forming what the founders' considered to be best pedagogical practice formed eight areas for consideration to include: (1) preparation; (2) management; (3) starting a TGfU lesson; (4) continuing a TGfU lesson; (5) teacher behaviours; teacher focus during a game; (7) teacher expectations; and (8) learning environment.

This paper aims to provide a starting point for further research, debate, and reflection as we engage with the founders' intentions – to provide students with teaching that is an overt social, cultural, and relational activity, as well as a set of plans, practices, and actions.

We start with the first of the cohort chapters with authors George Kanavos and Steve McGinley as they examine how a PE department in a medium sized urban secondary school in Canada undertook to revise their curriculum and teaching. An important element in this case was the way the HoD (Steve) could reconfigure the pattern of relations within the department that sustained current practices. He did this by enrolling in a Master's degree (opening a channel for new ideas and information to come into the department) and by inviting a district counsellor (George) from a nearby school to act as a 'critical friend' (creating a means to perturb current practice and enhance feedback). Another key element was the willingness of the HoD to develop a department culture that was more collaborative, democratic and focused on placing student learning at the heart of all planning and departmental initiatives. Creating a culture of support and trust where each member felt their contributions mattered required a shift in the usual hierarchical traditional approaches to leadership. Enabling this meant the HoD becoming less of a director and more willing to find ways to engage greater participation and sharing of ideas amongst his colleagues and students.

Chapter Two

ENACTING CHANGE IN A SECONDARY PHYSICAL EDUCATION DEPARTMENT

GEORGE KANAVOS & STEVE MCGINLEY

This chapter explores enacting change in a Physical Education (PE) department and the successful implementation of curriculum and pedagogical innovations (CPIs). The focus examines how to initiate effective pedagogical change using curriculum and pedagogical innovations such as: Teaching Games for Understanding (TGfU); Sport Education (Sport Ed.); Physical Literacy (PL); Personal and Social Responsibility (PSR); Movement Education (ME); and, Inventing Games (IG). This chapter attempts to answer the question; what are the experiences of secondary PE teachers enacting curricular and pedagogical change in a secondary PE department? Nine thematic sections are explored; these include: knowing, learning and teaching; TGfU, physical literacy and PE; pedagogical change in physical education; PE culture and curriculum innovation; technology as a change agent; PE depart-

ment cultural change; phenomenology as methodology; and movement. Our study has provided us with an understanding of how teachers can successfully implement CPIs in a secondary PE department. The findings have been categorized into five major themes: curricular and pedagogical innovations; cultural change; leadership and support; relationships and collaboration, and barriers to implementing change. This chapter aims to provide a starting point for future research, debate, and reflection on encouraging cultural changes that make PE departments relevant in the 21st century.

Much needed work is the next chapter where Charmaine Lum researches the experiences of Chinese teenage males and how curriculum developers needs to be sensitive and reflective of the populations they serve.

Chapter Three

CHINESE TEENAGE MALES' EXPERIENCES IN PHYSICAL ACTIVITY SETTINGS

CHARMAINE LUM

With the recent influx of immigrants from Hong Kong and Mainland China in Richmond, B.C. (Richmond Census Data, 2014), there has been a noticeable shift in the dynamics in school and community sports in the lower mainland. Several teachers in the Richmond school district reported that high schools that used to boast successful sports programs are struggling to form teams and community sports are noting lower registration rates, particularly amongst the Chinese population (AD, March 2014). To investigate these concerns, semi-structured interviews with six Chinese immigrant males (ages 15-16) from Richmond, B.C. were conducted with the central question, "What are the experiences of Chinese teenage males in physical activity settings?" as the focus. Two Richmond physical educators with 10+ years of teaching experience in the community were interviewed to obtain their perspectives of the impact of the rising immigration rates on the attitudes towards physical education and extra-curricular sports. Furthermore, the interviews with the students strived to unveil whether students' willingness to participate in physical activity were influenced by Chinese cultural ideals, parental support, dominant hegemonic masculinities, or past experiences in China. The students' responses were organized based on major themes that surfaced during the coding process and presented through narrative inquiry. By looking at the results, it is evident that their stories are complex and are highly influenced by not only their cultural upbringing, but by the past of the people in their lives. With the steady growth of the Chinese population in the lower mainland it is imperative that the voices of young Chinese males be heard. The aim of the study is to help educators and community members understand the cultural differences and to gain insight on the factors that motivate or de-motivate Chinese students to participate in sport. Educators are encouraged to con- sider these factors when planning physical education classes so that they are compatible and sensitive to the needs of this population. As suggested by researchers who have conducted similar studies on the intersection of Chi- nese culture and Chinese students' engagement in physical activity, further exploration of this population needs to take place.

Paisley Rankine continues to examine boys' experience but as a broader population within a more narrowed experience in TGfU.

Chapter Four

THE EXPERIENCES OF BOYS IN PE AS THEY ENCOUNTER THE TEACHING GAMES FOR UNDERSTANDING MODEL FOR THE FIRST TIME

PAISLEY RANKINE

The purpose of this study was to provide a voice to students engaged in the teaching games for understanding model (TGfU) for the first time. The partic- ipants of the study were a class of boys in the eighth grade engaged in a bas- ketball unit using the TGfU model. The study aimed to bring the importance of the affective domain to the foreground of research conducted on TGfU and other child-centered approach models. It is the sentiment of the author that much of the current available research is focused on the cognitive and psychomotor domain contributions of TGfU. It was the intent of the research to provide an avenue for the male participants to voice their experiences and feelings. The experiences are presented based on both quantitative and quali- tative data taken from questionnaires, interviews, and written comments. The results of which are paralleled with the voice of the teacher and researcher through observations and field notes presented in a confessional tale format.

The findings are described through emergent themes exposed through the data analysis. The six themes storied by the participants were: 1) Elemen- tary experiences, 2) Understanding of the game, 3) A sense of enjoyment for games and physical education, 4) Building confidence, 5) Feelings of im- proved abilities, and 6) Reflection of perceived limitations. The synonymous experiences and feelings of the teacher and researcher were storied through five emergent themes, 1) Levels of engagement, 2) Lesson flow, 3) Perceived learning, 4) Student behaviour, and 5) Difficulties in transition to TGfU.

Based on the research findings the concluding recommendations call for greater insight into the affective domain of students engaged in TGfU over a longer term. By providing a holistic approach to the research, the use of TGfU may grow and thrive in physical education programs on a grander scale because of its ability to meet the needs of a greater number of students.

The next two chapters research students' experiences, school scheduling, and underlying biases to explain the declining enrollment figures in senior PE. David Dunkin and Kara Wickstom compared populations across two secondary schools while Angela Bigiolli examines more deeply responses from a group of 22 girls.

Chapter Five

WHERE HAVE ALL THE KIDS GONE?
DECLINING ENROLLMENT IN
SENIOR PHYSICAL EDUCATION CLASSES

DAVID DUNKIN & KARA WICKSTROM

The purpose of this study was to explore reasons why students choose not to enroll in physical education past the mandatory year at their respective schools. The reasons for declining participation in physical education are many, and their complexity forces researchers to look at the variables that may lead students to not selecting physical education as an elective. Sallis (2000) suggests that there have been numerous descriptive and correlative studies that show physical activity levels decline as children age. Throughout the literature review, the focus is on declining enrollment in PE and what motivates students to elect to take physical education. The outcome of this research is to examine and analyze the reasons why our adolescents are not participating in a course that is essential for a healthy and well-balanced life.

Through participant interviews, the researchers gained an understanding of student feelings regarding their past enjoyment and participation in PE as well as the conflicts they face in registering for PE. In efforts to draw from a heterogeneous grouping allowing for a more diverse range of participants, purposive sampling was utilized. This type of sampling will allow researchers to gain a variation in perspectives to help identify common themes and gain greater insights into why these students are not electing to participate in physical education after they have completed their final mandatory year.

Chapter Six

WHERE HAVE ALL THE GIRLS GONE?
FEMALE CHOICE IN SENIOR ELECTIVE PE

ANGELA BIGIOLLI

Since the introduction of a new PE 11/12 Girls course, options have been increased for females who want to stay active but did not want the traditional senior coed PE elective at the school. By including female students in the curricular planning process for the year, students have been more engaged and understanding of why certain activities are happening when they do. Student voice really helped to create an overwhelming sense of ownership to the class.

Physical educators are responsible for evaluating the methods they use to teach our children and investigate ways in which to improve what they are doing in the gymnasium already. All students have needs that are required to be met in order to fully educate our children into physically, literate adults. Student centered methods of instruction like TGFU, Sport Education and Game Sense are proven methods of instruction that put the students first.

It is through this study that improvements have already been made in the delivery of curriculum at the junior PE level. My goal is to create a learning environment that will promote physical activity and instill values in all my students that movement is needed in order to balance lifestyle and health.

Brent Jackson continues the investigation into improving the learning experiences for girls by introducing both TGfU and a more authentic assessment tool. An ambitious study attempting to see if one, or both treatments made any difference in their learning experiences.

Chapter Seven

HELPING INCREASE GIRLS' PHYSICAL SELF-EFFICACY
THROUGH TGFU AND THE GPAI

BRENT JACKSON

The attrition rate of girls in physical activity is continuously higher than boys, and evidence points to the same conclusion in Physical Education. Still there is hope to reverse this trend as research has shown that an increase in physical self-efficacy will lead girls to higher levels of motivation and increased participation in physical activity. Using a quantitative research design, I studied the effect of Teaching Games for Understanding (TGfU) and the Game Performance Assessment Instrument (GPAI) on Grade seven girls' physical self-efficacy during game play. The data gathered from the Physical Self-Efficacy Questionnaire indicates that using a TGfU focus will lead to an increase in Grade seven girls' physical self-efficacy during game play. I cannot say with certainty that the GPAI had a positive effect, nor can I say that it was not a factor. However, the scope of the study group was quite modest.

Continuing the goal to improve the learning experiences of our students whether we are in the role of teacher or coach, Simon Dystra found himself in quite the transformational journey as he paid more attention to the context, learner and the teaching/coaching process.

Chapter Eight

REFLECTIONS ON PLAYER LEARNING: A SELF-STUDY OF COACHING PRAXIS

SIMON DYKSTRA

How can a school based basketball coach improve the learning environment for players and move forward the praxis of an educator? How might a coach move from direct instruction techniques, based on knowledge transmission, towards a process of increasing player centered participation and learning facilitation? How can I enable more player centred coaching through learning based on constructivist theories?

A qualitative self-study was used to investigate this inquiry. Data were sought that could further an understanding of my potential shift towards becoming an educator coach. Discussion and findings are connected to inquiry through a narrative, which examines the role of player journals, and coach reflections. A short autoethnography is also presented which sets in a cultural context, the constraint one faces as lifelong participant in school sport experiences. Shifting to constructivist informed coaching means becoming more aware of the player as an adaptive learner. In using four reflection journals during the season, important aspects of player motivation, relationships, metacognition and complexity emerged. Player journals helped enabled both individual growth and collective insight or intelligence.

The findings helped better adapt my constructivist methods and strategies to suit the unique learner. Examples of methods discussed include TGfU, Game Sense and the Growth Mindset approach. Findings challenge traditional behavioral assumptions that place the coach at the center of the learning environment. Social constructivist theories of learning help coaches imple-

ment the learning process that enables players agency in a complex process. Improving intrapersonal knowledge in teams may help connect players to hard to reach aspects of a situated nature and context of a basketball team. An intended outcome of the learning process was for players to better self-regulate and lead their improvement. This inquiry became an empowering journey for both participants and coach.

As the profession ponders the legitimacy of online PE, Susan Kimura carefully investigates the experience of two secondary students enrolled in OLPE.

Chapter Nine

NARRATIVE INQUIRY OF ONLINE PHYSICAL EDUCATION: WHAT IS THE EXPERIENCE OF ONLINE PE STUDENTS?

SUSAN KIMURA

There are a growing number of students who are taking PE online in order to meet graduation requirements in British Columbia; however, there is a lack of research about the student experience in online courses. This study asked the question, "What is the experience of online PE students?" and by using narrative inquiry as a methodology, this study interviewed two, lower mainland, high school students about their online PE experience. The small sample size is acknowledged as a limitation to this study and understands that these stories do not claim to be the only stories but offer a possibility of stories that may resonate with others. The researcher was able to discover themes of competition, communication and choice through interviews using guided, semi-guided and open ended questions. In the retelling of the participants' stories, the researcher realizes the collaborative nature of this study, which resulted in a shared narrative of online PE experiences.

This chapter is added with permission from a book titled 'Complexity thinking in Physical Education.' Minor changes have been made. Nevertheless, a final chapter for considering complexity thinking as a new way to think about the issues central to curriculum, pedagogy and research in physical education.

Chapter Ten

RECONCEPTUALIZING PEDAGOGY, CURRICULUM AND RESEARCH THROUGH COMPLEXITY THINKING.

ALAN OVENS, TIM HOPPER & JOY BUTLER

This chapter addresses two key questions: What is complexity? And what does it have to offer physical educators? In considering complexity as a source domain of analogies for understanding human action and practice in educational settings, the chapter outlines the key concepts central to complexity thinking.

Editor Qualifications

Dr. Joy Butler (Associate Professor) is Physical Education Teacher Education (PETE) Coordinator and Graduate Coordinator in the Department of Curriculum and Pedagogy at the University of British Columbia. She is active in the international scholarship, organization, and advocacy for Teaching Games for Understanding (TGfU): an innovative model for games education. Dr. Butler's research and teaching have developed around constructivist learning theory and focus on research and practice in curriculum and pedagogy. She convened the first International Teaching Games for Understanding (TGfU) Conference in 2001 in New Hampshire, US, and the fourth conference in 2008 at UBC, Vancouver, Canada. She founded the TGfU International Task Force in 2002, chaired it until 2009. She is now Chair of the TGfU International Advisory Board, which comprises of 17 countries across six continents. Joy has been invited to give presentations and workshops in many different countries, including Colombia, Finland, Singapore, Australia, Spain, Taiwan and Hong Kong. She is the co-editor of seven books on Teaching Games for Understanding and has authored many articles in the areas of physical education learning and teaching, curriculum innovations, and teacher education. More recently her research is centered around complexity thinking and situated ethics in games teaching and learning.

CHAPTER ONE

TGfU – Would you know it if you saw it? Benchmarks from the Tacit Knowledge of the Founders

BY JOY BUTLER

Introduction

In this paper, I ask a large question: 'How do you recognize a good Teaching Games for Understanding (TGfU) approach teacher when you see one?' I ask this particular question because I have heard the founders of TGfU, Rod Thorpe, David Bunker, and Len Almond, say on several occasions that what they see being taught and discussed at international conferences, particularly practical sessions, is not always the TGfU approach they had originally intended. Almond (2010) ascribes this situation to a divide between theory and practice. He believes that while TGfU has been accepted by academics, 'the rationale seems to have passed by practitioners without any major effect. TGfU currently thrives in only a few areas where practitioners are faithful to its original approach (2010: vii).' The other two founders agree. Thorpe and Bunker have suggested that (2010: xii) while there is '...exchange (between coaches, teachers and researchers at conferences),' these discussions don't transfer 'from the conference room into practical situations.' Elsewhere, I have suggested that this gap (Butler et al., 2008) between theory and practice or curriculum theory and instructional design (Petrina, 2004) has led to the continued, and disappointing, dominance of the traditional transmission approach in physical education. This paper attempts to bridge this gap, as it drills into the original beliefs, intentions, and actions of the founders in order to reconstruct the passionate vision that motivated and energized practicing teachers.

TGfU evolved from years of practice and reflection by teachers and teacher educators working collaboratively (through team teaching) to better the experience of learners. As Almond suggested, in recent email correspondence (March 13th, 2013),

> Ideas (practical or theoretical) were always open to scrutiny. We would read each other's words and discuss our interpretations of them, not to seek consensus, but a shared understanding of their possibilities. In the same way we sought the views of other practitioners and lecturers to test our understanding as well as to seek a different (or alternative) way of thinking or identify flaws in our perceptions. This process was important, and I believe stands out as a unique way of developing a curriculum.

The founders brought the approach to the attention of others largely through the 1982 paper: A model for teaching games in secondary schools, two special editions in the Bulletin of PE, i) Games teaching (1982) and Games teaching revisited (1983), and a slim booklet in 1986 called Rethinking Games

Teaching. The authors of the latter were primarily Physical Education Teacher Education (PETE) specialists – curriculum innovators rather than curriculum theorists (with the notable except of Len Almond). At the International TGfU Conference in 2012 (celebrating the 30th anniversary of 1982 landmark paper), Bunker suggested (in personal conversation substantiated by email in January 2013) that these seminal publications almost didn't make it into print. In the context in which these educators were working - a 1970s United Kingdom (UK) teacher training college with a strong focus on physical education (PE) - faculty publications were less frequent and less necessary to career development. 'We were too busy actually *doing it* to be bothered to write papers,' Bunker remarked and added with disguised affection, 'It would never have happened if Len hadn't bullied us!'

The early publications that introduced TGfU offered a new way to view the games curriculum through a four-category classification system supporting the related notion of transfer of knowledge across these classifications, a six-step cycle of teaching, and a set of pedagogical principles. The principles included sampling, exaggeration, representation and tactical complexity (Thorpe, 2005; Thorpe et al., 1986: 79). 'Importantly, a principles approach makes it possible for teachers and others involved in sports development to achieve a broad-based games education' (Thorpe and Bunker, 2010: xiii).

The approach was developed by practitioners for practitioners, rather than a broad, theoretically oriented teaching approach grounded in research. It was based on ideas and structures that would provide accessibility to all games, emphasize engagement for all learners at all stages of learning, and provide motivation for learners to be interested in games and to be involved in their own learning. Its pedagogical principles and planning fundamentals made excellent sense (and still do) but were not firmly attached to a larger world of curriculum theorizing – a field still in its infancy at that time. Thorpe and Bunker were mindful that future research was necessary (1986).

TGFU TASK FORCE (2002-2008) AND
AIESEP TGFU SPECIAL INTEREST GROUP (SIG) (2008-2014)

In the 21st century, TGfU has drawn attention from global educators. A TGfU task force was established in 2002, and its subsequent morphing into a Special Interest Group (SIG) of AIESEP (Association Internationale des Ecoles Superieures d'Education Physique or International Association for Physical Education in Higher Education) in 2008 has contributed to the production of a large new body of writing and research. I speculate that this new wave of theorizing has also been the result of a series of five international conferences (2001-US, 2003-AU, 2005 HK, 2008 CAN, 2012-UK, and the next in 2116-GER) that have generated proceedings, books, and articles, perhaps

3

at the expense over some of the other emerging alternative games approaches in the last three decades. Indeed, in July 2016, the TGfU SIG Executive will propose a name change for the SIG at the next TGfU International conference in Cologne, Germany. If approved the name will change from TGfU to Games Centred Approach (GCA) to provide a more inclusive term. Since this paper addresses the views of Almond, Bunker and Thorpe, the term TGfU will be used throughout to avoid confusion.

GAMES CENTRED APPROACHES (GCAs)

The theorizing of TGfU has centred around cognitive and social constructivism, based on the belief that learners construct meaning socially as well as individually (Bruner, 1966; Piaget, 1969; Vygotsky, 1978). However, there have been many interpretations and iterations of the original model offered by the founders. Approaches that had their origins in TGfU and share constructivist learning theories as their philosophical foundations are comprehensively reviewed in three helpful resources. The first, by Oslin and Mitchell (2006), covers the period from 1982 until 2006; the second, by Harvey and Jarrett (2013), reviews GCA research since 2006 and the third, by Stolz and Pill (2013), provides an excellent overview to anyone who is interested in learning more about the literature and research of TGfU and its major interpretations (GCAs). Stolz and Pill (2013) consider in depth a range of GCAs including Tactical Games (Griffin et al., 1997; Mitchell et al., 2003, 2006, 2013), Games Sense (Thorpe, 1996; Light, 2013), Play Practice (Launder, 2001; Launder and Piltz, 2013), Invasion Games Competency model (Tallir et al., 2004, 2005; Mesquita et al., 2012), Tactical decision learning model, (Grehaigne and Godbout 1997, 1998; Grehaigne et al., 2005, 2012), Games Concept Approach (Rossi et al., 2006).

The research project I discuss here consider might aptly be described as an experiment in 'retrospective theorizing,' as I invited the three founders of TGfU to identify and articulate their tacit knowledge (Collin, 2010) about their philosophy and pedagogy in games education. As the model is discussed, refined, disseminated, and theorized, I felt it might be timely to revisit, identify, and represent its intellectual and conceptual origins. I hoped to establish some philosophical benchmarks that might help identify some of the broad philosophical ideas underpinning TGfU and pedagogical strategies for teaching it. Rather than thinking in the 'virtual world' of theoretical abstraction (the 'why' of teaching), I wanted to try and capture the rather more elusive business of the 'what' and the 'how.' For this reason, I decided to focus on the beliefs, intentions, and actions of the founders. As I have said elsewhere (Butler et al., 2012), the belief that TGfU offers an alternative to traditional technique-based approaches rests upon theories and suppositions about knowledge and learning. In this sense an exploration of what this world looks like lie at the heart of discussions about teaching TGfU successfully.

RESEARCH CHALLENGES

The project posed some interesting challenges. Firstly, given the different cultural and pedagogical interpretations the model is now nested within, I was unsure if it might even be possible for the founders to retrospectively identify core beliefs that had not been a conscious focus for them at the time they were writing, since they were, as Bunker stated, 'too busy doing it.' Thirty years has passed since those early publications, and the model has evolved in varied global contexts (see Stolz and Pill, 2013). No teaching practice or model can be picked up wholesale and dropped into a different country or culture (Pinar, 2012) without being influenced by new epistemological and ontological beliefs and values that shape the ways in which it is understood and integrated.

Secondly, scholars are divided on the question of how possible it is to articulate tacit knowledge (Tsoukas, 2003). Some suggest that it is essentially ineffable, and at the very least, caution is required as we attempt to 'capture' or 'operationalize' non-conscious knowledge. Polanyi (1967) suggests that though expert teaching professors possess tacit knowledge of how they do their job they may struggle, like other expert workers, as they attempt to surface this knowledge and to explain it to others. Finally, collective tacit knowledge is filtered through and influenced by its socio-cultural contexts (Collin, 2010), in this case, a largely Caucasian and masculine profession in the UK.

Methods

RETROSPECTIVE THEORIZING

Rather than have the founders just describe their teaching philosophical perspectives, I used the Teaching Perspectives Inventory (TPI) developed by Pratt (1998), which I discuss in more detail below. The word 'perspective' derives from perspicere (to inspect, to look through, to look closely at). A perspective on teaching is an inter-related set of beliefs and intentions that gives direction and justification to our teaching actions (Pratt, 1998). As Pratt describes it is a lens that educators view their work through, and as such, it often becomes invisible. In this sense, our perspectives become a way of being (Hubball et al., 2005), and our pedagogical beliefs, intentions, and actions remain tacit (Polyanis, 1967). The word 'retrospective' means 'relating to' or 'contemplating' the past. It was my hope that as the founders used the TPI to 'look at' (rather than 'through') their teaching perspectives, they might be able to retrospectively theorize them. I provided opportunities for this in subsequent semi-structured interviews and a follow up questionnaire. These were designed to allow participants to relate their teaching perspectives to the ideas and principles of TGfU. As is apparent by now, this research is embedded in a qualitative paradigm.

PARTICIPANTS

As stated earlier, Len Almond, David Bunker, and Rod Thorpe have been largely credited with developing the approach at Loughborough University in England more than 30 years ago and were the participants for this research. All gave informed consent to participate in the study.

DATA COLLECTION

The three sources of data were as follows: *(1) the Teaching Perspectives Inventory (2) an online survey I created on SurveyGizmo* and *(3) informal interviewing.*

(1) THE TEACHING PERSPECTIVES INVENTORY

Participants were asked to complete the TPI and survey in the persona of their imagined 'ideal' TGfU teacher. I wanted to offer participants some critical distance from their own particular situations, in order to help them get to their beliefs more easily. Unexamined beliefs can lead to habitual pedagogical practices that serve to maintain the status quo rather than reflective, pedagogical practices that challenge it. Sparkes (1991) suggests that once teachers are presented with alternative visions of practice (with the tools to shape these alternative visions), they then often start to understand the dominant and stable practices of teaching as structures that have constrained them in schools. Once their beliefs are opened up for examination, they can provide a starting point for deep, sustainable teacher change. This examination of beliefs was especially important since a follow-up to this project will involve all GCA perspectives from a range of participants of various ethnic, cultural and educational backgrounds.

The notion of answering from the point of view of an imaginary ideal respondent came from the work of Pratt and Collins (the originators of the TPI), who recommended this technique as a way to gain greater clarity. This technique is also foregrounded by Bhabha's work in 1994 on 'Hybridity' and 'Third space' in post-colonial discourse.

Through extensive empirical and conceptual research, Pratt (1998) defined five teaching perspectives: Transmission (TR), Apprenticeship (AP), Developmental (DE), Nurturing (NU), and Social Reform (SR). There are some parallels with Ennis's value orientations (Chen et al., 1997) such as disciplinary mastery (similar to transmission), learning process (similar to developmental), self-actualization (similar to apprenticeship and nurturing), ecological integration (similar to social reform), and social responsibility (similar to social reform). I chose to use the TPI over Ennis' VOI for the following reasons: 1) I was able to compare the founders' profiles with over 100,000 profiles in the data bank developed by Collins and Pratt (2011) over 10 years, 2) I was to compare the founders' profiles with those of teachers in other subject areas 3) I was able to compare the founders' profiles with teachers working with different grade levels; 4) both architects and researchers of the TPI are affiliated with UBC and have been on-hand for consultations and data analysis advice, 5) the TPI can be easily accessed online.

The TPI includes nine questions for each of these five perspectives. These are further grouped into three sets of 15 items (1) biases in actions (how we teach), (2) intentions (what we are trying to accomplish), and (3) beliefs (why we consider that important or justified). A five-point likert rating scale that ranges from 'strongly disagree' (1) and 'strongly agree' (5) or 'never' (1) and 'always' (5) was used. Scores for each perspective could then vary from 9 to 45. A respondent's TPI scores are computed as plus or minus one standard deviation around the mean of each respondent's five perspective scores; this results in an individualized spread separating dominant from recessive scores (Collins and Pratt 2011).

DOMINANT AND RECESSIVE PERSPECTIVES

The sample profile (Figure 1) can be helpful in showing the kinds of data produced by the TPI. This particular respondent shows no dominant perspective and shows a recessive perspective in transmission. However, it is not unusual for a respondent to have more than one dominant perspective (perspective(s) that stand out as higher than the remainder). A dominant perspective indicates a leaning towards a 'style' or 'bias' in teaching. A recessive score indicates a perspective that is least drawn upon. Scores that fall in between are considered 'back-up' perspectives. The skills and strategies typical of these 'back-up' perspectives can be called upon when needed but are not necessarily the first response used. The teacher in this sample uses skills and strategies from four of the perspectives and tends to draw from transmission skills and strategies the least (recessive perspective).

(2) FOLLOW UP SURVEY (SURVEYGIZMO)

Parsaye (1988) believes that structured interviewing of experts provides the most effective way of teasing out their pertinent tacit knowledge. Since my three participants were in another country and I could not sit down with them in person, I turned to a second online instrument, the SurveyGizmo questionnaire. Made up of 29 questions (see Appendix A), the questionnaire was designed to help respondents reflect about their beliefs, intentions, and actions as these had been identified by the dominant and recessive perspectives in their TPI profiles. I field-tested and developed the questionnaire with 15 teacher educators. The questions included multiple-choice, short fill-ins, and open-ended questions. The first 12 questions captured each of the founders' responses to their TPI profiles and the last question asked for how close the ideal teacher description was to each of their own beliefs and practice. The remaining questions captured their educational philosophy and pedagogical ideas, and were divided into questions about their beliefs, intentions, and actions – the basis upon which the TPI is developed. So in summary, the questions were organized into the following groups (see Figure 2).

Figure 1. **Sample Teaching Perspectives Profile.**

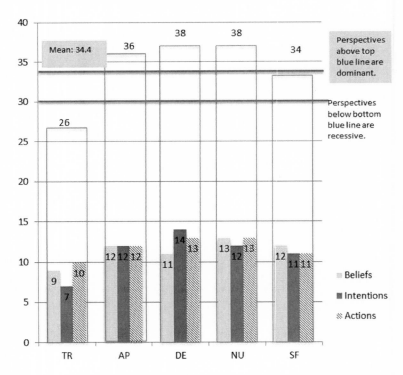

(Descriptions of each of the five perspectives and access to the instrument can be found at www.teachingperspectives.com.) Legend for horizontal axis. TR: Transmission; AP: Apprenticeship; DE: Developmental; NU: Nurturing; SF:Social reform

Figure 2. **Pyramid of Beliefs, Intentions and Actions.**

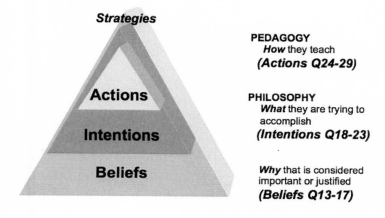

(3) INFORMAL INTERVIEWING

I followed up the SurveyGizmo with several telephone conversations and emails with each founder to clarify or probe further about particular responses to the two online instruments. I also met with each of the founders at the TGfU International conference in UK, July 2012.

SEQUENCE OF DATA COLLECTION AND ANALYSIS

1. The online TPI was completed. Copies of the profile were sent to the participants and to me for review (October 2010).

2. I followed up with each participant (through e-mails and phone calls) to discuss the composition of the profile and help make sense of the graph. This required pointing out the dominant and recessive perspectives and the internal scores for each perspective. Each 'agreed' or 'strongly agreed' that the profiles accurately represented the perspectives of his imaginary ideal TGfU teacher. Each also agreed that these profiles of the imaginary ideal teacher matched his own personal views (November, 2010).

3. The online SurveyGizmo was completed (January 2011).

4. Opportunity was provided for clarification and edits to the statements provided by each founder through e-mail and telephone communication (February-April 2011). SurveyGizmo survey questions 1-12 offered opportunities to comment on the validity of their TPI profile.

5. Responses to SurveyGizmo questions 13-29 were listed verbatim in three

columns in an Excel file. These questions were about educational philosophy: beliefs and intentions (questions 13-23) and pedagogical actions (questions 24-29). This was the first time that the founders were given the entire data set (June 2011).

6. Responses to questions 13-29 were coded for commonalities and key ideas (Summer 2011).

7. Benchmarks were developed from step number 6 (October 2011).

8. Benchmarks were distributed to the founders for editing (November, 2011).

9. Approvals for the benchmarks were given verbally or by email (March 2012).

Findings & Discussion

TEACHING PERSPECTIVES PROFILES

Since the founders have an 'n' of 3, no comparative statistics would be meaningful, either amongst the founders or between the two groups (founders and normative distribution scores). However these profiles (see Table 1 and Figure 3) provided a starting point for analysis in the SurveyGizmo and follow-up discussions.

BIASES AND DOMINANT PERSPECTIVES

This section focuses on the dominant perspectives or biases in the 'ideal' profile offered by each of the founders (see legend). For better understanding, each of the 'ideal' profiles has been mapped onto a normative distribution chart (see Figure 3) that was the product of over 170,000 TPI responses collected by Pratt and Collins (2011). For the purpose of comparison, the averages of three groups of teachers at the pre-school, elementary, and secondary levels from a further unpublished study by Collins and Pratt have been included. The pre-school and elementary profiles follow similar biases with a preference for the nurturing perspective (39/45) and is on the 70th percentile on the normative distribution, followed closely behind with social reform (30) and about 60th percentile for pre-school and elementary levels. The profile of the secondary school teachers varies from teachers of the younger grades, indicating an emphasis on transmission (34 and 60th percentile) and social reform (30 and 60th percentile).

As we view the 'ideal' TGfU profiles constructed by each of the founders, we see quite different profiles from the K-12 profiles referenced above. Almond's scores register considerably higher than all teacher groups with percentiles above 70% except for his recessive score for SR (23), which falls in

Table 1

Founders' ideal TGfU teacher's Teaching Perspectives Profiles.

	TR			AP			DV			NU			SR			TOTAL	
	Score	Rank	%	Score	Rank	%	Score	Rank	%	Score	Rank	%	Score	Rank	%	Score	%
Almond	38	4	87	43	3	96	45	1	100	44	2	98	23	5R	17	190	90
Bunker	36	4	75	37	3	60	38	=1	77	38	=1	60	32	5 R	73	181	76

TR: Transmission; AP: Apprenticeship; DV: Developmental; NU: Nurturing; SR: Social reform; D: Dominant perspective; R:Recessive perspective

11

Figure 3. Founders Ideal profiles and K-12 Norms.

Founder's TPI Scores Compared to Other K-12 Teachers' Norms

(N=21,828 Seasoned K-12 Teachers with 5 years or more experience.)
(P=750 Pre-School; E=5453 Elementary; S=7254 Secondary)
(Almond, **Bunker**, Thorpe)

%ile	Transmission	Apprenticeship	Developmental	Nurturing	Social Reform	Belief	Intent	Action	Total	%ile
%ile	43		45 A		42	70	72	71	209	%ile
98%	42	44	43	44 A	40	68	70	70	204	98%
	41	43 A	42		39	67	69	69	202	
95	40	42		43	38	66	67	68	197	95
	39		41		37	65	66	66	193	
90		41	40	42 T	36	63	65	65	190	90
	38 A				35	62	64	64	188	
85		40						63	186	85
	37		39	41	34	61	63		185	
80			38 B			60	62	62	183	80
		39			33				182	
75%	36 B			40		59	61	61	180	75%
		38	37	39	32 B			60	179	
70	35				P / 31	58	60		178	70
				E					177	
65					E,S		59	59 P	176	65
						E,P			175	
60	34 S	37 B	36	38 B	30	57	58	58	173 E	60
						S			172 P,S	
55	m / E	f / S	f / 35 E,S	f / 37	29f T	56f	TS,E / S	S / 57	171f	55
50%	33f	38 m	m	S	m / 28	m / 55	57 / mP	57 / 56m	170 / 169 / 168m	50%
45	32		36	36			56		167 / 166	45
40	p	35	34	m / 35	27	54	55	55	165 / 164	40
35	31		33 T		26	53	54	54	163 / 162	35
30		34	32	34	25	52	53	53	161 / 160	30
25%	30	33	31	33	24	51	52	52	159 / 158	25%
20	29	32 T		32	23 A	50	51	51	157 / 155	20
15	28	31	30	31	22	49	50	50	154 / 152	15
10	27	30	29	30	21	48	48	48	150	10
	26 T		28	29	20	47	47	47	147	
5	25	29	27	27	18	46	46	46	144	5
	24	28	26	26	17		45	45	141	
2%	23	26	25	24	15	43	43	43	137	2%
1%	21	25	24	22	14	41	41	41	132	1%

	Transmission	Apprenticeship	Developmental	Nurturing	Social Reform	Belief	Intent	Action	Total
Scores	Tr ___	App ___	Dv ___	Nu ___	SR ___	B ___	I ___	A ___	T ___
Norms: minant:	13%	37%	19%	51%	3%	(None=5%; One=68%; Two=27%)			

the 17th percentile. Thorpe's scores register lower than the 3 teacher groups except for his dominant perspective in nurturing (42). Bunker's scores fall between Rod's and Len's and are closer to the means of the teachers. While it is informative to compare individual profiles with normative scores to understand variations from norms in teaching, it also important to remember that the scores are most meaningful in the context provided by the other scores within that individual's profile. For example, though four of Thorpe's scores are much lower than Bunker and Almond's, the variations in his scores are still significant. Thorpe's highest score is 33 in development and is his second biased perspective. See rank scores in Table 1.

SIMILARITIES AMONGST THE FOUNDERS' 'IDEAL' PROFILES

As we consider each of the founders' ideal TGfU teacher's strongest scores, we find that they follow almost the same pattern of bias, with nurturing and developmental perspectives as their top two perspectives (see shaded area on table 1). Their TPIs appeared in this ranked order: (1) Nurturing-NU, (2) Developmental-DV, (3) Apprenticeship-AP, (4) Transmission-TR, (5) Social Reform-SR.

The significance of Nurturing and the Development perspectives being at the top of their lists is not immediately apparent until a comparison is made with the normative distribution scores of 170,000 respondents. The nurturing perspective scores, when compared with normative distribution fall into the 60th, 90th and 98th percentiles respectively. The Developmental scores fall into the 100th, 77th and 36th percentile respectively (although low by comparison – this is Thorpe's second highest perspective score). Inasmuch as the TPI offers insight into individual biases and trends around practice, these contrasts do speak to the founders' differences from the norm.

NURTURING PERSPECTIVE

What remains consistent through TPI studies of PE educators (Jarvis-Selinger et al., 2007) and now of the TGfU Founders is that the Nurturing perspective remains strong or dominant in their profiles, as might be expected from educators with a strong focus on student empowerment (Thorpe, 2005).

> Nurturing: Effective teaching assumes that long-term, hard, persistent effort to achieve comes from the heart, as well as the head. People are motivated and productive learners when they are working on issues or problems without fear of failure. Learners are nurtured by knowing that (a) they can succeed at learning if they give it a good try; (b) their achievement is a product of their own effort and ability, rath-

er than the benevolence of a teacher; and (c) their
efforts to learn will be supported by their teacher and
their peers. The more pressure to achieve, and the
more difficult the material, the more important it is
that there be such support for learning. Good teachers promote a climate of caring and trust, helping
people set challenging but achievable goals, and providing encouragement and support, along with clear
expectations and reasonable goals for all learners.
(Pratt, Collins, & Jarvis Selinger, 2001)

As suggested earlier, what sets the founders apart from the cultural norm
for PE teachers and PE teacher candidates (Selinger et al., 2007) is their pro-
pensity toward the developmental perspective. While the transmission approach has its roots in behaviourism, the developmental perspective has its
roots in constructivist learning theory in that knowledge is constructed by
learners from the ground up, with the help of teachers who understand and
adapt to each learner's level of understanding. Given this belief, effective decision-making is a sought for outcome of the TGfU approach (Thorpe, 2005).

Developmental: Effective teaching must be planned
and conducted 'from the learner's point of view.'
Good teachers must understand how their learners
think and reason about the content. The primary goal
is to help learners develop increasingly complex and
sophisticated cognitive structures for comprehending
the content…Good teachers work hard to adapt their
knowledge to each learner's level of understanding and ways of thinking. (Pratt, Collins, & Jarvis
Selinger, 2001)

RECESSIVE OR NON-DOMINANT PERSPECTIVES

Knowing one's dominant TPI perspective is helpful, but knowing one's
recessive perspective (that one draws from least) can be equally important. As
indicated by table 1, the ideal profiles recessive perspectives were transmission for Thorpe and social reform for Almond and Bunker. Thorpe stated that
the recessive perspective of his ideal TGfU teacher is in transmission since 'in
TGfU the pupil learns from the problems posed by the game, ergo indirectly
from the teacher (SurveyGizmo.)' It is interesting to note that while transmission was the style most favoured by PE teachers and often still is (Jewett, Bain,
& Ennis, 1995; Penney & Evans, 1995; Capel & Blair, 2013), it is the one perspective least drawn from by Thorpe and second least by Bunker and Almond.
Almond and Bunker's recessive perspective was in social reform. They both
found one or two statement items in the TPI for the social reform category to

be too strong and off-putting, pointing to the example 'effective teaching seeks to change society in substantive ways.' Almond concluded that it was 'not a major concern for TGfU.'

PHILOSOPHY AND PEDAGOGY OF IDEAL TGFU TEACHERS

What follows is a summary of the statements made by the founders initially through the SurveyGizmo and then confirmed or expanded upon through email or phone calls through a process of members checking. These were further coded and summarized. I then reframed these as bullet points in Figures 2-4.

The SurveyGizmo questions regarding games education were grouped into Beliefs, Intentions, and Actions, to reflect the TPI questions. The following summary is divided into two broad categories – philosophy and pedagogy. The philosophical responses were further divided into beliefs and intentions. The beliefs included statements that the founders considered to be 'important or justified,' and the intention statements included statements that indicated 'what they are trying to accomplish.' The pedagogical responses include the Action question responses and describe 'how' the founders think their ideal TGfU teachers should teach.

Figure 4. **Benchmarks for TGfU Beliefs.**

BENCHMARKS FOR BELIEFS (Butler, 2012)
(TGfU Teachers' beliefs *about...*)

	Learners and Learning
B1	Start from the learner's knowledge base and build on what children already know
B2	Emphasize play
B3	Children learn more from situations, other children, and experimenting with roles (e.g. referees) than from teachers
B4	Children enjoy learning
B5	Children are curious
B6	Effort should be encouraged and acknowledged at all times
	Content
B7	Use the logic of progression
B8	Recognize the timing and level of modifications needed to provide challenge, interest, and success for all
B9	Games should be built on the principles of play
B10	Games that build learning are designed to pose questions
	Teacher's Role and Responsibilities
B11	See every child as a learner – there are no barriers
B12	Value the game as teacher
B13	Explore content with energy and enthusiasm
B14	Lead through guided discovery
B15	Nurture different kinds of learning
B16	Encourage inter-student interactions to promote social skills
B17	Allow friends to play together at appropriate levels
B18	Ask questions to set up problems to be solved in game play; ask questions in game context and ask questions to aid reflection

Philosophy

1) BELIEFS (WHY STATEMENTS FROM QUESTIONS #13-15)

As indicated in Figure 2, beliefs take up residency in the bottom layer of the pyramid, a position that represents beliefs as the bedrock – those underlying values that underpin our conscious teaching behaviors (actions) and our teaching and learning intentions. The why statements were those that the founders considered to be important or justified and have been labelled as 'beliefs.' Similar statements were grouped together (in a grounded theory approach) until a workable list was developed. The 18 beliefs in Figure 4 are categorized into beliefs about (1) Learners and Learning, (2) Content and (3) Teacher's Role and Responsibilities.

INTENTIONS (Q 16-17 WHAT ARE THEY TRYING TO ACCOMPLISH)

'Intentions are general statements that point toward an overall agenda of purpose' (Pratt & Associates 1998: 18). The 13 intentions listed in Figure 5 include statements about the purpose and commitment towards learners; content, contexts and professional development and growth. These were divided into rationales for assessment and teacher strategies.

PEDAGOGY (ACTION)

Actions are described as the 'routines and techniques we use to engage people in content' (Pratt & Associates 1998: 17). Actions are the most concrete and accessible aspect of a teaching perspective and are the means through which we activate intentions and beliefs to help people learn. These actions are the product of tacit knowledge. The 48 summary statements of action found in Figure 6 are divided into seven areas for consideration: *(1) Preparation (2) Management; (3) Starting a TGfU lesson; (4) Continuing a TGfU lesson; (5) Teacher Behaviors; (6) Teacher Expectations; (7) Learning Environment.*

Though many of the statements seem simple and obvious, I believe that as they are clearly articulated and presented here, they do speak to a common tacit worldview held by the founders of TGfU – a set of benchmarks that generate and guide pedagogical practices. Unpacking or drilling deeply into these statements is the next obvious and most immediately needed research, but beyond the scope of this paper.

Figure 5. Benchmarks for Intentions (Butler, 2012)

BENCHMARKS FOR INTENTIONS
(what TGfU teachers are trying to accomplish)

	Assessment Rationale	
I-1	Discover what learners can do and what they know	WHY
I-2	Help students understand their progress	
I-3	Assess learners' progress relative to their starting points for skill development (not just technique) and understanding game play	
I-4	Engage students in own learning	
I-5	Assess knowledge of tactical concepts in context (declarative & procedural)	WHAT
I-6	Assess skill development (not just technique development) – learners develop more practical options and refine these	
I-7	Observe individuals during game play and as they create games	WHEN
	Teacher Strategies	
I-8	Identify contexts that will stimulate what students need to learn	
I-9	Explore ways to engage with learners	
I-10	Clarify beliefs and test them against known research evidence	
I-11	Work with at least one other teacher - debates will clarify beliefs and provide some objectivity to B, I and A	
I-12	Assess whether approaches used result in intended outcomes - review this against beliefs	
I-13	Enable all students to develop the necessary skills required when fulfilling the role of referee, umpire, coach, player	

Figure 6. Benchmarks for Actions (Butler, 2012)

BENCHMARKS FOR ACTIONS
(how TGfU teachers teach)

	Preparation
A1	Plan ahead but with flexibility
A2	Design coherent units
A3	Prepare lessons based on what has gone before
A4	Plan stimulating learning points
A5	Be ready to move the lesson in a different direction, if it leads to important learning
	Management
A6	Consult with students
A7	Be firm (expect attention) but flexible
A8	Be prepared to change if things aren't going well
A9	Be inclusive, interactive, and democratic
A10	Let students set up games and equipment
A11	Ask questions and allow non verbal answers ('Show me how')
	Starting a TGfU lesson
A12	Observe students playing small sided games
A13	Start with modified games, generic games, invented games
A14	Keep explanations and rules to a minimum
A15	Emphasize play
A16	Check for safety and engagement
A17	Provide fun mental warm ups
A18	Use Q and A to connect this lesson with the last
A19	Use short video clip of play
	Continuing a TGfU lesson
A20	Play games that provide new challenges as well as reinforcing learning
A21	Work in small groups
A22	Ask learners to suggest next stages
A23	Highlight good practice from individuals and teams
A24	Conclude with competition between evenly matched teams / players

Figure 6. **Continued.**

	TGfU Teacher Behaviors
A25	Give positive feedback
A26	Be playful
A27	Ask effective questions
A28	Be patient and encouraging
A29	Work with individuals and small groups whilst others play the game
	• Skill development is rarely appropriate to the whole class
	• Take students out of the game to offer positive challenges ('Can you show me how to..?')
	• If skill interjection can be introduced within the game context, so much the better
A30	Try to improve (own practice)
A31	Consult (with colleagues)
	TGfU Teacher focus during a game
A32	Deciding when to interject to all or some, to prompt thought
A33	Tactics
A34	Observe if all players are involved
A35	Safety
	Teacher Expectations of students in a TGfU class
A36	Enthusiastic
A37	Gives high effort
A38	Involved: physically and mentally
A39	Interactive
A40	Makes progress and seeks to improve
A41	Smiles on faces – if time!
	Learning Environment
A42	Inclusive
A43	Busy, interactive and energetic
A44	Joyful
A45	Organized
A46	Spontaneous
A47	Safe, playful and reflective
A48	Facilities and equipment match ability

Conclusion

Clearly research, theory and practice need to be considered simultaneously, and remain in constant dialogue, each with the other. As Kirk and Tinning (1992) put it, the two need to '…refine and redefine each other in a continuous process of organic change (p. 4).' That said, ideas and beliefs are fundamental to the way we teach, and whether they are aware of it or not, all teachers operate from a framework of ideas and beliefs (including beliefs about the nature of knowledge) that Apostel (in Aerts et al., 1994) has called a 'worldview' or ontology that serves as a descriptive model or schema of the known world. A worldview is by nature interpretative, and we draw upon it constantly to evaluate, to act, and to put forward prognoses and visions of the future. Teachers draw upon such schemas as they make hundreds of quick decisions every day – acceding or denying requests, or deciding when to step in and when to let the game unfold. As I consider these findings, I conclude that both the TPI results and the statements made in the online survey indicate that Thorpe, Bunker and Almond do share certain pedagogical and ontological beliefs that were not clearly articulated in their early publications.

Firstly, all three founders belief that the focus of the successful TGfU teacher is upon the emergent understanding of learners. In this regard, their beliefs about teaching and learning reflect contemporary research. They believe that students learn as they work toward common goals and when they are engaged passionate and interactive, as do contemporary commentators working with complexity thinking and constraints led practices (Chow, Davids, Button, Shuttleworth, Renshaw, & Araujo, 2007). The focus of the successful TGfU teacher, they suggest, is upon the emergent understanding of learners rather than predictable outcomes or predetermined curriculum or lesson plans. Again, this view is similar to those expressed in current research, including my own, that argues for an ecological complexity worldview, incorporating dynamic systems theory (Butler et al., 2012; Davis et al., 2008).

Secondly, the benchmarks created from the founders' survey responses (listed in Figures 4, 5 and 6) are largely embedded in the developmental and nurturing perspectives. The founders' TPI results reflect their belief that successful TGfU teachers are more likely to focus on nurturing and developing than on transmitting content. These results are consistent with many teacher education programs, which have a learner-centered constructivist focus (Jarvis-Selinger, Collins, & Pratt, 2007). As a means of diagrammatic summary, this information has been synthesized into Figure 7, which represents beliefs, intentions, and actions shaped by a developmental perspective and on into Figure 8, which represents beliefs, intentions, and actions shaped by a nurturing perspective.

Figure 7. **Developmental Perspective in TGfU**

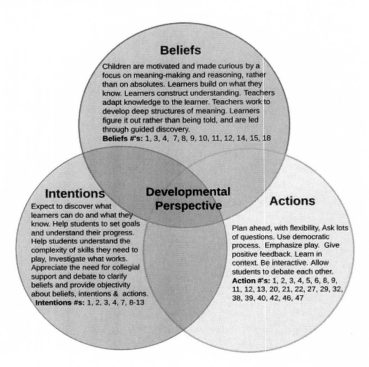

I hope and expect that these results will generate further discussion and analysis as well as being of practical help to researchers, teachers, and teacher educators who wish to consider what TGfU is and is not. I also hope to expand upon this research as I conduct similar studies with practicing GCA teachers in Canada and with GCA teachers and advocates across the world in order to consolidate and refine a comprehensive worldview that provides a philosophical home for effective practice. I do so in the belief that effective teaching practice cannot be separated from the beliefs and intentions that lie at its heart, even though these are not always easy to articulate. Teaching involves both the chicken and the egg, in that the ways we plan teach and assess reveals what we believe about knowledge and learning and what we believe about knowledge and learning inevitably influences what we offer our students in the way of learning experiences. It is thus important that teachers delve into their tacit knowledge and understanding of teaching and learning in order to identify their beliefs and intentions and to investigate their congruency with their pedagogical actions. As GCA approaches attract the interest of new prac-

Figure 8. Nurturing Perspective in TGfU

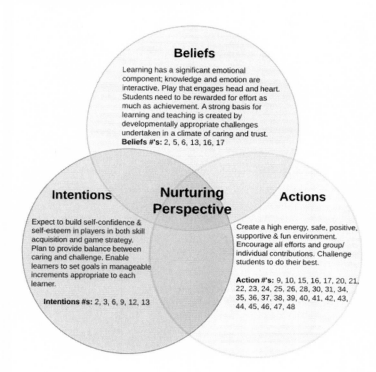

titioners (and practitioners who are looking for something new), it will be increasingly important to remember that teaching is a social cultural and relational activity as well as a set of plans practices and actions.

Acknowledgements

I would like to extend my sincere thanks to Len Almond, David Bunker and Rod Thorpe for their limitless sources of tacit knowledge, refinements of this manuscript and patience over the course of three years of this study. I would also like to acknowledge the helpful and expansive comments of two anonymous reviewers. My final thanks are for Claire Robson who provided inexhaustible and invaluable editorial assistance.

With permission from Ken Green, Editor: European Physical Education Review, May 6th 2015.

References

Aerts DL, Apostel B, De Moor S, Hellemans EM, H Van Belle and J Van Der Veken (1994) Worldviews: From Fragmentation to Integration. Brussels: VUB Press.

Almond L (1986) Asking teachers to research. In: Thorpe R, Bunker D and Almond L (eds) Rethinking Games Teaching. Loughborough UK: Department of Physical Education and Sport Sciences University of Technology, pp. 35 – 44.

Almond L (2010) Forward: Revisiting the TGfU brand. In: Butler J and Griffin L (eds) More Teaching Games for Understanding: Moving Globally. Champaign, IL: Human Kinetics, pp. vii-x.

Bhabha H K (1994) The Location of Culture. London: Routledge.

Bruner J (1966) Toward a Theory of Instruction. Cambridge, MA. Belknap Press of Harvard University.

Butler, J. (1993) Teacher change in sport education. Dissertation Abstracts International, 54 02A, (UMI No. 9318198).

Butler, J. Oslin, J. Mitchell, S. and Griffin, L. (2008) The way forward for TGfU: Filling the chasm between theory and practice. Physical & Health Education Journal, 74(2): 6-12.

Butler, J. (2012, July 14). Conceptualizing teaching games for understanding by revisiting foundations. Keynote presentation given at: International Conference (5th) of Teaching Games for Understanding, Loughborough University. UK.

Butler, J., Storey, B., Robson, C. (2012). Emergent learning focused teachers (ELF's) and their ecological complexity worldview. Sport, Education and Society, DOI:10.1080/13573322.2012.680435.

Bunker D and Thorpe R (1982) A model for teaching games in secondary schools. British Journal of Physical Education 13: 5-8.

Bunker, D., & Thorpe, R. (Eds.). (1983). Games teaching revisited [Special issue]. Bulletin of Physical Education, 19(1).

Capel S and Blair R (2013) Why do physical education teachers adopt a particular way of teaching? In: Capel S, Whitehead, M (eds) Debates in Physical Education. London and New York: Routledge, pp. 120-139.

Chen A Ennis C D and Loftus S (1997). Refining the value orientation inventory. Research Quarterly for Exercise and Sport, 68(4): 352-356.

Chow J Y Davids K Button C Shuttleworth R Renshaw I and Aruaujo D (2007) The role of nonlinear pedagogy in physical education. Review of Educational Research, 77(3): 251-278.

Collin H (2010) Tacit and Explicit Knowledge. Chicago: University of Chicago Press.

Collins J and D Pratt (2011) The teaching perspectives inventory at 10 years and 100 000 respondents: Reliability and validity of a teacher self-report inventory. Adult Education Quarterly 61(4): 358-375.

Grehaigne J and Godbout P (1997) Performance assessment in team sports. Journal of Teaching in Physical Education 16: 500–516.

Grehaigne J and Godbout P (1998) Formative assessment in team sports in a tactical approach context. Journal of Physical Education, Recreation & Dance 69(1): 46–51.

Grehaigne JF, Richard JF and Griffin L (2005) Teaching and Learning Team Sports and Games. New York, NY: RoutledgeFalmer.

Grehaigne JF; Richard JF and Griffin LL (2012) Teaching and Learning Team Sports and Games. New York: Routledge.

Griffin L, Mitchell S and Oslin J (1997) Teaching Sport Concepts and Skills: A Tactical Games Approach. Champaign IL: Human Kinetics.

Harvey S and Jarrett K (2013) A review of the game-centred approaches to teaching and coaching literature since 2006. Physical Education and Sport Pedagogy DOI: 10 1080/17408989 2012 754005.

Hubball H, Collin J and Pratt D (2005) Enhancing reflective teaching practices: Implication for faculty development programs. The Canadian Journal of Higher Education: 35(3): 57-81.

Jarvis-Selinger S, Collins JB and Pratt DD (2007) Do academic origins influence perspectives on teaching? Teacher Education Quarterly 67-81.

Jewett AE, Bain LL and Ennis CD (1995) The Curriculum Process in Physical Education. Dubuque IA: Brown and Benchmark.

Kirk, D and Tinning, R. (1992). Physical education pedagogical work as praxis. Paper presented at the annual meeting of the American Educational Research association, San Francisco, CA.

Launder A (2001) Play Practice: The Games Approach to Teaching and Coaching Sport. Adelaide: Human Kinetics.

Launder A & Piltz W (2013) Play practice: Engaging and Developing Skilled Players from Beginner to Elite. Champaign IL: Human Kinetics.

Light R (2013) Game Sense: Pedagogy for Performance Participation and Enjoyment. Routledge Studies in Physical Education and Youth Sport. Oxen Abingdon: Routledge.

Mesquita I, Farias C and Hastie P (2012) The impact of a hybrid sport-education-invasion games competence model soccer unit on students decision making skill execution and overall game performance, European Physical Education Review 18(2): 205-219.

Metzler M (2000) Instructional Models for Physical Education. Boston: Allyn and Bacon.

Mitchell S, Oslin J and Griffin L (2003) Sport Foundations for Elementary Physical Education. A Tactical Games Approach. Champaign, IL: Human Kinetics.

Mitchell S, Griffin L and Oslin J (2006) Teaching Sport Concepts and Skills: A Tactical Games Approach. Champaign, IL: Human Kinetics.

Mitchell S J Oslin and L Griffin (2013) Teaching Sport Concepts and Skills: A Tactical Games Approach for Ages 7 to 18 (3rd edn). Champaign, IL: Human Kinetics.

Oslin J and Mitchell S (2006) Game-Centred Approaches to Teaching Physical Education. In: Kirk D, MacDonald D and O'Sullivan M (eds) The Handbook of Physical Education. London: SAGE, pp. 627–651.

Parsaye K and Chignell M (1988) Expert Systems for Experts. Hoboken NJ: Wiley.

Penney D and Evans J (1995) Changing structures; Changing rules: The development of the 'internal market' School Organisation 15(1): 13-21.

Petrina S (2004) The politics of curriculum and instructional design/theory/form: critical problems, projects, units and modules Interchange 35(1), 81-126.

Piaget J (1997) The Child's Conception of the World: Selected Works. Abingdon, Oxen: Routledge.

Pinar W (2012) What is Curriculum Theory? New York: Routledge.

Polanyi M (1967) The Tacit Dimension. London: Routledge and Kegan Paul.

Penney D and Evans J (1995) Changing structures; changing rules: the development of the internal market. Social organization 15: 13-21.

Pratt DD and Associates (1998) Five Perspectives on Teaching in Adult and Higher Education. Malabar FL: Krieger Publishing Company.

Pratt DD, Collins JB and Jarvis-Selinger S (2001) Development and use of the teaching perspectives inventory (TPI). Presented at the annual meeting of the American Educational Research Association, Seattle, Washington, April.

Rossi T, Fry JM, McNeill M, Tan CWK (2006) The games concept approach (GCA) as a mandated practice: views of Singaporean teachers Sport Education and Society 12(1): 93-111.

Sparkes A (1991) The culture of teaching, critical reflection, and change: Possibilities and problems Educational Management Administration & Leadership 19(4): 4-19.

Stolz, S. A., & Pill, S. (2013) Teaching games and sport for understanding: Exploring and reconsidering its relevance in physical education. European Physical Education Review, Epub ahead of print 6 Aug, 2013. DOI: 10.1177/1356336X13496001

Tallir IB, Musch E, Lenoir M, et al. (2003) Assessment of game play in basketball. Paper presented at: The 2nd International TGfU Conference: Teaching Sport and Physical Education, Melbourne, University of Melbourne.

Tallir IB, Musch E, Valcke M, et al. (2005) Effects of two instructional approaches for basketball on decision making and recognition ability. International Journal of Sport Psychology 36: 107–126.

Tsoukas H (2003) Do we really understand tacit knowledge? In: Easterby-Smith M, and Lyles MA (eds) The Blackwell Handbook of Organizational Learning and Knowledge Management. Malden MA; Oxford: Blackwell, pp. 410–427.

Thorpe R and Bunker D (1986) Where are we now? A games education. In: Thorpe R, Bunker D and Almond L (eds) Rethinking Games Teaching. Loughborough UK: Department of Physical Education and Sport Sciences University of Technology, pp. 35 – 44.

Thorpe R (2005) Rod Thorpe on teaching games for understanding. In: Kidman L (ed), Athlete-Centred Coaching: Developing and Inspiring People. Christchurch, NZ: Innovative Print Communications Ltd, pp. 229–244.

Thorpe R and Bunker D (2010) Preface: In Butler J and Griffin L (eds) More Teaching Games for Understanding: Moving Globally. Champaign, IL: Human Kinetics, pp.vii-xv.

Vygotsky L S (1978) Mind in society: The Development of Higher Psychological Processes. Boston: Harvard University Press.

CHAPTER TWO

Enacting Change in a Secondary Physical Education Department

BY GEORGE KANAVOS & STEPHEN MCGINLEY

Introduction

Much of the past and current research surrounding enacting change and the successful implementation of curriculum and pedagogical innovations (CPIs) identifies that there are a number of barriers to overcome in the process (Hetherington & Underwood, 2010). Specialist PE teachers, such as Hetherington and Underwood, have examined the experiences of PE teachers surrounding the unsuccessful implementation of curricular and pedagogical change. With this in mind, the focus of this study will be to examine how to initiate effective pedagogical change using curriculum innovations such as Teaching Games for Understanding (TGfU), Sport Education (Sport Ed.), and Physical Literacy (PL).

These perceived barriers and their implications led to our research question: What are the experiences of secondary school teachers as they implement curricular and pedagogical innovations?

GOALS OF THE STUDY

The goals of our study were to:

1)   *address some of our own questions surrounding the successful curricular and pedagogical change in PE,*

2)   *to successfully implement CPIs, and*

3)   *to enact changes in a PE department.*

Based on our goals, we identified the following five major themes: curricular and pedagogical innovations; cultural change; leadership and support; relationships and collaboration, and barriers to enacting change in a PE department through the successful implementation of CPIs as encountered by our colleagues. Using these themes, we provided indicators of change that each teacher displayed when they were moving through the implementation of curricular and pedagogical change in their respective PE departments. This allowed us to identify what is required for change to occur in a secondary PE department and how to overcome barriers to change. We believe that these themes and indicators are the key to successful change in a PE department.

Our study also has implications for the entire PE profession in that it identifies reasons why change is difficult to implement in PE. These insights have led to recommendations for the successful implementation of CPIs through a step-by-step process of stages and phases for teachers to reference and follow, collectively and collaboratively, along their journey to improvement. Such suggestions will aid teachers professionally and encourage students to take ownership of their learning and to be more engaged in the PE classroom. The implications of our project will help with the adjustment of successful PE implementation for the 21st century and for PE teachers to align good practice with clearly identified philosophy and goals for PE.

COLLABORATIVE TEACHER INQUIRY (CTI)

Collaborative Teacher Inquiry (CTI) is the methodology that was used to investigate the experiences of teachers implementing curricular and pedagogical change in a physical education department. This process is also known as Action Research (AR) with the participants engaged to plan, implement action, observe, and reflect on enacting change in the PE department. We adopted this cyclical perspective for our research and concentrated on its three main stages: focus and planning; implementation; and reflecting and evaluating. This cycle involved several stages of collaboration, which aided in a wide variety of support networks amongst participants and from the department head and the administration team.

SETTING

Research was conducted within a physical education department at a secondary school in British Columbia, Canada. In order to maintain confidentiality in the study, the pseudonym Game School (GS) will be used. Currently, GS has approximately 600 students enrolled in Grades 8 to 12. GS is organized in a linear timetable with a total of eight classes on a four-block rotation in a day-one and a day-two format.

Classes are 70 minutes in length and on average students in grades eight to 10 take mandatory physical education two to three times per week. In addition, there are two PE 11 and two PE 12 courses offered at the school every year as elective courses. All PE classes at GS are co-ed. PE classes are currently organized into 10 units, with each unit comprised of seven to eight classes.

CO-RESEARCHERS AND PARTICIPANTS

The two main co-researchers and active participants in the study were Steve and George. Steve was head of the physical education department and an employee at GS in his eighth year of teaching. Steve was also very active in the athletics program and coaching at GS.

George, while a non-employee of GS, participated in the study in his role as a critical friend. George has been a counsellor for 15 years, a vice principal for three years and special education and summer school teacher. George's role at GS was unique in the sense that he was able to inform and provide valuable feedback to the Collaborative Teacher Inquiry (CTI) community. He was also able to provide a neutral element and bring fresh perspectives to the table. George's role as a co-researcher also overlapped into consultant and counsellor, focusing on how the participants felt and acted during the study and offering insights into how students benefit from a constructivist perspective. Due to his years of counselling in the school environment, working with students and adults in stressful situations, George was able to offer support to teachers during some trying times as they wrestled with the implementation of curricular and pedagogical innovations. The co-researchers, George and Steve, guided and led the participants through the CTI process, provided information on instructional strategies and feedback that helped to successfully introduce and implement new curriculum and pedagogical innovations at GS.

Participants

As part of a collaborative teacher inquiry, all teachers in the PE department at GS were given the opportunity to participate in the study. The secondary physical education department consisted of six physical education teachers who vary in years of teaching experience from one year to over thirty years of teaching PE.

CTI IMPLEMENTATION PLAN OF CPIs:
Phase One - Creating the Environment

1.1 PLANNING

During phase one of our research we set out to create a nurturing and supportive environment in which to establish and explore common ground for our participants. We began stage one by interviewing the principal of GS regarding her input and opinions about the suggested curriculum and pedagogical innovations (CPIs) that we planned to introduce to the PE department and how we hoped to enact sustainable change in the PE department. Our research coincided with a school growth plan being implemented by the principal for the entire GS. The principal was very receptive to our Collaborative Teacher Inquiry (CTI) plan. The changes called for by the school growth plan were compatible with the CTIs we proposed. We began with an earnest discussion within the department, comparing PE of the past and PE innovations of the present.

1.2 IMPLEMENTATION

The department action plan was set in motion in the second stage of "Implementation" during Phase One. The CPIs shared by the researchers were embraced by the department, and department members contributed to healthy discussions about them. The development of the PE department growth plan included the input of all the department members. As a result, our teachers were invested in CTIs and took an interest in implementing PE department growth plans through PE yearly plans, units, and lessons.

1.3 REFLECTION AND EVALUATION

We began meeting regularly to reflect and evaluate progress through discussion. These discussions were recorded. We also incorporated regular discussions with our supervisor, Dr. Butler for continued reflection and guidance. These discussions allowed us to delineate clear phases and stages in our research study.

Phase Two - Building the Foundation

Stage one set the stage so that we too would grow and progress with the development and evolution of our study. To implement the curricular and pedagogical innovations, the phases of our plan had to be flexible. Adaptation and evolution were critical for successful implementation of our plan.

2.1 PLANNING

We began with an introduction to the curricular and pedagogical innovations in question. To help students improve Physical Literacy in the PE department, we initially began with the goal of implementing TGfU above the other innovations. However, during the initial phases we opened up more and more to each other during department meetings, we found that teachers were drawn away from TGfU. The safe environments that we had created in Phase One and continued to foster allowed for ideas to be shared. This further allowed the participants to evolve and develop their professional practices independently with support and guidance along the way from the co-researchers and from colleagues in the PE department. This set the stage for the "implementation" of the plan in Phase Two.

2.2 IMPLEMENTATION

At the next department meeting, teachers were invited to rank a list of PE philosophy statements. This helped to articulate many of the individual feelings and thoughts of the participating teachers with regard to PE. As they discussed the ideas they felt safe to express themselves on philosophy and their thoughts on the introduced CPIs.

As a result, we planned our first "temperature check" questionnaire. The teacher participants were given a questionnaire where they responded to various questions privately. The results revealed to us the energy and intent of the department. We saw that the innovations would be taken seriously, but we still needed to put into practice the positive affirmations that were made publicly to the department.

2.3 REFLECTION AND EVALUATION

The teachers reflected on and reported their findings and experiences back to the department at the next department meeting via verbal discussions and written temperature check questionnaires.

Phase Three - Lesson Plan Development & Implementation with Support

The third phase of the study focused on the development of CPIs through lesson planning. This was done individually or in pairs, as teachers chose, and with support on hand from Steve and George.

3.1 PLANNING

Lesson planning: Teachers, individually or in collaboration with other department members, planned their trial lessons.

3.2 IMPLEMENTATION

Teachers trialled their lesson plan(s) with continued support of the department members involved in the study.

3.3 REFLECTION AND EVALUATION

Teachers reflected and reported findings back to the department after implementing curricular and pedagogical innovation lesson(s). Revealing and rich discussions emerged from the findings. Teachers were encouraged to provide further data contributions through online blog contributions and a second temperature check questionnaire.

Phase Four - PE Release Time Workshop

Phase Four centered on the PE workshop planned at the school for the entire department, with the support of the administration through approved release time to participate in the workshop and develop the CPIs. The purpose of the PE workshop was to give the teachers a hands-on practical session with the CPIs and a knowledgeable guest speaker. The teachers were also able to have a discussion about the CPIs in a debriefing session at the conclusion of the workshop with the guest speaker. This proved to be an excellent source of data.

4.1 PLANNING

The planning stage focused on the workshop day. Steve secured PE release time from the administration so that the teachers would not have to invest coaching, preparation and marking time to receive the training for the CPIs.

4.2 IMPLEMENTATION

The workshop day began with a temperature check of previous CPI implementations and expectations for the workshop. We followed this up by revisiting the school and PE department goals and school growth plans to gently remind the teacher participants of the goals set out for the department by the School Board.

Overview of the gym session by guest speaker Professor Joanna Sheppard from the University of Fraser Valley: Joanna gave an opening lesson on the Sport Ed. unit infused with TGfU and Personal and Social Responsibility (PSR) curriculum and pedagogical innovations. This was immediately followed by a practical gym session of the lesson conducted by one of the teacher participants and Professor Sheppard in a grade 8 PE class (28 students). The first lesson of the invasion games unit was basketball and used curricular and pedagogical innovations.

The workshop debrief focused on the practical session with an emphasis on reflection and feedback. We followed by redistributing the CPI information and resources. We intended to keep the support there to implement the CPIs, which would make lasting change possible.

The action plan focused on the teacher participants implementing new CPIs in an upcoming unit for their classes. Teachers were encouraged to collaborate with other PE department teachers or teachers sharing the same teaching block.

4.3 REFLECTION AND EVALUATION

Teacher participants reflected on whole unit implementation of curricular and pedagogical innovations as presented by Professor Sheppard and how the Sport Education model, or CTI of their choice, can lead to effective change in their practices. We followed up by reporting back in group discussions and peer conversations.

Phase Five - Unit Plan Development & Implementation with Support

Phase Five focused on unit plan development and implementation with support from all the teacher participants.

5.1 PLANNING

The intention was to have teacher participants, individually or in collaboration with other department members, set out their unit plan with CPIs.

5.2 IMPLEMENTATION

To implement this stage, the teacher participants tested their created unit plans by carrying them out with the support of all participants. The action plan was organized and planned by the participants and it helped that implementation was carried out with collegial cooperation.

5.3 REFLECTION AND EVALUATION

After the units were planned and carried out by the teacher participants, they reflected and reported findings back to the department. The CPIs were then evaluated by the teacher participants in department discussions and followed by written responses in the temperature check #4 questionnaires.

Phase Six - Developing a Collective PE Department Philosophy & Mission Statement

Phase Six of the study revealed the shared perceptions and interpretations of CPIs within the PE department. We revisited an old philosophy statement, reflected and made any necessary changes, and began to develop a new collective PE department philosophy and mission statement that reflected current practices.

6.1 PLANNING

The teacher participants start planning and developing a PE department philosophy and mission statement for the department. They may plan to develop a workshop on the PE philosophy and mission statement to present to other PE departments who are interested in enacting similar change.

6.2 IMPLEMENTATION

Implementation of this stage began with the teacher participants discussing the topic – essentially a verbal version of the temperature check. This is followed with a revision of the school growth plan and PE department goals. As in the initial phases, the teacher participants will once again rank, reflect, and discuss their personal philosophies of physical education. This will help to establish an atmosphere that will enable participants to collaboratively create a PE department philosophy. The collective PE philosophy will direct the creation of a mission statement for the PE department. The long run intent of the action plan is for the teacher participants in the PE department to continually implement individual and collaborative CPIs. As a result, the PE department will be receptive to new curricular and pedagogical innovations in the future.

6.3 REFLECTION AND EVALUATION

It is the teacher participants' professional duty to constantly reflect and evaluate their own practice for the betterment of the students.

Results & Discussion of the Five Major Research Themes

We received responses from most of our participants in the PE department in the form of questionnaires, blogs, interviews, and temperature checks. These themes were revealed as a result of coding all the data sources, the details of which can be found in Figure 1 and summarized in Figure 2.

Figure 1. **Major Research Themes.**

Figure 2. **Summary of Major Research Themes.**

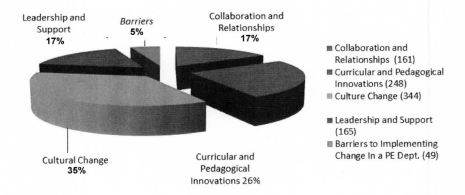

Figure 3. **Collaboration and Relationship Data Summary.**

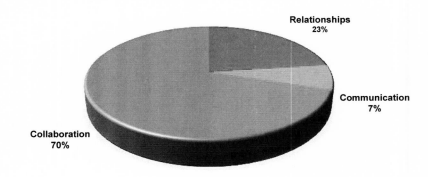

THEME ONE: COLLABORATION AND RELATIONSHIPS

Collaboration and relationship building was a significant key to curriculum and pedagogical innovation implementation. Collaboration, communication and relationships were all referred to by the teachers as the building blocks that constructed the connections and partnerships. Each successful teacher who implemented change repeatedly listed collaboration as important.

All the teacher participants needed collaboration to successfully implement the CPIs. The initial weeks and months of the study revealed department members that had been provided support and leadership to apply new instructional strategies but were still reluctant to collaborate with each other. The collaborative PE workshop was the turning point where teachers began their process of collaborating with each other to implement changes.

We immersed ourselves in this living change through collaboration with specialized PE teachers. We began by creating a common ground that the entire PE department identified with, leading them to feel safe and attached to part of a greater whole. This was achieved by effective communication, which led to the creation and establishment of PE department growth plan goals and a discussion surrounding our philosophy of physical education. This creation of a common ground amongst our teachers created a solid foundation for emergent change to occur, and all members of the department heard each member's voice. This framework encouraged cultural change that made this PE department relevant in the 21st century and consistent with the new BC PE curriculum that is currently being drafted and implemented in 2015.

The theme of collaboration and relationships revealed itself time and time again in the data. Had the leadership and support not been present, the communication between department members would not have developed as quickly, which in turn would not have nurtured the relationships built. We believe that, as a result, the collaboration would not have taken place. The CPIs were successful because the changes were not imposed from the top down. They worked due to the interaction of all the parties and because all parties were invested in the changes. As a result of the strong relationship building and collaborative discussions, a new PE department vision, mission and philosophy statement was developed.

THEME TWO: LEADERSHIP AND SUPPORT

The research data showed that the leadership (Figure 4) differed from the conventional perception of leadership as being hierarchical in nature where commands are top-down. Through years of observations and immersion in the British Columbia education system, George and Steve observed a clear connection between this type of leadership and perpetual failure of goals and initiatives. George and Steve have observed and experienced that this hierarchical leadership style has failed to cultivate a collaborative environment; and with an absence of a culture change, the initiatives also failed. At GS, we aimed to avoid a top-down hierarchical command system. George's previous experience as a vice-principal and department head in counselling made him privy to very sensitive issues at schools where leaders failed to lead, as they mistakenly viewed culture change as obedience.

Figure 4. **Leadership and Support Data Summary.**

LEADERSHIP

As a young department head, and one of the principal researchers, Steve provided leadership that was well-planned and instilled with vision and purpose. The culture change he sought was not blind obedience by teachers. Feedback by the department members provided some of our most valuable data on the theme of leadership. When asked in the exit interviews, "what were the greatest factors that contributed to change occurring in your teaching practice?" the answers repeatedly referred to the leadership and support the department received. Oscar responded that, information and resources were provided by the department head at meetings, and there was a clear connection between the theory and practice of delivering PE with the implementation of new instructional strategies. He continued by stating "it wasn't just lip service" and that "resources were provided to support and enable change to happen" (Oscar, exit interview/questionnaire, May 2, 2014).

RESOURCES

A subheading that appeared within this theme was the need for resources to be readily available to successfully implement CPIs into the teacher's toolbox. The resources that the teachers referred to the most were time and space.

SUPPORT

Our data revealed that all the teachers who were successful in implementing CPIs made repeated references to leadership and support from the department head. Oscar and Charlie made references to a safe environment that was created by the department head. The leadership and support led to a culture change that encouraged healthy risks to be taken that improved teachers professionally and therefore directly benefitted the students. However, the leadership provided isn't necessarily enough to enact successful change. Irene and Eric were still struggling with a cognitive dissonance with the changes they needed to make to adopt CPIs. This was when our collaborative workshop was introduced in late November to provide support for those teachers who were struggling with the confidence and competence to implement the CPIs.

PE WORKSHOP

The data from the collaborative PE workshop indicated that this was one of the most supportive and successful initiatives the department head showed as a leader. Furthermore, Steve lobbied for administrative support for the workshop and the principal agreed to provide release time to all the PE department teachers for a half-day collaborative workshop. According to our data, this workshop is where Charlie's transformation took place as he worked with Dr. Sheppard (guest speaker) in his PE 8 class and collaboratively taught a hybrid model using a combination of Sports Ed., PSR, and TGfU models in a basketball lesson. This collaborative effort by Dr. Sheppard and Charlie influenced Irene and Eric as they used the workshop to learn the "how to" and also bought into the cultural shift the leadership provided. Ultimately they decided to collaborate on an upcoming Tchoukball Sport Ed. unit.

The leadership nurtured a cultural shift to collaborate, but it did not reach everyone. Julie attended the workshop but appeared distant at times and her body language showed that she did not particularly want to participate nor did she want to collaborate. Later in the workshop, during the debrief session with Dr. Sheppard, Julie left the collaborative workshop to help set up a school assembly. Although we agreed that the assembly was important to the school, this action indicated to us that she did not view the workshop as important. Julie's actions might have undermined the goals of the day, yet, in the end, the only member of the department who did not successfully change was Julie. The other department members all contributed feedback and pointed to the significant importance of the workshop.

THEME THREE: CURRICULAR AND PEDAGOGICAL INNOVATIONS (CPIs)

Initially, we anticipated that the teachers would gravitate towards TGfU as the CPI of choice. The teachers used their knowledge of TGfU to reflect on their current teaching practices. However, our findings revealed that TGfU was not the primary model of choice to begin the change in their teaching practices (Figure 5). They discovered that there were many other innovations available to them, which offered them choice and comfort. The data revealed that all members of the department demonstrated a specific

Figure 5. **Curricular and Pedagogical Innovations (CPI's) Data Summary.**

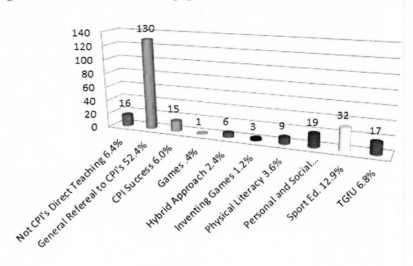

pattern to initiate change in their teaching. The pattern revealed that the CPI of choice was the Sport Ed. model which also served as a platform from which to develop their teaching and implement other CPIs.

SPORT ED. MODEL

We found in our data that the teachers' gravitation towards the Sport Ed. model was due to it being more palatable to teachers. They viewed it as an easier transition from their previous practice of direct teacher-centered methods. One area that was cited revealed that it was "easy to implement due to the fact that the teachers were still in control of the overall direction of the class as they facilitated the various roles of the team members" (Oscar, blog/questionnaire, Dec 5, 2013). Eventually the students assumed more responsibility of their roles, which contributed to the transition to a more student-centered approach. It also made the teacher workload lighter and less stressful, and as the unit developed, the students took more control of the direction of the class and their own learning.

Our research data indicated another pattern that emerged, as the teachers became more "confident and comfortable with the CPIs they began to use a hybrid approach that incorporated various strategies from TGfU, PL, IG, and PSR models throughout the unit and within each lesson" (McGinley, 2014).

Figure 6. **Cultural Change Data Summary.**

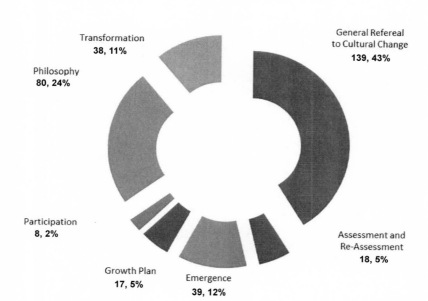

Transformation
38, 11%

Philosophy
80, 24%

General Refereal
to Cultural Change
139, 43%

Participation
8, 2%

Assessment and
Re-Assessment
18, 5%

Growth Plan
17, 5%

Emergence
39, 12%

Overall, the Sport Ed. model was the CPI of choice and was used as a vehicle to transform change in classroom practice and the curriculum, moving ulti-mately from direct teaching methods to more student-centered approaches.

THEME FOUR: CULTURAL CHANGE

Cultural change was overall the strongest theme that came out in teachers implementing CPIs into their teaching practices. The data revealed that this theme of cultural change was the crux for the success of teachers' transforma-tion as they all stated this at various points of the study and it is evident in the final data numbers.

GENERAL REFERRAL TO CULTURAL CHANGE

The PE department clearly realized that in addition to making structural changes, it was paramount that be complete buy in by teachers to change the culture of the PE department. This was the most important factor to imple-ment and sustain longer-term cultural changes (Figure 6). As Schlechty stated, "structural change that is not supported by cultural change will eventually be overwhelmed by the culture, for it is in the culture that any organization finds meaning and stability" (Schlechty, 2001, p. 52). Teachers revealed in the data that to overcome barriers in implementing change, the structural changes needed to include: more time, flexibility in the schedule, and more facility space. These were barriers that impeded successful change. Each of the teachers was able to overcome these barriers as they were committed to cultural change and this in turn helped them to overcome barriers to structural change. Irene and Eric were able to combine their PE classes so they had twice the facilities to use. They also combined two units together, a total of sixteen classes, to successfully implement the Sport Ed. model as it was stated that for the successful implementation of this model, more time was needed and more flexibility required in the schedule. Irene and Eric demonstrated that the structural changes that took place were successful because they were supported and were part of the bigger cultural change.

Oscar quotes Dr. Muhammad in his exit interview, "it starts with cultural change for people to change. Cultural change will eat structural change for breakfast" (Oscar, Exit interview, May 2, 2014). Our data revealed that all the teachers that were successful in implementing CPIs mentioned that cultural change was a key component to the overall change that was occurring in their own practices and within the PE department as a whole. The PE workshop was mentioned by all the participants as the real turning point for personal and PE department cultural change. The PE workshop demonstrated leadership and support by the department head and administration; collaboration and relationship building were occurring and the curricular and pedagogical innovations implementation followed in their PE classes. Furthermore, the department's commitment to reflect on the current state of the PE department at GS and to develop new PE mission, vision, and philosophy statements will go a long way to achieve a cultural change that can sustain itself for years to come.

INTERDEPENDENCY OF THEMES TO CREATE CULTURAL CHANGE

The theme of cultural change overlapped with all the other themes of: leadership and support; collaboration and relationships, barriers to enacting change in a PE department; and curricular and pedagogical innovation. They are all interdependent on one other. Firstly, cultural change was established when there was strong leadership and support from the PE department head, the administration and from teachers within the PE department. This is supported by Oscar stating "that there was an acceptance of change from the administration and leadership team" (Oscar, Exit interview/questionnaire, May 2, 2014). Secondly, this strong leadership and support provided the building blocks for the nurturing of relationships amongst all the educators. This fostered a cohesive and constructive cycle of successful collaboration that ended in successful cultural change. Eric supported this effort by stating some of the greatest factors that contributed to change occurring in the PE department were that there was an "acceptance among teachers to change with a clear focus and a plan in place to make changes and this was successful by the collaboration of the department" (Eric, Exit interview/questionnaire, May 2, 2014). Finally, once the leadership and supports were in place, the relationships and collaboration developed and grew, and the curricular and pedagogical innovations were implemented successfully by overcoming the barriers to change in a PE department. "George and Steve were able to use their knowledge and expertise from their Master's program, move the entire department through change and to showcase the department as a leader in PE throughout the school board and district" (Charlie, Exit interview/questionnaire, May 2, 2014). As the study developed, it became apparent that these themes were like an ecosystem. All the themes were interdependent and were responsible to each other for the successful implementation of new instructional strategies. If one theme failed, the rest would fail and therefore the changes would not be successful. This interdependence was the common ground for cultural change to occur.

THEME FIVE: BARRIERS TO ENACTING CHANGE IN A PE DEPARTMENT

With change there are always going to be barriers that make progress challenging. Teachers in our study mention that CPI challenges, space, and time are all barriers to implementing change (Figure 7).

Figure 7. **Barriers to Enacting Change and Implementing CPIs.**

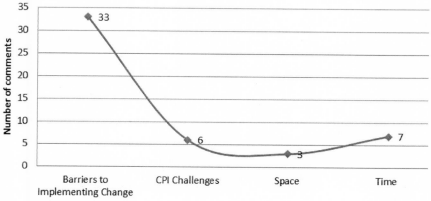

GENERAL REFERRAL TO IMPLEMENTING CHANGE

Most often when teachers referred to any of the barriers, they included the general concept of barriers to implementing change.

SPACE

The lack of space and facilities at Games School presented itself as a challenge to the teachers. Eric was concerned with the amount of space in terms of facilities and the consistency of space was an issue to implementing CPIs because it limited what he was able to achieve when facilities were not available. To help alleviate this problem and others, Eric and Irene combined classes to utilize and share all the facilities during the same time period when conducting a combined Grade 8 and Grade 9 tchoukball unit using the Sport Education model.

CPI CHALLENGES

Implementing CPIs into the PE classroom comes with various challenges. At the early stages of the study there is a "huge learning curve for the both the students and the teachers when implementing CPIs" (Oscar, Exit interview/questionnaire, May 2, 2014). "Some classroom dynamics makes it difficult to implement some CPIs as some classes are not ready to try riskier models. More student responsibility is required in the Sport Ed. Model" (Charlie, Exit interview/questionnaire, May 2, 2014). Charlie continued by revealing that the teachers themselves shared in the responsibility of the challenges they faced. He indicated that "ignorance by some teachers, the lack of awareness and knowledge of the various CPIs, and the personal reluctance to change for some teachers" (Charlie, Exit interview/questionnaire, May 2, 2014) contributed to the barriers of implementing change.

TIME

The lack of time to implement change was a recurring concern, referred to directly and indirectly, to many of the teachers during our study. Steve and George overcame this by providing collaboration time, a PE workshop, and ongoing active support to successfully implement CPIs. Irene acknowledged that this support of time was provided. She stated "that there was time given, but there was still a lack of time" (Irene, Exit interview/questionnaire, May 2, 2014).

Conclusion & Recommendations

BARRIERS TO IMPLEMENTING CHANGE

Our first four themes are very positive in nature and contributed to making successful curricular and pedagogical implementations in the GS PE department. However, another theme that our research revealed revolved around the barriers to change. The teacher participants exposed their concerns to risk change due to the learning curve required by teachers and students alike to implement CPIs successfully. Furthermore, the limited resources of time and space made for challenges to apply CPIs. The teachers acknowledged time was given, and appreciated it; but they reported that more time was necessary. Limited space at GS also caused a barrier to implementing change. The facilities were too limited to deliver the CPIs in a manner they felt comfortable with. As a result, teachers combined classes as it allowed them to share limited space.

PHYSICAL LITERACY

Physical Literacy was the ultimate goal in our study for all our students. We introduced the concept of PL and began to develop it in the PE setting at GS. We did this by introducing, and helping to implement, TGfU and other innovations. We anticipated an increased level of PL with students immediately in the study and anticipate an increase over the long term. We foresee these changes also benefiting society as a whole because the transformations of the students today will positively affect the economy in future years. We anticipate a healthier population of students if CPIs are implemented across Canada. A predominantly healthy population can potentially save taxpayers billions of dollars in health care costs.

SIGNIFICANCE AND CONTRIBUTIONS

This research is significant because it has provided us with a better understanding of the successful implementation of CPIs in a PE department and of overall positive cultural change. As stated above, our study has identified the five major themes of successful change. It is also important to state here that our teachers, with the exception of one, have changed to some degree. An important impact our study has to offer centres on the fact that there are very few studies about departmental change. Therefore we hope that our research will pave the way for other departments to take on wholesale change. The results of our study will contribute to the growing amount of research aimed at implementing successful and sustainable changes in PE by overcoming barriers and embracing cultural change. With a clearer understanding of cultural change, future researchers may be able to share more success stories and their strategies to implement change in PE.

STRENGTHS TO OUR RESEARCH

Strengths of our research revealed that when changes were implemented in the PE department it fostered an environment of camaraderie and inclusion, which had previously been lacking. In the end we found that we could not force teachers to change. Successful change in a PE department could only be achieved through support, positive leadership, and providing support and encouragement for teachers as they worked to change their teaching practices. We felt that our teachers' responses were honest in nature when they personally reflected on their journey and shared their responses with us. We were able to approach our research question through the experiences of our teachers and construct new knowledge through this relationship. We validated our teachers' contributions as much as our own knowledge and therefore were able to create a higher level of knowledge of change collectively as a department. As the department changed, the students also significantly benefited from the new CPIs. Oscar stated that the CPIs were "a huge benefit to the students" (Oscar, Temperature check #1, October 18, 2013). "…students did increase accountability and ownership…" (Oscar, Blog/questionnaire, Dec 5, 2013). Furthermore, our relationship building and support of working relationships was the key to the success of every teacher in the department. Teachers declared that they felt safe as they collaborated and offered their insights and struggles to the rest of the collective group.

LIMITATIONS TO OUR RESEARCH

As with many studies where the accuracy of the personal experiences and information is paramount in collecting rich data, ours depended on the truthfulness of our teachers' accounts, our field notes, and our interpretation of this data. Another limitation is the fact that we only studied one school in this research and potentially the findings may not compare with other PE departments. Time may also prove a limitation as our research in the study only took place over a span of several months.

POSSIBLE FUTURE RESEARCH DIRECTIONS, RECOMMENDATIONS

The implications of our project can potentially help with the successful implementation of CPIs for 21st century learners. Our findings have the potential to inform PE teachers, administrators, student teachers looking to enact curricular and pedagogical change.

There are a number of recommendations we advocate to foster successful change in teaching approach and the implementation of CPIs in physical education.

Teachers need more of a sound understanding and knowledge of the curriculum and pedagogical innovations models. This can be achieved through: 1) CPIs being placed into teacher education preparation programs for teacher candidates to be exposed to and sample in their practicum schools (Petrie,

2007) CPIs being placed in professional development program days to maximize chances of improved performance and change within teachers (Patton & Griffin, 2008b).

Teachers need to be supported in their efforts through a collaborative investigation, and to receive backing from colleagues with expertise in curricular and pedagogical innovations. Confidence to persist in efforts to change will prevent teachers returning to prior practice.

PE is in danger of losing significance in the 21st century as it has retained outdated practices by many of its practitioners (Penney & Chandler, 2000). Our engagement of CPIs in the PE department at GS was aimed at making change from skill testing, or as Kirk accurately coined "physical education-as-sport-techniques" (Kirk, 2012) to CPIs that look at developing the whole student into one who cultivates their physical literacy. We believe that the CPIs, once introduced, will bring the relevance back to the skills in a games context and the social, emotional and physical benefits of Physical Literacy will be made clear to a generation of learners in a PE setting.

Conclusion

In conclusion, we feel that for sustainable change to occur, educational leaders must collaboratively enact change following the cyclical collaborative teacher inquiry's three main stages of: focus and planning; implementation; and reflecting and evaluating. This cycle involves several stages of collaboration, which also aids in a wide variety of support networks. We have drawn up a list of change indicators in Table 2, which summarize indicators to recognize that a teacher is going through the various stages of change.

Table 2

Stage indicators of CPI change.

STAGE 1 - BEGINNING AND ATTEMPTING	
1-1	Discovered knowledge and gathered resources of new CPIs
1-2	Exposed to new instructional strategies
1-3	Attempted to implement CPIs into lesson plans
1-4	Accepted that change was necessary and reflected on personal PE philosophy
1-5	Attended professional development workshop on new CPIs
1-6	Teachers invested in planning lessons and unit planning
1-7	Teachers asked questions and struggled with CPIs
1-8	Articulated and discussed philosophies of PE and implemented them
1-9	Support received by teachers and department head
1-10	Time allocated to develop CPI lesson plans
1-11	Identified and anticipated barriers and attempted to overcome
1-12	Collaborated with teachers in the department

STAGE 2 - EMERGING AND LEARNING	
2-1	Emerged knowledge of CPIs
2-2	Confident to try CPI while learning them.
2-3	Attempted to implement CPIs into unit plans
2-4	Identified barriers into CPIs and attempted to overcome them
2-5	Relationships emerged between department members
2-6	Collaboration increased between department members.
2-7	Resources between department members shared more readily
2-8	Felt safe to attempt CPIs in class
2-9	Attended PE workshop on CPIs
2-10	Teachers felt supported and not scared to fail if CPIs were not successful
2-11	Continued support received by teachers and department head
2-12	Time given to develop CPI unit plans

Table 2

Continued.

STAGE 3 - TRANSFORMING	
3-1	Transformed knowledge of CPIs
3-2	Continued reflection and re-implementation of unit
3-3	Collaborated with department members on implementing new unit
3-4	Educated other teachers on CPIs
3-5	Developed new personal/departmental PE philosophy
3-6	Teachers felt confident and competent with CPIs
3-7	Continual support received by teachers and department head
3-8	Time given to develop, reflect and redevelop CPI unit plans
3-9	Barriers were overcome prior to unit beginning
3-10	Continued collaboration with teachers in the department

References

Hetherington, K. & Underwood, S. (2010). Is TGfU for you? A study to determine the barriers of implementing TGfU. (Masters graduating paper, University of British Columbia)

Patton, K., & Griffin, L.L. (2008). Experiences and patterns of change in a physical education teacher development project. *Journal of teaching in Physical Education,* 27 (3), 272-291.

Penney, D., & Chandler, T. (2000). Physical education : What future (s)? *Sport, Education and Society*, 5 (1), 71-87.

Petrie, K. (2007) Physical education in primary schools: Holding onto the past or heading for a different future? Retrieved from http://www.educaitoncounts. govt.nz/publications/schooling/25294/25331. 67-80.

Schlechty, P. C. (2001). *Shaking up the schoolhouse.* San Francisco: Jossey-Bass.

CHAPTER THREE

Chinese Teenage Males' Experiences in Physical Activity Settings

BY CHARMAINE LUM

Introduction

1.1. AN AUTOETHNOGRAPHY: THE ROOT OF MY INTENTIONS

For most of my life, I lived in Richmond, B.C., a multicultural city with a dominant Chinese population that continues to rise. Since I was nine, I have been highly involved in recreational and high school sports, and competitive softball as a player and coach across the Lower Mainland in B.C. Throughout these experiences, I have always noticed an absence of Chinese female athletes in community and high school-based sports programs and wondered why this was the case. Of the few Chinese female participants I encountered, rarely did they play at the senior high school level and there were even fewer who played softball. Being involved in sports has provided me with an immense amount of joy and an extensive list of incredible life opportunities. Why were Chinese females not present in these physical activity environments?

As I was working towards my Physical Education degree at the University of British Columbia, I began to spend more time listening to my Chinese (immigrant and Canadian-born) friends', cousins' and players' experiences. Many of them claimed that their parents were not supportive of them pursuing sport, especially at a higher level, because it would interfere with their academics. Some explained that their parents felt that sports were too dangerous and feared that they would be injured. Their responses prompted me to reflect on my personal journey and the factors that shaped my experiences. In addition to timely opportunities and encouraging mentors, I concluded my parents and their personal perspectives on sports and academics were the main influencers on shaping who I am today. Although they were both encouraging and committed to helping me pursue my passion in sports, there were moments in time where my parents disagreed on where sports should be prioritized amongst my academic responsibilities and other extracurricular activities (piano lessons, Chinese school classes, and Kumon math). At the age of 11, my father immigrated to Canada and completed his schooling in East Vancouver and eventually at Simon Fraser University. He played high school and recreational sports and was the one who would give me permission to skip Chinese classes for softball tournaments and coached my teams. My mom, on the other hand, completed her education in Hong Kong and never participated in physical activity outside of her PE classes. In the early years, she was not as supportive of my athletic endeavors as she feared it would interfere with my academics. However, over time she realized that my involvement with sport provided me with numerous opportunities and in fact, instilled a work ethic that benefited my education. With these realizations, I became motivated to learn more about the experiences of Chinese students in my community and whether their level of involvement with physical activity and sport are influenced by Chinese culture or their parents' perspectives. These feelings were further amplified when I began teaching elementary PE four years ago and had the privilege of gaining more insight on students' perspectives towards physical activity and sport.

1.2. THE ISSUES

With the recent influx of immigrants from Hong Kong and Mainland China in Richmond, B.C. (City of Richmond, 2011), there has been a noticeable shift in the dynamics in school and community sports in the Lower Mainland region. The two teachers involved in the study reported that schools in Richmond that used to boast successful sports programs are now struggling to form teams and community sports are noting fewer registrants, particularly amongst the Chinese population (AD, personal communication, March 4, 2014; Mr. Teach, personal communication, March 4, 2014). These teachers claim the lack of participation in extra-curricular sports is evident through the Chinese students' absence of fundamental skills and knowledge of games strategies in sports covered in the high school PE curriculum (Mr. Teach, March 2014; AD, March 2014). Without these abilities, they are less likely to pursue new activities or take part in traditional team games such as volleyball, basketball, or hockey (Mr. Teach, March 2014). While this problem is not unique to PE classes and probably existed prior to the influx of Chinese immigrants to Richmond, the intersection of rising Chinese immigrants and the decreasing enthusiasm for school and community-based physical activity programs and PE captured my attention.

Considering physical activity rates amongst young females have recently gained more attention, there has been a surge of research (Sepp, Nelssaar, & Kull, 2013; Pauline, 2013; Shen, 2014) and energy placed towards creating PE programs that are inclusive of girls with diverse abilities and interests. Despite the existence of similar issues, such as declining enrollment, motivation, and rising obesity rates amongst young males, they have yet to be fully acknowledged. According to Connell's hegemonic masculinity theory, there are hierarchies of masculinity that are embraced and valued in a society (Connell & Messerschmidt, 2005) that create unrealistic expectations for young males. Moreover, many boys who embody non-dominant masculinities go unnoticed, are oppressed by their peers and at times their teachers.

1.3. RATIONALE

With these concerns, a study on the experiences of immigrant Chinese teenage males (ages 15-16) was designed. The overemphasis and overvalue of dominant masculinities that often most Chinese males do not embody leave them marginalized and de-motivated to be active participants (Millington,

Vertinsky, Boyle, & Wilson, 2008). Could this be a contributing factor to the lack of presence amongst Chinese participants in Richmond, B.C.?

With the steady growth of the Chinese population in the Lower Mainland, it is imperative that the voices of young Chinese males (and females) be heard, and that educators utilize their input to foster physical activity programs that are sensitive to cultural differences and the hidden biases that may discourage young Chinese males to participate in sports programs. Their experiences and stories are complex and are highly influenced by not only their cultural upbringing, but by the past of the people in their lives.

1.4. RESEARCH GOAL

The goal of my work is to not change the minds of Chinese immigrants, rather to lend a voice to a group of Chinese teenage males in order to assist educators, coaches, and community members in understanding the cultural perspectives that may influence the decisions of Chinese male teenagers to participate in physical activity. In addition, this project strives to provide insight on the factors that motivate or inhibit Chinese male secondary PE students to participate in sports at their schools or community.

2. Literature Review

While there has yet to be a specific study on what motivates or de-motivates Richmond's Chinese immigrant males (ages 15-16) to join school sports teams, several related studies have taken place (Minichiello, 2001; Millington, 2006; Millington, Vertinsky, Boyle, & Wilson, 2008; Johnson, 2010; Dandy & Nettelbeck, 2010). Collectively, these investigations not only indicate that further research of this particular demographic needs to take place, but they also bring awareness to the experiences of Chinese immigrant teenage males in physical activity settings.

2.1. EDUCATIONAL VALUES

Sue and Okazaki (1990) argue that for most Asians, education becomes the primary means of achieving social status and that immigrants are attempting to attain opportunities that are not available in their home countries. In the Lower Mainland, there are Chinese international students studying on Canadian soil to acquire a university degree and intend to return home upon completion of their education (Minichiello, 2001). Considering academic success is their focus, it is not surprising that PE is not prioritized. In fact, participants in Ha et al.'s (2010) study revealed that many Hong Kong Chinese students were willing to sacrifice physical activity participation for the sake of high academic achievement in subjects such as Math, Sciences, and English. Considering students in B.C. have the option to not participate in PE in Grades 11 and 12 and health concerns continue to increase for children and youth, it is critical that further investigations be made to find solutions on how to encourage Chinese students to be physically active.

2.2. PARENTAL INFLUENCES

Upon reviewing multiple related studies, it is clear that parents' own previous experiences and attitudes towards sports is strongly correlated with their own child's level of participation (Kalakanis, Goldfield, Paluch, & Epstein, 2001; Cheng, Mendonca, & Farias Junior, 2014; Li, 2001; Li, 2004; Ha et al., 2010). In Li's (2001) study, it was unanimous amongst all of the interviewed parents that education was their top priority and "emphasized that their children must obtain a quality university education" (p. 481). This strong desire for academic achievement and value for post secondary education, is at times influenced by their parents' own educational experiences. Mrs. Lin, a participant in Li's (2001) study shared, "The source of our expectations is deeply embedded in our family roots and our life experiences..." (p. 483). Other parents claimed that their high expectations came from a place of concern for their child's well being and their desire to ensure that their child would avoid any misfortune they endured due to their lack of education.

This emphasis on attaining a quality education by parents not only places pressure on their child, but it also impacts their child's physical activity levels. A student from Li's (2004) study said, "My parents told me that I should prepare for my math contest, so the time for ping-pong was cancelled for a few weeks" (p. 171). Aside from one parent in a sample size of 22 parents in Ha et al.'s (2010) investigation, the parents believed that increased time devoted to PE would "adversely affect students' academic studies" (p. 342).

2.3. OBESITY RATES AND PHYSICAL INACTIVITY IN CHINA AND HONG KONG

Similar to other countries around the world, physical inactivity and rising rates of obesity amongst children and youth in Hong Kong and China are concerning (Ha et al., 2010; Bradsley, 2011; Morgan, 2014). In addition to parental influence, schools' PE programs in Hong Kong and China are major contributors to the epidemic. In 2002, it was reported that only 5-8% of the entire school curriculum is allocated to PE where at both primary and secondary levels, students receive less than an hour of instruction per week (Ha et al., 2010). When students immigrate to Canada, particularly at the high school level, these habits that they have acquired from their home country have already been so deeply ingrained that it poses major challenges for their current physical educators.

2.4. PHYSICAL ACTIVITY AND PURPOSE: CONTRASTING PERSPECTIVES

Researchers shed light on Chinese parents' and students' perspectives on the purpose of physical activity (Wang et al., 2010; Dandy & Nettelbeck, 2010). For instance, some researchers argue that Asian cultures are more focused on the prevention of illness through physical activity but do not view physical activity as a means to maintain health (Johnson, 2010; Dandy et al., 2010). Thus, Asians tend to take on individual pursuits such as swimming, badminton, or Tai Chi rather than team sports where social involvement occurs. Considering our current PE curriculum highly emphasizes team sports, these contrasting interests needs to be considered.

2.5. DOMINANT HEGEMONIC MASCULINITIES

Past studies have examined this relationship have found the existence and favouritism towards dominant hegemonic masculinities have a negative impact on the PE experiences of marginalized males (Braham, 2003; Kehler, 2010; Millington, 2006; Millington, et al., 2008; Tischler & McNaughtry, 2011). Kehler (2010) argues, "School-based PE continues to reinforce traditional masculine values associated with competitive team sport" (p. 155). According to Millington et al. (2008), these biases are further amplified for some Chinese males in Vancouver high schools. Their work revealed that some Chinese males feel marginalized by their Caucasian peers and experience historical racial stereotypes of being feminine or incapable of demonstrating athleticism (Millington et al., 2008).

3. Participants and Procedures

To acquire an understanding of Chinese teenage males' experiences in physical activity settings, two Grade 9 and 10 PE classes were approached to gather participants. After sharing the details of the study, six 15-16 year old Chinese immigrant students volunteered to be interviewed. The interviews consisted of semi-structured questions created by the researcher and inquired about students' PE experiences in Richmond, B.C. and in China. To provide perspectives on the landscape of PE and extracurricular sports programs over the last 10-15 years, teachers from two Richmond high schools were invited to take part in the study. Two male PE teachers who attended a Richmond secondary school and have 10+ years of teaching experience in Richmond, B.C. volunteered to be interviewed. One teacher taught at the same high school as the student participants and the other taught at another Richmond high school. To maintain confidentiality, the participants selected pseudonyms for the study.

Table 1

Overview of Student Participants.

NAME	John	George	Nick	Ping Pong	Steven	Tommy
GRADE	10	10	10	10	10	9
BIRTHPLACE	Shanghai, China	Guangzhou, China	Shenzhen, China	Shenzhen, China	Guangdong, China	Suzhou, China
YEAR OF IMMIGRATION	2010 (Grade 6)	2006 (Grade 2)	2014 (Grade 10)	2006 (Grade 2) Returned to Hong Kong for 2 years	2013 (Grade 9)	2013 (Grade 9)

4. Results & Discussion

This section provides readers with the participants' interview responses that are organized based on major themes that surfaced during the coding process. This process involved reviewing the interviews and clustering similar perspectives and experiences.

4.1. STUDENTS & PHYSICAL ACTIVITY

This component addresses the students' attitudes towards physical activity and their current level of involvement in school-based physical activities and organized sport teams.

4.1.A. PERSPECTIVES & EXPERIENCES

When asked if they enjoy physical activity, all six participants claimed that they liked being physically active and shared how it benefited their health. Steven said that physical activity makes him strong and elaborated by explaining, "I'm very skinny and I think I need to exercise to be stronger. Because I'm a male and I think that I should be bigger and stronger (Steven, personal communication, February 26, 2014)." While describing some of his favourite activities, one participant claimed he liked basketball because it makes him taller (Nick, personal communication, February 26, 2014). These perspectives on the importance of physical activity to build strength and height echo the dominant hegemonic values that have been found to be present in North American PE and sport settings (Braham, 2003; Kehler, 2010; Millington, 2006; Millington, et al. 2008; Tischler et al., 2011). Past researchers claim that hegemonic masculinities are present in our society and these ideals create a divide for those individuals who do not embody these qualities. Millington (2006) and Millington et al. (2008) explain that these values are particularly concerning for Chinese-Canadian males or Chinese immigrant males as they often embody masculinities that are not typically recognized in Canada. Although neither participant made any claims of discrimination or being ostracized by their peers, their comments support the belief that strength and physical appearance are dominant determinants of masculinity.

4.1.B. ACTIVITY PREFERENCES

When asked to share which sports they enjoyed doing on their own time, John, George, and Ping Pong reported that they prefer badminton and Nick and Steven claimed they enjoy playing basketball with their friends occasionally. Ping Pong also said that he enjoys weightlifting at home and doing martial arts and Tommy reported that he likes Taekwondo and cycling.

4.1.C. EXTRACURRICULAR ACTIVITIES & FREQUENCY OF INVOLVEMENT

Interestingly, despite expressing enjoyment for physical activity, the participants' level of involvement was not indicative of this. When asked to describe the time they spent engaging in physical activity after school hours, four participants reported that they were active one day a week for less than 30 minutes each time. Three of the four participants who were only physically active one day per week attributed their lack of involvement to focusing on homework. Given the fact that they acknowledged that physical activity is important and that they enjoyed being active, I was prompted to investigate further on their perceptions of their abilities and accessibility to sports programs at school and in their community.

4.1.D. PERCEIVED ACCESSIBILITY & COMPETENCE

In response to AD and Mr. Teach's reports of lack of participation in organized sports in the community and at school, the students were asked if they would like to be more involved with team sports. Four participants agreed while the other two said no. Two of the four participants, Steven and John, said that they would try out for their school teams but were not confident that they would be selected. Moreover, they felt that they were not equipped with the necessary skills and did not feel that they had enough practice to improve. Ping Pong and John expressed that they were interested in joining community soccer but were unsure of how to register.

The two students who said they would not like to be more involved said it was because they were not very good at sports. "I don't think I'm good enough…look at those people, they are taller and stronger than me," (personal communication, February 26, 2014) explained Ping Pong when discussing trying out for the school soccer team. However, when asked if they would reconsider their decision if they were more skilled, both participants said that they would want to take part in school or community sports leagues.

4.2. EXPERIENCES IN CHINA

This component is divided into two parts and draws awareness to the influence of the students' exposure to PE and physical activity in China.

4.2.A. EXTRA-CURRICULAR SPORTS & ACTIVITIES

When questioned about their involvement in extra-curricular activities while in China, three participants said they went to tutoring classes and Tommy and John claimed they were active outside of school hours. None of the mentioned activities were organized sports and only one participant, Tommy, took part in sports-related activity regularly. Three participants (John, Nick, and Tommy) mentioned the absence of school sports teams at their school. "My school don't have any teams so I don't play anything," Nick (personal communication, February 26, 2014) explained. Apart from the student who took part in Taekwondo, the other participants did not discuss opportunities to be a part of organized activities in their communities.

When asked about why they were not more involved in sports-related activities, all participants explained that most of their time after school was devoted towards their studies. "We have a lot more homework in China so no time to play after school" (Nick, personal communication, February 26, 2014). Another student said, "In China, we don't have that. We don't have time. Sometimes we play during lunchtime...I have to do lots of homework in China" (Tommy, personal communication, February 21, 2014). Academic pressures in China are high, thus it is not uncommon for students to spend after school hours studying or receiving additional tutoring to improve their academic performance (Li, 2001). Considering most participants were not involved in extra-curricular sports at their school or community, this may explain why they continue to be inactive while they are in Canada.

4.2.B. PE EXPERIENCES

All six participants expressed that their PE classes were absent of structure and specific instruction by their teachers. "They don't teach, it's just free. We do what we want," (personal communication, February 21, 2014) Tommy explained. Another student echoed the freedom to choose their activities:

> We have some choice; sometimes we can play badminton or basketball. We have a playground so we can play there...your friends teach you how to play. They just gave us free time, do whatever you want. (Nick, personal communication, February 26, 2014)

One student remembered some similarities between his classes in China and here in Canada.

> Well, we pretty much do what we do right here. But um...there was no gym. There was basically just a big field. A big track and field. We'd basically just play outdoor games but they don't teach us how to play. (George, personal communication, March 13, 2014)

When asked about the types of sports in their curriculum, the students reported little diversity. All six participants mentioned badminton and table tennis being played regularly while others mentioned occasionally playing basketball and volleyball, and doing track and field.

4.3. PE EXPERIENCES IN CANADA

The students' perspectives on PE classes in Canada will be addressed in this section through three sub-sections: 1) Attitudes towards PE, 2) Marginalization and hegemonic masculinities and 3) Perspectives on senior PE.

4.3.A. ATTITUDES TOWARDS PE

Three students mentioned that they liked PE because they preferred it to their academic subjects. "We get to play sports...the other classes are boring," said Steven (personal communication, February 2014). Tommy explained, "Because we just have fun...I don't feel very nervous in this PE class. I feel very nervous in Social Studies or Science class, but I feel comfortable in PE class," (personal communication, February 21, 2014).

Four students mentioned that they enjoyed the wide range of activities and sports offered in their PE classes. In contrast to their experiences in China, students claimed that they not only played more sports in Canada, they learned how to play the games. Steven said that they really enjoyed learning to play hockey because they did not play the sport in China.

4.3.B. MARGINALIZATION AND HEGEMONIC MASCULINITIES

During the process of constructing the interview questions and reading of relevant literature, I learned there was ample concern for marginalized Chinese males who do not embody the often-glorified hegemonic masculinities of our society. Although it was anticipated that some students' experiences would reflect the findings of Millington (2006), none of the participants in the study reported any incidents of exclusion by their classmates or teachers.

4.3.C. PERSPECTIVES ON SENIOR PE

Considering senior PE is not a graduation requirement in B.C., many students choose to not take it as an elective in order to release time for an additional academic subject (AD, March 2014; Mr. Teach, March 2014). In fact, it has been reported that there is a declining enrollment in senior PE in Canada (Physical & Health Education Canada, 2007). With a heavy emphasis on academic pursuits, particularly amongst Chinese families (Li, 2001; Ha et al., 2010; Li 2004; Yan et al., 2004), there was an expectation that the sample group would choose to opt out of taking PE in their senior years. However, five of the six participants claimed that they were planning on taking PE in Grade 11 and Grade 12. John claimed he does not plan to take senior PE because he would be focusing on Math and English rather than electives.

George mentioned the de-emphasis of language in these learning environments as an influential factor when deciding on whether to take PE when it was no longer mandatory. He appreciated the absence of homework and the pressure of having to keep up with the English language amongst many other things. Three students mentioned they would rather take PE during school time because they don't have time after school to be active. "I don't have time after school so if I take PE, I can play during school time," John explained (personal communication, March 13, 2014). These responses were not anticipated as many physical educators are struggling to fill their classes (AD, March 2014; Mr. Teach, March 2014). Whether these students will follow through with their intentions cannot be guaranteed but it is uplifting to learn that students who are not highly active appreciate having PE classes to help them stay active.

4.4. PARENTAL INFLUENCE

The final section provides information on the students' perspective on the role of their parents in their physical activity experiences. Moreover, the influences of their parents' educational and cultural values are discussed.

4.4.A. PARENTAL SUPPORT AND INVOLVEMENT

Parents play a major role in their child's exposure to activities, particularly at a young age whether it is athletics, art, or music. This is especially true for Chinese families as decisions are often based on what is best for the family, rather than placing the needs of the individual at the forefront (Li, 2001; Li, 2004). Thus, parental support and involvement are critical determinants of whether a child takes part in extra-curricular activities or not. While none of the participants reported that their parents were opposed to them taking part in sports, there was little mention of encouragement to be active. All six participants believed that if they had asked their parents to register them for an activity, they would be willing to do so. However, little discussion about physical activity takes place at home for the participants. Only one participant, John, reported that he occasionally played sports (badminton and table tennis) with his parents.

Although the participants reported that their parents would support their decision to participate in extra-curricular sports, the combination of the students' hesitance to join sports, and the parents' lack of encouragement resulted in inactivity. Thus, it is imperative that educators and community partners reach out to not only the children, but their parents as well to encourage them to register their children in sports and senior PE classes.

4.4.B. EDUCATIONAL VALUES

Striving for academic success is not a concept that is unique to Chinese parents, as all parents want their children to receive a good education. However, research has demonstrated that the Chinese culture tends to place higher value in academic achievement, so much that non-academic subjects, such as PE, are not taken seriously (Li, 2001; Li, 2004; Ha et al., 2010). The responses from the participants support this idea as they all reported that their parents were not concerned about their progress in PE. "They most care about math because I'm Chinese student and I should be good at it. Second is ESL. These two are very important" (Tommy, personal communication, February 21, 2014). With the pressure of being accepted into university, some academic sacrifices have to be made and PE is often at risk.

Although many Chinese parents may not value PE, it should be acknowledged that these parents might not understand the benefits associated with regular physical activity. Rather, they can be guided by Confucian ideals where academic success leads to opportunities. Perhaps the solution starts with making changes at the secondary school level where senior PE courses are graduation requirements. For many students, they want to take senior PE; however, timetables and entrance requirements make this challenging.

5. Conclusion

Prior to my involvement with this study, I was convinced that the rising immigration rates of Chinese immigrants were the "problem" with the lack of school and extracurricular sports programs in Richmond. However, as I spent more time researching this topic and analyzing the results of my study, my perspective on this issue has evolved.

The six interviews with 15-16 year old Chinese male immigrants not only provided an understanding of their school-based physical activity and PE preferences, but also addressed their support systems, perceived accessibility, and how their previous PE experiences in China impacted their perspectives. All six participants claimed to enjoy being physically active, while four demonstrated an interest in taking part in school and community sports. With increasing academic pressures at the Grade 9 and 10 levels, these responses are refreshing and encouraging for physical educators as oftentimes, it appears as if they don't want to be there.

According to Ha et al. (2010), Yan et al. (2004), Li (2001), and Li (2004), pressure for academic achievement was a major factor contributing to a diminished value of sport and PE by Chinese families. However, my study's results indicate that perceived lack of encouragement and opportunities by their schools, community, and parents are the contributing factors to their lifestyle choices. Although the students expressed they learned more in Canadian PE classes, they still believed that they were not equipped with enough skills to have the confidence to take part in a school or community team. For some, their decision to try-out for a team was based on whether they felt they were more competent than the current members of the team. Considering there is usually only one team per sport per grade where teams are typically comprised of 10-12 players, the students' sense of hopelessness is understood. When asked if they knew how to become more involved in sports, most were unsure of how to access these opportunities. Some participants also indicated that their parents did not enroll them in sports. However, they did mention that they felt their parents would not oppose them doing so. Given parental perspectives and personal involvement have been linked to children's physical activity patterns (Kalakanis et al. 2001), perhaps more efforts should be placed towards educating parents on how to and why they should encourage their children to participate in extra-curricular sports.

The participants' responses also suggest that our current, school-based approach to increasing physical activity levels amongst this population needs to be reviewed. This is not to say that teachers and community centres have neglected this population or that they have not attempted to include Chinese teenage males. Rather, further consideration and research on their activity preferences, cultural influences, and past experiences should be explored for PE and sport program development. Instead of asking, "Why are they not taking part in the programs we are currently offering?" we as PE teachers and community coaches should re-frame our thinking by asking, "How can we encourage them to take part? Are there obstacles impeding their ability to participate?" We should also consider the types of activities that are being promoted. Are they conducive to their interests or skill assets?

While only a small group of students were interviewed and their opinions are not reflective of all Chinese teenage males, their responses support the suggestion that Chinese people tend to prefer individual, non-competitive, or recreational sports (Yan et al., 2004). Moreover, the results of this study support the notion that Chinese immigrant male students are more inclined to play racket sports because they have had more experience playing in their home country. Thus, we should not expect this student demographic to possess the fundamental skills to participate successfully or assume they are not motivated due to their inability to execute the skills. PE teachers may want to include a wider range of activities to appease the diverse interests and abilities of Chinese students and consider the cultural upbringing of their students that may affect their activity preferences. Immigrant students may not have been exposed to traditional team sports that typically comprise the majority of the PE curriculum for many North American schools (Bramham, 2003; Millington et al., 2008) and this could affect their motivation to take part. Abandoning traditional sports entirely is not necessary as two students indicated that they really appreciated learning baseball and hockey after arriving in Canada.

5.2. LIMITATIONS OF THE RESEARCH

While the stories of the participants were similar to one another and support the findings of researchers who studied topics related to my focus, the small sample size does not reflect the opinions and experiences of all Chinese male immigrant students and PE teachers in Richmond. Instead, the information should be viewed as examples of perspectives that exist amongst these populations.

5.3. POTENTIAL APPLICATIONS OF RESEARCH FINDINGS

My hope is that this project draws awareness to PE teachers and the Richmond, B.C. community with regards to the experiences and cultural values that many of the Chinese immigrants identify with. Rather than forcing change on the Chinese students and parents who are reluctant to take part in physical activity, one strategy may be to understand their culture first. From there, we as physical educators should then look at our programs and evaluate whether they are suitable to the needs of the growing Chinese, teenage male population. Parental support was noted as an important factor when it comes to students' PE and physical activity involvement. As discussed in this study, Chinese parents tend to place great value on academic achievement and undervalue PE and extracurricular sports. If we want to encourage more of the growing Chinese immigrant population to take part in sport, we need parents to be supportive and we must first understand the underlying reasons for their aspirations for their child. Since parental attitudes are strong determinants of their child's involvement in physical activity (Cragg et al., 1999), perhaps investigation of parents' perspectives on accessibility to programs for their children should take place. We should not assume that all parents are fully aware of the programs that exist in their communities, especially those who are new immigrants.

Like Millington (2006), Millington et al. (2008), Minichiello (2001), Wang et al. (2010), and Yan (2004), this study aims to provoke further investigation into the PE and physical activity experiences of Chinese male students in secondary schools. While my research focused on males, the same approach could be applied to Chinese teenage females as well. Research suggests that Chinese girls' physical activity participation rates are consistently lower than that of boys as they lack support from family members (Ha et al. 2010; K.Y. Cheng, P.G. Cheng, & Mak, 2003). Lastly, my experiences as a teacher in the Surrey school district prompts me to believe a similar investigation on the influences of the prominent Indo-Canadian culture on students' perspectives on physical activity would be of value. Given the fact that the lower mainland is increasingly multi-cultural, physical educators should not ignore the impact of this shift and be open to change in curriculum delivery. Through this paper, I hope physical educators are further encouraged to learn about their students' histories, and how their experiences have shaped their outlook on PE and physical activity.

References

Bradsley, D. (2011). Childhood obesity is on the rise in China. Retrieved March 10, 2014, from http://www.thenational.ae/news/world/childhood-obesity-on-the-rise-in-china

Bramham, P. (2003). Boys, masculinities and PE. Sport, Education and Society, 8(1), 57-71.

Cheng, K.Y., Cheng, P.G., & Mak, K.T. (2003). Relationships of perceived benefits and barriers to physical activity, physical activity participation and physical fitness in Hong Kong female adolescents. *Journal of Sports Medicine and Physical Fitness,* 43, 523–529.

Cheng, L.A., Mendonca, G., & Farias Junior, J.C (2014). Physical activity in adolescents: analysis of social influence of parents and friends. *Jornal de Pediatria* (Versão em Português), 90(1), 35-41.

City of Richmond: Policy Publishing Division. (2011). Population & Demographics. Retrieved from City of Richmond: http://www.richmond.ca/discover/about/demographics.htm

Cragg, S., Cameron, C., Craig, C. & Russell, S. (1999). Canada's children and youth: a physical activity profile. Ottawa, Canadian Fitness and Lifestyle Research Institute.

Connell, R. W., Messerschmidt, J.W. (2005). Hegemonic masculinity: Rethinking the concept. *Gender & Society,* 19(6), 829-859.

Dandy, J., & Nettelbeck, T. (2010). The relationship between IQ, homework, aspirations and academic achievement for Chinese, Vietnamese and Anglo-Celtic Australian school children. Educational Psychology: *An International Journal of Experimental Educational Psychology*, 22(3), 267-275.

Ha, A.S., Macdonald, D., Pang, B.O.H. (2010). Physical activity in the lives of Hong Kong Chinese children. The interplay of postcolonialism and Confucianism. *Sport, Education and Society,* 15(3), 331-346.

Hong Kong Department of Health (2001). Annual Departmental Report by the Director of Health 2000-2001 (Hong Kong, Hong Kong Department of Health).

Johnson, M. R. (2010). Perceptions of barriers to healthy physical activity among

Asian communities. *Sport, Education and Society,* 5(1), 51-70.

Kalakanis, L. E., Goldfield, G. S., Paluch, R. A., & Epstein, L. H. (2001). Parental activity as a determinant of activity level and patterns of activity in obese children. *Research Quarterly for Exercise and Sport,* 72(3), 202-209.

Kehler, M. (2010). Negotiating masculinities in PE classrooms: Boys, body image and -want[ing] to be in good shape. (pp. 143-165). In M. Kehler & M. Atkinson (Eds), Boys' bodies: Speaking the unspoken. New York, N.Y.: Peter Lang.

Li, J. (2001). Expectations of Chinese immigrant parents for their children's education: the interplay of Chinese tradition and the Canadian context. *Canadian Journal of Education,* 26(4), 477-494.

Li, J. (2004). Parental expectations of Chinese immigrants: a folk theory about children's school achievement. *Race, Ethnicity and Education,* 7(2), 167-183.

Millington, B. (2006). Learning masculinities: youth, media and physical education. MA thesis, University of British Columbia.

Millington, B., Vertinsky, P., Boyle, E., & Wilson, B. (2008). Making Chinese-Canadian masculinities in Vancouver's physical education curriculum. *Sport, Education and Society,* 13(2), 195-214.

Minichiello, D. (2001). Chinese voices in a Canadian secondary school landscape. *Canadian Journal of Education,* 26(1), 77-96.

Morgan, S. L. (2014). Growing fat on reform: Obesity and nutritional disparities among China's children, 1979-2005. *The China Quarterly,* 220, 1033-1068.

Pauline, J. S. (2013). Physical activity behaviors, motivation, and self-efficacy among college students. *College Student Journal,* 47(1), 64-74.

Shen, B. (2014), Outside-school physical activity participation and motivation in physical education. *British Journal of Educational Psychology,* 84, 40–57.

Sue, S. & Okazaki, S. (1990). Asian-American educational achievements. *American Psychologist,* 45, 913–920.

Tischler, A. & McCaughtry, N. (2011). PE is not for me: when boys' masculinities are threatened. *Res Q Exerc Sport,* 82(1), 37-48.

Wang, C. J., Liu, W., Sun, Y., Coral Lim, B., & Chatzisarantis, N. L. (2010). Chinese students' motivation in physical activity: goal profile analysis using Nicholl's Achievement Goal Theory. *International Journal of Sport and Exercise Psychology,* 8 (3), 284-301.

Yan, J.H. & McCullagh, P. (2004). Cultural influence on youth's motivation of participation in physical activity. *Journal of Sport Behaviour,* 27(4), 378-391.

The Experiences of Boys in PE as they Encounter the Teaching Games for Understanding Model for the First Time

BY PAISLEY RANKINE

Introduction

Jacob was very kind and quiet, but there was a sense of sadness that seemed to follow him. The other boys in his physical education class rarely spoke to him, and his presence on a team was hardly acknowledged. He struggled with coordination and somehow his running looked almost painful. He was the smallest of his Grade 8 classmates, but perhaps it was not his physical size that made him appear small, but the way in which he held his body. His presence in class felt somewhat invisible. He avoided contact with the other boys at all costs. He forgot his gym strip more often than not and usually made some attempt at not having to participate. I could tell that PE class was not his favourite place to be and I felt that I was somehow failing him. I tried to encourage him to participate and socialize with his classmates, and would place him on teams with other boys that might have a positive influence. I often wondered how he would tell his story of high school physical education. What were his experiences and how could giving them a voice help?

This experience with Jacob had a profound impact on how I viewed physical education early in my career as an educator. Throughout my own education and teacher training I became very familiar with the teacher-centered, technique based method to teaching PE and had been emulating this as a novice teacher. I soon realized that this approach was not meeting the needs of all my students. This was especially true for boys such as Jacob who illustrated an ongoing failure of physical education in promoting the importance of lifelong physical activity.

During my journey to address the failures of physical education in schools and continue my learning as a physical educator, I was exposed to the teaching games for understanding (TGfU) model while engaged in the beginnings of my graduate studies. I was immediately drawn to its student-centered approach that focused on concepts using small-sided games. I felt that TGfU might have the potential to reach a greater number of students and promote a joy of games in physical education. It was at this time and upon reflecting on my experience with Jacob, that I decided to conduct a study that focused on the experiences of boys engaged in a basketball unit using the TGfU approach. The research narrates the experiences of the boys to determine if TGfU provided a positive learning environment that encouraged their participation in games and potentially a desire for a lifetime of physical activity.

A literature review found that student experiences while engaging in physical education has been the focus of numerous education related studies over the last several decades. Many of these studies have highlighted different models of teaching physical education including teaching games for understanding (Bunker & Thorpe, 1986), tactical games approach (Griffin,

Mitchell, & Oslin, 1997), and Sport Education (SE) (Siedentop, 1994). It has been noted that negative experiences in physical education can impact levels of participation in physical activity (Cardinal, B., Yan, Z., & Cardinal, M., 2013). Perceived competency in games by students can have a large impact on their desire to participate in sport and their levels of motivation (Kirk, 2005).

Games are an integral part of many physical education programs around the globe (Holt, Strean, & Bengoechea, 2002). The typical games learning situations presented have a structured emphasis on technique (Holt et al., 2002). Research suggests that this approach to teaching games is not meeting the needs of a large number of students and perhaps affecting their levels of enjoyment and learning outcomes (Brooker, Kirk, Braiuka, & Bransgrove, 2000; Holt et al., 2002). If games are to continue to make up the majority of physical education programs, it is important that we continue to study and support the meaningful learning potential of games. TGfU encourages game appreciation, develops decision-making skills, and builds competent game players (Griffin & Patton, 2005). TGfU has also been perceived as more en-joyable by students, therefore encouraging greater motivation for game play (Kirk & MacPhail, 2002). This study aims to continue the drive to incorporate approaches to teaching PE that is student-centred and pedagogically sensitive to the needs of all students. This chapter will focus on addressing the research question: "What will be the experiences of boys engaged in the TGfU model for the first time?"

Methods

The purpose of this research was to engage in an ethnographic study that critically analyzed the experiences of boys engaged in a TGfU approach to physical education (PE). The experiences were shared using interviews, questionnaires, written comments, and observations in an attempt to provide a voice to boys participating in PE class. To complement the voices of the students, I also kept a researcher journal that reflects my experiences as the teacher and researcher during the study period. It was my intent to design a study that empowered both my students and myself to purposefully engage in a narrative of our experiences while participating in a student-centred method that breaks the mould of more common teacher-centred skills based approach to teaching PE. The following paragraphs are a brief description of the partici-pants, planning, and research tools used throughout the study.

PARTICIPANTS

The participants of this study were enrolled in a single gendered eighth grade physical education class at a secondary school in the Surrey School District. The school is in an upper middle socioeconomic class neighbourhood. The class reflects the overall school composition: 50 percent of the students of Asian decent; 50 percent Caucasian. All the boys in the class are between the ages of 12 and 14. Twenty-nine of the 30 boys in the class joined the study to participate in questionnaires after providing both parental consent and assent forms. From this group of 29 participants, five boys were also chosen randomly to participate in a post unit interview.

Because I am both a researcher and teacher in this study, I am also somewhat of a participant. I am a female teacher with over five years of experience teaching PE to both male and female students in grades 8 through 10. I spent the year prior to the commencement of the study engaged in a master's program dedicated to exploring student-centred approaches to physical education highlighted through TGfU.

PLANNING

Prior to the study, I planned a TGfU unit concentrating on basketball. The unit was composed of 12 lessons; 11 lessons focused on different concepts unique to basketball and invasion games, and one lesson that had a team focused tournament at the end of the unit with teams that were teacher selected. The total length of the unit was four weeks of class on alternating days for a total of three lessons each week.

The basketball unit and research period started in October 2013. The study began with an age appropriate explanation of the research and the TGfU model (Bunker & Thorpe, 1986) that was the focus. Students were made aware that their participation would be held confidential from the public and myself as their teacher. By participating in the study, students' marks would not be affected. A colleague in the PE department would collect all of the questionnaires, interviews, and requested written information in an attempt to elicit candid responses and uphold the participants' anonymity from the teacher and researcher.

RESEARCH TOOLS

Data for the research was collected using a variety of methods including questionnaires, student interviews, written comments, and teacher observations. Two questionnaires were performed during the study, one prior to the start of the TGfU unit, and an identical questionnaire at the end of the unit. The questionnaires contained 12 questions using a 5-point Likert scale for each response. The questions ranged in emphasis from motivation and engagement, to enjoyment of activities and games. Each response from the questionnaire was then given a numerical value and these values were compared using statistical analysis to highlight any differences from the pre- to post-unit questionnaires. Results from the statistical analysis are further discussed in the quantitative data section.

Five students were interviewed after the completion of the unit. The interviews consisted of open-ended style questions in regard to their experiences and feelings throughout the unit. A few examples of questions include: "What has been your experience during this basketball unit? Discuss the positive and negative experiences you have had," and "Describe any changes in your confidence during the basketball unit." Interviewed students were then asked to complete additional written comments after reading through the transcripts from their interviews. Interview transcripts, written comments, along with the teacher observations were all coded and placed under emergent themes. The coding process placed key words, similar feelings and ideas, and complementing opinions and expressions together. The emergent themes were drawn from the collections of coded data. The data and subsequent emergent themes are discussed further in the qualitative data section.

Results & Discussion

INTRODUCTION

The following section will describe the analysis of the quantitative data taken from the students' questionnaires. Secondly, there will be a detailed discussion of the quantitative and qualitative data.

The quantitative data that resulted from the questionnaire will be outlined by the statistical tests and the results presented in table format. The results of the pre- and post unit questionnaires have been separated to analyze the statistical difference for each individual, as well as the difference of the total numerical averages from all 12 questions. The quantitative results lead into a detailed discussion of the qualitative data.

The qualitative data generated from the written comments, interviews, and observations have been coded and grouped based on common themes. The themes have been divided into those generated from the students' data, and those generated from the teacher observations. The students' data resulted in six different themes: *1) elementary experiences, 2) understanding of the game, 3) a sense of enjoyment for games and physical education, 4) building confidence, 5) feelings of improved abilities, and 6) reflection of perceived limitations.* The themes extracted from the coding of the observations and field notes are: *1) levels of engagement, 2) lesson flow, 3) perceived learning, 4) student behaviour, 5) difficulties in transition to TGfU.* The final section of the results and discussion will triangulate the data (Denzin & Lincoln, 2011) and discuss the emergent themes that are consistent through all the data. The triangulation results in a final discussion of two major recurrent themes in the student and teacher/researcher data: *1) learning through TGfU* and *2) engagement and enjoyment of games.*

Quantitative Results

The pre- and post results from the TGfU unit questionnaires have been assigned numerical values and analyzed on a spreadsheet for significant differences, using a paired sample t-test (Cohen, Manion, & Morrison, 2000). The average values for (a) each question and (b) the total test scores from all 12 question questionnaires were analyzed individually. The data were analyzed by testing each pair of individual question's value for statistical significance, using a paired sample t-test. This method was repeated using the individual values for the twelve questions. The tests were used in describing the experiences of boys engaged in TGfU and answering the two research statements:

1) *Will boys engaged in the TGfU approach for the first time report increased feelings of joy and excitement?*

2) *How will the data support changes in students understanding of the game and perceived abilities?*

Table 1

Paired-samples t-test results for individual questions.

Pair	Pre-unit mean	Post-unit mean	diff	t-value	p-value
1	4.96	5.25	-0.29	-1.69	0.10
2	4.54	4.89	-0.36	-1.29	0.21
3	5.32	5.29	0.04	0.24	0.81
4	5.04	5.04	0.00	0.00	1.00
5	4.93	5.14	-0.21	-1.06	0.30
6	4.93	5.54	-0.61	-2.92	0.01
7	5.14	5.43	-0.29	-1.61	0.12
8	4.89	5.25	-0.36	-2.29	0.03
9	4.64	4.75	-0.11	-0.43	0.67
10	3.96	4.25	-0.29	-0.90	0.38
11	4.50	5.00	-0.50	-2.56	0.02
12	4.96	5.10	-0.14	-0.75	0.46

Table 1 represents the paired samples t-test results for the individual questions. Pre- and post results showed 10 questions with an increase, where individual questions 6, 8 and 11 held statistically significant difference among values: $p<0.05$. This indicates that the difference in the values is a result of a change and not solely chance.

The total pre- and post question averages of all twelve questions were also tested to see if there were any significant statistical differences. Table 2 shows the results from the paired sample t-test using the total averages.

Table 2

Paired-sample t-test results for total average from all questions.

Pair	Total pre-unit mean	Total post-unit mean	diff	t-value	p-value
1	4.82	5.09	-0.26	-2.69	0.01

The results from the paired t-test show that there is a statistically significant difference between the total averages (4.82, 5.09). Table 2 shows the results from the paired sample t-test for the total scores from the pre- and post questionnaires. The sampled pair (M=0.26) of the total values can be interpreted, as the change from the total values was the results of an observable change and not solely by chance (p=0.01).

The results from the statistical analysis provided an important set of data that reveal a self-identified change in mind-set by some of the participants before and after their experience with the TGfU teaching practice in PE. The following discussion will further explore the interpretation of these results and their relation to the emergent themes drawn from the interviews, field notes and observations.

Qualitative Results

The results of the interviews and written add-ons provided by the five students who participated in the TGfU basketball unit were analyzed and categorized into six emergent themes. These six themes are organized into separate sections. I then used a confessional tale (Sparkes, 2002) to connect my observations as the teacher and researcher with the feelings and experiences of my students. The observations are also organized into five emergent themes. The themes are identified and described using the voices of the students and the researcher through quotes, feelings, and emotions expressed throughout the data.

EMERGENT THEME 1: ELEMENTARY EXPERIENCES

In order to gain a greater understanding of the students' previous knowledge and experience in PE, the first few interview questions were focused on their elementary PE classes. The student responses produced a myriad of, at times, provocative answers. The common thread though the majority of the interviews identified that elementary school physical education was not taken seriously and fell short of teaching beyond the basics. Student 1 stated, "We honestly didn't do much, it was almost a joke. We would go there, there was almost no schedule. We wouldn't work on really anything" (Interview, November 20, 2013). All five students interviewed found (a) high school PE more challenging and (b) they were enjoying the opportunity to learn more advanced concepts and skills.

EMERGENT THEME 2: UNDERSTANDING OF THE GAME

TGfU has been repeatedly praised (Griffin et al., 2005; Hastie & Curtner-Smith, 2006) for its ability to engage students in meaningful learning through games. This foundation of TGfU is evident in how many of the boys interviewed commented on feeling a greater understanding for the game of basketball. One student reported, "I have started to understand the rules better and how to get to the basket better instead of just dribbling to one spot" (Student 11, interview, November 20, 2013).

A number of student comments not only related to a better understanding of the game, but also reflected a positive change in decision-making abilities. For example Student 1 stated, "Now people like knew what to do and they weren't just aimlessly shooting and passing the ball" (Interview, November 20, 2013). Along with a greater understanding, students also discussed how knowing the game lead to feelings of enjoyment based on their perceived improvement in the cognitive domain. One student admitted, "It is more fun if you know the game well and then you play it" (Student 19, interview, November 21, 2013).

EMERGENT THEME 3:
A SENSE OF ENJOYMENT FOR GAMES AND PHYSICAL EDUCATION

TGfU places an emphasis on learning games through play (Kirk & McPhail, 2002). Tactical problems and strategies are addressed through modified games where students are engaged in an environment that encourages problem-solving skills. This study supports current research findings (Webb, Pearson, & Forrest, 2006; Stran et al., 2012; Brooker et al., 2000) that a focus on play using modified games not only encourages cognitive development and game sense, but also creates an inclusive environment that results in reported feelings of fun and enjoyment by both students and teachers.

"I was always excited to go to PE during this unit because I had a genuinely good time," wrote Student 1 (Written comments, December 4, 2013). The boys interviewed described experiences using such words as "fun", "excitement", "enjoyable" and "happy". Many students also spoke of how the TGfU approach created an environment that encouraged learning and was enjoyable at the same time. Student 19 described this environment when he said, "I think doing games in PE is a good thing because we can enjoy playing and enjoy learning" (Written comments, December 4, 2013). The students in this study supported previously reported data (Kirk & McPhail, 2002; McNeill et al., 2011) that validate the ability of TGfU to enhance learning and foster an enjoyment of games and physical activity.

EMERGENT THEME 4: BUILDING CONFIDENCE

Building confidence within the PE setting can be instrumental in shaping attitudes and behaviours towards future physical activity (Cardinal et al., 2013). Student 1 supported the ability of the TGfU approach to promote confidence when he said, "With this games based teaching method, I gained more confidence while playing basketball" (Written comments, December 4, 2013). He continued this sentiment in his interview by discussing his new found confidence in a number of basketball related skills, explaining, "I'm more confident that I can pass and shoot, and dribble the ball. So I'm more confident about that" (Interview, November 20, 2013).

EMERGENT THEME 5: FEELINGS OF IMPROVED ABILITIES

Not only did students express gains in confidence, but also improvement in abilities and skills related to basketball. Although lessons were not focused on one particular skill, but rather concepts or tactical theories related to invasions games, many students expressed a perceived improvement in basketball skills. One student acknowledged, "Before I did not feel that comfortable with my cuts and stuff, and now I'm really good at it" (Student 19, interview, November 21, 2013). Students expressed seeing an overall improvement in the abilities of their classmates over the course of the unit. One student praised his classmates and said, "Now people like knew what to do and they weren't just aimlessly shooting and passing the ball" (Student 1, interview, November 20, 2013).

EMERGENT THEME 6: REFLECTION OF PERCEIVED LIMITATIONS

After the completion of the TGfU unit, the students interviewed reported some negative experiences and areas they felt could have been improved. The majority of the concerns expressed by the boys pertained to the repeated use of modified games and the written assessments. A number of the boys interviewed felt that the modified versions of basketball used to highlight different tactics and concepts were boring at times and they felt a need to play the "real game", specifically 5-on-5 basketball instead of the smaller sided games. Student 4 made this point by saying, "I think the modified version of basketball is boring. It's a good idea, but some people would just like to play the legit game" (Written comments, December 4, 2013).

Student 26 was particularly vocal in his dislike of the written assessments, which occurred in the last 3-5 minutes of most lessons. He said, "The activity that I found most painful was writing after we had played" (Written comments, December 4, 2013). He describes the written assessments as taking away from exercising in PE:

> I don't really like the way you do a lesson, she teaches you how to do it, and then you actually go and do it, and then you have to write about what you did. I don't really like that. I guess it kinda takes away from the actual exercise part. (interview, November 20, 2013)

The reported concern about the written assessments from this student may be the results of not having experienced more formal types of assessments during PE in elementary school.

CONFESSIONAL TALE

This study required that I take on the roles of researcher, teacher, and finally author. The use of a confessional tale allowed the telling of my personal research experiences in hopes of promoting a greater understanding of the research journey (Sparkes, 2002). Playing multiple roles during this journey proved to be a complex experience. I found it challenging to blend the roles in one space. For example, at moments while teaching the TGfU basketball unit, I found myself losing sight of the role of the researcher. When I focused on the role of the researcher, I found it difficult to maintain my expectations as a teacher. The following paragraphs highlight my voice as a teacher, researcher and author. My intent is to personalize my story as I have done for my students, and discuss my experiences in implementing and researching TGfU. I have organized my experiences through the emergent themes of my observations.

EMERGENT THEME 1: LEVELS OF ENGAGEMENT

As a teacher I feel as though I continuously monitor the level of engagement throughout a lesson. This was especially the case with this study, as I was implementing a relatively new practice with which I had limited previous experience. I was nervous and excited to fully immerse in an approach I believed to be more inclusive and student-centred than the technique based and teacher-centred approach I was more familiar with. I could not avoid asking the question, "What would the students' level of engagement be when experiencing the TGfU approach for the first time?"

During the first half of the unit students were highly engaged in the small-sided modified games. "Students were engaged throughout most of the lesson. They were especially engaged during gameplay" (Teacher observations, October 16, 2013). I felt that using the small-sided games kept all the students active over a greater period of time. The small-sided games also created an environment where students were much more focused on the gameplay happening on their court.

Overall I felt that the TGfU approach was successful in engaging a larger number of students over a greater period of time. The activities and assessments kept students focused and engaged at a greater level than I have experienced using a more technique based teacher-centred approach. "The lesson seemed to engage a greater number of students. They were highly involved in the actions of playing and assessing" (Teacher observations, October 24, 2013).

EMERGENT THEME 2: LESSON FLOW

The sequencing of activities and questioning that is fundamental to TGfU (Bunker & Thorpe, 1986) was one of my greatest concerns prior to the commencement of the unit. How would the students react to stoppages related to the questioning periods associated with TGfU, and instruction time associated with changes to game conditions? It required patience and trust in the process on my part, as the students became accustomed to the new lesson flow. I remember writing, "Students were more attentive this lesson than the previous one. Perhaps they are getting used to the starting and stopping routine required for the questions, instructions, and assessments" (Teacher observations, October 24, 2013). By the end of the unit students were comfortable with the sequencing of the lessons and my practice improved with experience as I gained confidence and became more comfortable with my timing for questions and instructions.

EMERGENT THEME 3: PERCEIVED LEARNING

Throughout the course of the TGfU unit it was noticeable that the students' movement on the court reflected the concepts that were being presented in the lessons. I reflected, "I am finding that the concepts like moving to open spaces, making quick cuts, and giving lead passes are starting to show more in their games" (Teacher observations, October 30, 2013). The concepts and tactics highlighted in the lessons were being transferred to the students' small-sided games:

> What I did notice right away was the teammates were spread out and using open spaces. There was much more movement off the ball than I had observed in previous classes. There were also a lot less errant long shots, and most of the shots occurred from within the 3-8 feet zone. (Teacher observations, November 14, 2013)

The engagement during the question periods and assessments indicated that students were making connections with the concepts being presented as well as linking with their previous knowledge. Although the students were not accustomed to written assessments in physical education, it was evident that they were effective:

> The students were aware of the different types of basketball passes and could even describe scenarios of when to use each one. I think that this GPAI complemented their previous knowledge well with what they were trying to produce on the court. It helped make them connect their knowledge with the movements, and decision-making in "real time" which was interesting to watch. (Teacher observations, October 24, 2013)

EMERGENT THEME 4: STUDENT BEHAVIOUR

Using the TGfU approach, I was required to release control of many aspects of the lessons. By this I mean that students were actively involved in small-sided games instead of controlled drills and technique practice. The use of small-sided games meant that the environment was decentralized (Davis, Sumara, & Luce-Kapler, 2008) which is a change from the teacher-centred technique based approach I have been using for a number of years. This was a difficult transition early in the unit: to let go of the control and place a greater responsibility on the students for their own learning. After working through the transition from a centralized to a decentralized structure using the TGfU approach, the inclusivity of this model was further supported by a greater number of students, and presented opportunities for students of multiple abilities to embrace different roles within the unit.

EMERGENT THEME 5: DIFFICULTIES IN THE TRANSITION TO TGFU

When attempting to implement a new model to teaching one can expect challenges. The initial challenge was for my students and myself to become accustomed to the interruptions in gameplay for questioning and instructions. I took a few lessons to refine my timing in stoppages, and embrace the time spent questioning and encouraging the students to think critically about the lessons' concepts. By the end of the unit the sequence of activities and questioning was routine for the students and a noticeably essential part to the TGfU model.

Another challenge that I was faced with while presenting the TGfU model was getting students to 'buy in' to the importance of the assessment and, in particular, the written assessments presented. The act of writing in PE may require a longer period of adjustment. It should be noted that meaningful assessment is a valuable tool for all PE programs, and not solely a part of TGfU. The belief held by a number of the students in regards to the act of written assessments in PE as taking away from physical activity may be a result of having little to no previous experience with valid assessments in PE in earlier years. Future studies could include followup with students after they have experienced a greater number of assessments in PE. It would be interesting to assess if the students' sentiments of their validity have changed.

Finally, I felt that to effectively utilize the TGfU model in its full potential required a deeper awareness of the students' level of understanding and abilities. It is more complex to comprehend a game's concepts and tactics, than it is to grasp or demonstrate a static skill. The TGfU model required that the teacher be more in tune with how and if the concepts and tactics transfer to the students' game play.

CONNECTING THE DATA

In reviewing all of the data and compiling the emergent themes from each source there are some compelling connections, pertaining to the themes, between the results of the questionnaires, the interviews and written add-ons from the students and the teacher/researcher observations. The triangulation of the results in this section is meant to add validity through the cross examination of the data across multiple sources (Denzin & Lincoln, 2011).

LEARNING THROUGH TGFU

The results of this study found that students experienced a self-reported gain in understanding for the game of basketball. This supports findings from Hastie et al. (2006) and Griffin et al. (1997). In their study of a hybrid approach to teaching games using TGfU and Sport Education, Hastie et al. (2006) reported that students made significant gains in competency, literacy and improved technical skills during a batting and fielding unit. Griffin et al. (1997) concluded from multiple studies that using a tactical games approach similar to TGfU was effective in improving students' overall game performance. Questions 6, 7, 8 and 9 from the questionnaire relate to the enjoyment of games based on abilities, and an understanding of concepts and tactical awareness. In the post unit questionnaire all four questions showed an increase in numerical values where questions 6 and 8 produced increases of statistical significance.

This connects directly to the interview results, where all five students expressed learning more about the game and having a greater understanding of the rules and tactics associated with basketball. The supporting component to the students' experiences is the teacher/researcher observations that noted on several occasions witnessing the use of concepts and tactics highlighted in lessons during game play. The triangulation of the data sources support enhanced learning by students while engaged in TGfU (McNeil et al., 2011).

ENGAGEMENT AND ENJOYMENT OF GAMES

Key factors that are associated with a students' participation in physical activity are (a) their perceived level of competency and (b) experiencing feelings of enjoyment while engaged in PE (Gray et al., 2008). The results of this study present statistically relevant evidence that students experienced feelings of enjoyment while engaged in TGfU for the first time. Furthermore, questions 1, 5 and 11 specifically address feelings of excitement in attending PE, participating in competitive activities, and playing small-sided games. All three questions highlighted an increase in numerical values from the pre-unit to post-unit questionnaires where the increase shown in question 11 held statistical significance. The results from the questionnaires were supported by the interview comments shared by the five boys from the class. The boys shared that they experienced feelings of enjoyment, excitement, happiness and fun while engaged in the TGfU unit. The teacher/researcher observations also reported high levels of engagement especially during the small-sided games. Some students also were reported to have enjoyed having active leadership roles within their teams.

In summary, the supporting literature pertaining to TGfU and like models, continue to recognize this method of teaching practice as pedagogically sound. Students, teachers, and researchers not only report classroom environments filled with excited and engaged students, but also experience heightened learning and physical literacy of games (Brooker et al., 2000; Chatzopoulos et al., 2006; Gray et al., 2008; Hastie & Curtner-Smith, 2006; McNeill et al., 2011). This study supports TGfU as a delivery method, which promoted experiences that students find enjoyable and encourage greater competency of games and physical ability.

Conclusions & Recommendations

This paper focused on answering the research question "What will be the experiences of boys engaged in the TGfU approach for the first time?" The experiences of the boys were discussed using emergent themes, which included higher levels of confidence and perceived ability, as well as a greater understanding of the game of basketball. Students also expressed feelings of fun, enjoyment, and happiness while engaged in TGfU. Student feedback results were supported by teacher/researcher-recorded observations that included greater perceived learning and higher levels of engagement. The following sections conclude this study with discussions on the role of TGfU in a balanced physical education program and recommendations for current and prospective educators.

TGFU AND PHYSICAL EDUCATION

Physical education has been, and will continue to be, an important aspect of young people's education portfolio. The learning that occurs within physical education (PE) includes all domains; psychomotor, affective, and cognitive. PE contributes to the growth and development of physically and emotionally healthy individuals, and promotes the value of lifelong physical activity. However, just as the nature and needs of our students are evolving, the way in which we present PE must also evolve to support our changing student demographic. TGfU presents an approach that centres on the students and nurtures their multidimensional learning needs.

TGfU advocates support the philosophy that PE is an important avenue not only for enhanced physical activity and social development, but also to engage students in critical thinking and decision-making. The approach places students at the forefront of their learning while encouraging their positive participation in games. Studies have concluded that using the TGfU approach not only encourages game appreciation, but also develops tactical awareness, and decision-making skills (Griffin et al., 2005). Moreover, recent studies point to the approaches ability to foster feelings of enjoyment, fun, and confidence (Stran et al., 2012; Hastie & Curtner-Smith, 2006; Holt et al., 2002).

The future of PE programs and curricular changes should reflect the positive research developments of TGfU and similar models. Penny and Chandler (2000) further support and identify that TGfU should hold a position in the future development of initiatives in PE as it shows a valuable ability to build connections between classroom learning and the greater lives of our students. This study supports previous research in that TGfU is a valuable model when used as part of a balanced physical education program.

RECOMMENDATIONS FOR CURRENT AND PROSPECTIVE EDUCATORS

This section focuses on recommendations to teacher practitioners beginning to implement the TGfU model. Changing a pedagogical approach in physical education classes is challenging. It is a process that requires time, dedication, discipline, patience, effort, and knowledge before feeling confident that a beneficial change for the students and teachers has been made. By choosing to adopt TGfU in PE programs, teachers are also accepting to revisit their values and beliefs that have been their previous pedagogical foundation. It also required that we take steps to further connect theory to practice (Butler, Oslin, Mitchell, & Griffin, 2008).

As professionals we need to be conscious of the importance of reflective behaviour in our practice. We should embark in the process of questioning our methods and their outcomes on a regular basis. The process of reflection and questioning in our practice ensures that our students are receiving a quality, relevant and connected education. This may be an individual professional journey, but it can serve as a positive way to engage other members of the education community including colleagues and administrators. Support from these communities is critical to a successful implementation of TGfU in PE programs (Butler, 2005). Once educators engage in the process of reflection and questioning of their methods it is important that they seek out professional development opportunities. Gaining hands-on experience in using the TGfU model is tremendously advantageous while making a transition to a new model of teaching. Finally, the transition period may seem long and at times uncomfortable. Striving to create change is a journey that requires time and patience. Educators need time to process and practice using the model before success may be fully recognized.

References

Brooker, R., Kirk, D., Braiuka, S., & Bransgrove, A. (2000). Implementing a game sense approach to teaching junior high school basketball in a naturalistic setting. *European Physical Education Review,* 6(1), 7-26. doi:10.1177/1356336X00006103

Bunker, D., & Thorpe, R. (1986), The curriculum model. *Rethinking games teaching,* 7-10.

Butler, J. I. (2005). TGfU pet-agogy: old dogs, new tricks and puppy school. *Physical Education & Sport Pedagogy,* 10(3), 225-240.

doi:10.1080/17408980500340752

Butler, J., Oslin, J., Mitchell, S., & Griffin, L. (2008). The way forward for tgfu: Filling the chasm between theory and practice. *Physical & Health Education Journal,* 74(1).

Cardinal, B., Yan, Z., & Cardinal, M. (2013). Negative experiences in physical education and sport: How much do they affect physical activity participation later in life? *Journal of Physical Education, Recreation & Dance,* 84(3), 49-53.

Chatzopoulos, D., Drakou, A., Kotzamanidou, M., & Tsorbatzoudis, H. (2006). Girls' soccer performance and motivation: Games vs technique approach. *Perceptual and Motor Skills,* 103(2), 463-70. Retrieved from http://www.ncbi. nlm.gov/pubmed/17165411

Cohen, L., Manion, L., & Morrison, K. (2000). *Research methods in education* (5th ed.). London: Routledge Falmer.

Davis, B., Sumara, D., & Luce-Kapler, R. (2008). *Engaging minds: Changing teaching in complex times* (2nd ed.). New York, NY: Routledge.

Denzin, N., & Lincoln, Y. (2011). The discipline and practice of qualitative research. In Denzin & Lincoln (Eds), *The sage handbook of qualitative research* (4th ed). (pp.1-19). Thousand Oaks, CA: Sage.

Gray, S., Sproule, J., & Wang, C. K. J. (2008) Pupils' perceptions of and experiences in team invasion games: A case study of a Scottish secondary school and its three feeder primary schools. *European Physical Education Review,* 14(2), 179-201. doi:10.1177/1356336X08090705.

Griffin, L., & Patton, K. (2005). Two decades of teaching games for understanding: Looking at the past, present, and future. In Griffin & Butler (Eds), *Teaching games for understanding; theory, research, and practice.* (pp.1-17). Champaign, IL:Human Kinetics.

Griffin, L., Brooker, R., & Patton, K. (2005). Working towards legitimacy: Two decades of teaching games for understanding. P*hysical education and sport pedagogy,* 10(3), 213-223.

Griffin, L. L., Mitchell, S.A., & Oslin, J. L. (1997). *Teaching sports concepts and skills: a tactical games approach.* Human Kinetics Publishers (UK) Ltd.

Hastie, P. A., & Curtner-Smith, M. D. (2006). Influence of a hybrid sport education- teaching games for understanding unit on one teacher and his students. *Physical Education & Sport Pedagogy,* 11(1), 1-27. doi: 10.1080/17408980500466813.

Holt, N. L., Strean, W. B., & Bengoechea, E. G. (2002). Expanding the teaching games for understanding model: New avenues for future research and practice. *Journal of Teaching in Physical Education,* 21(2).

Kirk, D. (2005). Physical education, youth sport and lifelong participation: The importance of early learning experiences. *European Physical Education*

Review, 11(3), 239-255.

Kirk, D., & MacPhail, A. (2002). Teaching games for understanding and situated learning: Rethinking the Bunker-Thorpe model. *Journal of teaching physical education,* 21, 177-192.

McNeill, M.C., Fry, J. M., & Hairil, M. (2011). Motivational climate in games concept lessons. I*CHPER- - SD Journal of Research in Health, Physical Education, Recreation, Sport & Dance,* 6(1).

Penney, D., & Chandler, T. (2000). Physical education: What future(s)? *Sport, education and society,* 5(1), 71-87.

Siedentop, D. (1994). S*port education: Quality PE through positive sport experiences.* Human Kinetics Publishers.

Sparkes, A. (2002). T*elling tales in sport and physical activity: A qualitative journey.* Champaign, IL: Human Kinetics.

Stran, M., Sinelnikov, O., & Woodruff, E. (2012). Pre-service teachers' experiences implementing a hybrid curriculum: Sport education and teaching games for understanding. *European Physical Education Review,* 18(3), 287-308. doi 10.1177/1356336X12450789.

Webb, P., Pearson, P. & Forrest, G. (2006). Teaching games for understanding (TGfU) in primary and secondary physical education. Paper presented at ICHPER- SD International Conference for Health, Physical Education Recreation, Sports and Dance, 1st Oceanic Congress Wellington, New Zealand, 2006 (1-4 October), www.penz.org.nz

Where have all the Kids Gone? Declining Enrollment in Senior Physical Education Classes

BY DAVID DUNKIN & KARA WICKSTROM

Introduction

Over the past twenty years, there has been a substantial amount of research conducted that indicates significant declining enrollment in elective physical education not only in British Columbia, but also internationally.

> Students are required to take physical education from Kindergarten to Grade 10, at which point they can opt to take physical education as an applied skills graduation requirement. Ministry of Education data show that enrollment in physical education has been steadily declining throughout the 1990s. (Deacon, 2001, p. 23)

Deacon's research suggests that declining physical education enrollment rates indicate a need for certain changes in curriculum delivery, pedagogical assumptions and/or resulting classroom atmospheres to ensure a positive, worthwhile experience where students feel motivated, engaged and safe. The reasons for declining participation in physical education are many, and their complexity forces researchers to look at the variables that may lead students to not selecting physical education as an elective. Throughout our literature review, we limited our focus to declining enrollment in PE and what motivates students to elect to take physical education. It is our intent to determine the reasons that lead students to select other courses instead of physical education. While there is existing research in this area, the majority of it has been conducted via surveys. Although informative, survey data can be limiting as respondents may not want to take the time to provide a detailed written response. To gather more detailed information, we elected to interview students in hopes that they could enlighten us as to why this non-enrolment is occurring.

RESEARCH QUESTION

What are the contributing factors to students not electing to enroll in formally scheduled physical education after completing the mandatory Ministry of Education requirement in British Columbia?

RESEARCH GOAL

Through this research, it was our goal to examine the physical education experiences of students who chose not to enroll in elective PE. Through this examination, we attempted to determine the contributing factors that lead to low enrollment in senior physical education. Having determined the causes of this issue, we are now in a better position to make recommendations about how students, parents, teachers, schedulers and administrators can change their current thinking about physical education. By raising a greater awareness of the issues, it is our hope that the result will be a greater enrollment in PE by all. We hope to connect with potential readers to generate conversations that will lead to change. Literature from 1991 is not that different from what we have found with our recent data, and this is frustrating, as it is hard to believe that not much has changed in physical education for over 20 years. We feel passionate that change needs to occur in order to keep our youth active and healthy participants who want to continue to be active after required physical education classes cease.

We speculated that the issues surrounding the non-enrolment of students in elective PE were systemic in nature. Though all of our participants did not elect to enroll in senior PE, there were a great deal who reported that they would have if it were available to them. The reasons surrounding the difficulty accessing this course are deep and complex. From the stress of competing for entrance to post-secondary institutions, to having important core courses scheduled opposite PE in high school timetables, students are being forced to make a difficult choice. Why should these students have to make such an unhealthy choice? We believe they shouldn't.

Literature Review

The focus of our literature review was on declining enrollment in physical education and what motivates students to not select senior physical education. This research allowed us to examine and analyze the reasons why our adolescents are not participating in a course that is essential for them to develop the skills to lead a healthy and well-balanced life. Unfortunately, there is not one simple explanation of why students choose not to continue with organized physical education. We have found several contributing factors that serve as barriers to students interested in selecting elective PE.

THEMES

We used five themes identified by Sinclair and Luke (1991) that determine attitudes towards physical education to organize our literature review. These five themes include: "curriculum content, teacher behavior, class atmosphere, student self-perceptions, and facilities" (p. 44). While the themes used to organize our literature review provided a framework for our understanding around the matter, they did not exclusively shape our interview questions. The resulting interview data is explained below.

Methodology

Data generation occurred through a structured interview of the sample participants. The reason structured interview methodology was utilized was to ensure all participants focused on the ideas that presented themselves within the literature review. For this study, we invited two sets of six participants from two different schools (n=12) who had not selected a physical education course for the current school year. In efforts to draw from a heterogeneous grouping to allow for a more diverse range of participants, both female and male participants were invited based on athletic program participation, low achievement in previous physical education class, and high achievement in previous physical education classes.

These participants answered twelve open-ended questions asked orally by the researchers. The use of these questions was determined through discussions with our professors, our coursework, our literature review and our interest. It was our hope that through responding to the list of questions, students would be able to share with us their experiences in PE and the factors that led to their non-enrolment. Each interview was audio recorded with the sound recorder on password-protected school district laptops and transcribed upon completion. Once the researchers transcribed the data, each interview participant was invited to meet with the researcher to confirm the accuracy of the transcription.

To increase potential understanding, we decided to utilize Fictional Ethnography (Rinehart, 1998), in hopes that readers would draw upon their own experiences to connect with those of our research participants. From here we examined our emerging themes of curriculum, timetable, academic achievement, student enjoyment, student voice and choice, and physical activity versus physical education, through a lens of Critical Ethnography (Hardcastle, Holmes, & Usher, 2006) in hopes that a critical examination of the participant information can positively affect systemic change. Additionally, we feel that using Self-Determination Theory (Deci & Ryan, 1985) as our theoretical framework helps illuminate a number of important reasons why students are not motivated to continue with physical education after it is no longer mandatory.

Results & Discussion

The following is a fictional ethnography that represents the information shared by the participants in our study. Each detail provides significant and important clues as we attempted to unravel the issues surrounding declining numbers in elective PE enrollments.

Mark grew up in a small town in northern British Columbia. The location provides the opportunity for participation in several outdoor pursuits including skiing, biking, horseback riding and hiking. Additionally, the town is well equipped with programming for youth through the local recreation center and pool. Mark enjoys being active through community sports, high school sports and time spent at the rec center. He has participated enthusiastically with excellence in physical education throughout his schooling. When it came time to select courses for the 2013-2014 school year, Mark found little flexibility in the schedule and was disappointed that he could not find time in his timetable to include PE 11. It seemed that PE was scheduled in direct conflict with the courses he needed to ensure his successful acceptance to a significant number of post-secondary institutions across Canada. No matter how many times he reworked his timetable with his academic counsellor, the result was always a schedule loaded with academic courses and a spare to support them. While he was convinced the spare was not necessary, he found there was no way to fill it with his love for activity. Unfortunately, he would have to settle for getting his activity at the recreation center and with his high school basketball team. He did take advantage of the opportunity to drop in to PE classes going on during his spare, but this was not the same and he was only able to participate on occasion. He was deeply disappointed that this was the only way he could spend time with his favorite teachers and like-minded peers.

While this fictional ethnography lists some of the difficulties students in our study have had with the various issues surrounding PE enrolment, it is not exhaustive. Through the coding process, transcript data was examined to determine a more extensive list of issues. The following six themes have been examined further given the frequency of their occurrence in the transcript data: academic achievement, scheduling, curriculum, student voice and choice, other relevant physical activities and student enjoyment.

THEME ONE: ACADEMIC ACHIEVEMENT

It is clear from our interviews that students from both research school sites valued the completion of academic credits over the completion of physical education credits. This occurred regardless of whether or not they reported enjoying physical education. One participant was very forthcoming about how she saw academics and PE at odds, "This year, I have decided to focus on my classes" and "when I am at school, I will focus on studying" (Cammy, Interview #9, December 17, 2013). This type of comment was typical, as if involvement in physical education would come at the expense of academic achievement. Another student simply commented, "I thought that my time would be better used in a more academic setting" (Holley, Interview #10,

January 16, 2014). In addition to the fact that participants put a high value on core academic courses, many also felt that they benefited from the extra study time at school provided by a spare block of time in their timetable. Those who had the option to choose a spare over PE did so. One student explained that, "I could have taken gym as a seventh course, but left it open to do other work" (Tom, Interview #1, December 12, 2013). Another student made this statement, "Because of all my other classes, I had a pretty full schedule already" (Cammy, Interview #9, December 17, 2013). Ratey (2008) comments on how one study "showed that cutting gym class and allocating more time to math, science, and reading did not improve test scores, as so many school administrators assume it will" (p. 42).

The issue of having to choose been academic courses and studying versus enrolling in physical education lies in the misperception by many students, parents and educators that extra time and effort is better spent on academics and studying. Trudeau and Shephard (2008) comment on the importance of physical education, physical activity, and sport team involvement with respects to achievement when they state, "such activities are likely to increase attachment to school and self-esteem which are indirect but important factors in academic achievement" (p. 18). Coe, Pivarnik, Womack, Reeves and Malina (2012) showed that the fittest children got the highest test scores and the best grades, regardless of gender or whether they'd yet gone through puberty. Additionally, Trudeau and Shephard (2008) provide an interesting commentary regarding negative views of PE involvement stating that, "parents concerned about decreases in study and homework time may be better advised to question the time their children spend on TV and computer games rather than the time that they devote to PE, PA or sports in school" (p. 18). While we realize this brings about an entirely different issue, we thought it bore enough poignancy to include here. Educating our student body on the importance of physical activity along with the potential health and academic benefits may be something we need to do earlier in their schooling when they are not pressured with these high academic expectations.

STUDENT MOTIVATION FOR HIGH ACADEMIC ACHIEVEMENT

In terms of student motivation for high achievement, we discern that it comes from the very real pressure students feel to achieve top marks in the core academic subjects required for acceptance to most post-secondary institutions. This sentiment was shared by participants who cited the importance of having time to study in hope of improving their chances at higher academic achievement. Physical education does not typically factor into this equation as most universities do not recognize PE as one of the six core courses they use to calculate an applicant's grade point average. Unfortunately, we believe this can devalue the importance of physical education and continue to hamper efforts to keep students enrolled in PE 11 and 12. One participant echoed this sentiment, "No universities really accept (PE), so it didn't seem beneficial to take it" (Larry, Interview #4, December 16, 2013). We feel that when students perceive the lack of importance of PE, as determined by post-secondary institutions, their motivation to enroll drops off.

While some students struggled with choosing PE over academics, there were those students who despite being motivated to take PE, were not able to find room in their schedule.

THEME TWO: SCHEDULING

Scheduling was another barrier that emerged as a major theme standing in the way of students enrolling in elective physical education. Physical education often conflicts with core academic subject times, making it difficult to schedule into student timetables. Though this situation is often less an issue in larger schools, both researchers at their respective sites noticed the problem given their relatively smaller populations. One student reported that, "It didn't fit into my schedule and I had more important courses that I needed to take" (Allison, Interview #7, December 16, 2013). When asked if she would have taken physical education if it had not conflicted, she offered that "yah" she would have. Mark, commented that, "I really wanted to take phys ed, but unfortunately due to that course load, it was impossible" (Interview #6, December 16, 2013). Still another participant offered that, "For me, it was a scheduling issue, it didn't have anything to with not wanting to schedule it." (Kirk, Interview #12, January 29, 2014). Finally, the simplest statement, "I just didn't have enough space in my timetable" (Allison, Interview #7, December 16, 2013) encapsulates the issue completely.

It became clear that at this particular school (School A) PE only conflicted with Advanced Placement (AP) courses. While this was encouraging to us, it turned out four of the six students interviewed at school A were all enrolled in AP courses, so they could not take PE. Additionally, 84 senior students (Grade 11 and 12) were enrolled in AP courses at this school. Some of these students were taking multiple AP courses, while others only enrolled in one. While this particular school works to avoid conflicts between PE and core academic subjects, academics are highly valued, and the numbers show that those who enroll in AP are unable to participate in PE as well. Of the four students interviewed who were taking AP at school A, all enjoyed PE but stated that they needed the time to study.

Some of our participants did not even have to factor in their past feelings towards PE as their scheduler/administrator had not given them a choice. Without the apparent scheduling barriers, would these same students have chosen PE? All students were asked if they would have taken PE if there had not been conflicts and 75% (9/12) said they would have. One student stated, "It is not that I did not like PE but I really wanted to take AP Human Geography and it took priority as well as conflicted with PE" (Holley, Interview #10, January 16, 2014). It seems fairly consistent with our participant responses that the majority had a conflict with PE. Many also did not know what they wanted to do at university and felt like they needed to keep their options open by taking the extra academic course instead of PE.

THEME THREE: CURRICULUM

Sinclair and Luke (1991) identify that "curriculum is the most influential factor in the development of both positive and negative attitudes toward physical education, regardless of students' gender and regardless of whether they elect or avoid school physical education" (p. 37). During the interview process, participants were questioned as to the nature of the curriculum they participated in while enrolled in mandatory PE. While there was some sentiment that these activities were enjoyable, there were telling comments that lead to the emergence of what we considered a troublesome trend. Students provided evidence that not all teachers selected activities based on criteria that potentially benefit students or the field of physical education; rather, they were selecting activities based on criteria that either satisfied their own interests or were traditionally scheduled.

With this in mind, we believe it is crucial that students are offered a balanced curriculum that allows them to build the skills and appreciation necessary to foster continued positive feelings and competence in their physical learning. Through our interviews, it became very apparent that a balanced curriculum was not common. While there is some indication that the curriculum our participants experienced was well rounded in its offering of varied activities, most students explained that their curriculum was heavily tied to popular team sports such as basketball, volleyball and soccer. Bryan and Solomon (2012) comment that curricula of this nature "do not provide a motivational climate that is appropriate for students who may not like sports, who do not feel competent or successful, or those who are physically inactive and/ or unfit" (p. 10). Other students did not comment directly about their sports-heavy curriculum or structure but were disenchanted with their experiences, as highlighted by the following comment: "Every day we would do warm ups and then stretches and either sit ups or push ups and then we would all decide on a game we wanted to play" (Allison, Interview #7, December 16, 2013). Yet another student commented that he "remembered she [the teacher] liked volleyball, so we did a lot of volleyball" (Devon, Interview #3, December 16, 2013). Even in a small sample such as this research group, there are differing opinions that provide insight into the types of curriculum being offered by various teachers.

Immediately, this brings forth a concern for the authors. By not choosing meaningful or novel activities and presenting them in an appropriate manner, many students are unmotivated to continue to participate in elective PE. Mandigo and Holt (2002) explain that "humans have an intrinsic desire to seek out and participate in optimally challenging activities that foster their self-development," and "when individuals are successful at an optimally challenging activity (i.e., not too easy, not too hard), their competence is enhanced" (p. 22). By ignoring this opportunity to match curriculum to the learners it is intended to serve, students are done a disservice and are made to simply go through the motions.

Unfortunately, this is where the injustice can surface for many PE students. Teachers, for the most part, have the autonomy or power in selecting curriculum they want to deliver. This does not necessarily mean that the curriculum is best for learning, suitable for all students, or associated with student interest. This sentiment is echoed by Sinclair and Luke (1991): "because most teachers have considerable choice over the curricular content of their PE programs, this is an area where the teacher plays a vital role in the process of attitude change" (p. 41). Some students were disappointed that the curriculum didn't change over their years in PE. Comments such as "I found it somewhat repetitive some years" (Kirk, Interview #12, January 29, 2014), and "it kinda was the same every year. It would be like soccer then basketball then badminton." (Sally, Interview #11, January 27, 2014).

Still others reported feeling inadequate in their PE classes, "I felt like some things were if I wasn't on the basketball team I felt like I had a disadvantage in it so I didn't really enjoy it" (Sarah, Interview #5, December 16, 2013). This inadequacy has been examined by Mitchell (1996) and Cloes (2005), who both found that students' intrinsic motivation increases if they perceive the learning environment to be non-threatening to their self-esteem. When traditionally scheduled sport dominates a curriculum, students compare themselves with other students who may be proficient by way of participating on a competitive team in those sports. Thus, the students deem themselves less worthy in their abilities compared to someone who spends hours practicing a given sport. With the choice of activities being such a determining motivator in students' attitudes towards PE, it becomes increasingly important that physical educators are equipped with the skills to make appropriate decisions based on the types of curricular activities that will foster important learning and enjoyment of PE.

THEME FOUR: STUDENT VOICE AND CHOICE

As we collected information regarding student voice and choice, it became increasingly clear that there was inconsistency in how this option may have been offered by teachers. There was a relatively even split between students who experienced the option to have input about their curriculum and those who did not. On one hand, a student commented that "she [the teacher] also listened to the students to make sure that we were doing something we all liked" (Holley, Interview #10, January 16, 2014). Allison commented that "[the teacher] would give us the choice of what we wanted to do that day" and "[there was] consideration [of] what everybody wanted to do and not just the top athletes in the class, because it's only fair to think of everyone" (Interview #7, December 16, 2013). On the other hand, one student found that, "The students' opinions weren't really heard, we didn't really have a decision in what we wanted to do." (Tom, Interview #1, December 12, 2013). Others echoed this sentiment with comments such as, "I would've enjoyed if it was more like what the kids wanted to do," "I liked it better when there was more choice," and "no, [the class] was very standardized" (Sarah, Interview #5, December 16). All that said, none of the participants provided information that confirmed the presence of voice and choice in creating their own games or curriculum; all related to merely choosing a particular activity for one class. While the existence of student voice and choice is encouraging, the opportunity to choose and plan with teachers ahead of time would have likely had more impact on the recognition that real choice was being offered in a collaborative setting.

The opportunity for students to make decisions about what type of curriculum they might participate in is not a new idea. Sinclair and Luke (1991) reported that "the opportunity to make choices and decisions were cited as important determinates of positive attitudes" (p. 42). By allowing students the chance to provide input about the types of activities they are interested in, or enjoy participating in, the resulting dynamic can increase positivity towards the class as a whole. Students are increasingly interested in having autonomy within their learning and providing this opportunity makes sense. Ryan and Poirier (2012) agree that providing choice to students is a considerable way to increase interest:

> One great way to put this motivational method into practice is to create a survey to begin to understand what type of activities they would enjoy doing during the semester. The teacher can learn from the data and build a physical education course around the interests of the students. (p. 186)

This shift towards acknowledging student interest is something that is taking place in several schools across Western Canada. Specifically, several of our colleagues have engaged in creating courses that cater to the interests of females in hopes of increasing their enrollment in senior PE. These classes enroll only female students and provide the opportunity for those girls to take part in activities they enjoy. By utilizing the opportunity for choice, these educators have found a way to increase the enjoyment of the females who likely would not have enrolled were this choice not available.

THEME FIVE: OTHER RELEVANT PHYSICAL ACTIVITY

Each student we interviewed felt that, in the absence of a scheduled PE class, they were benefiting from other relevant physical activity. While there are those who consider their involvement in competitive sport as a reasonable replacement for PE, "I play for team BC for rugby, I know fitness is not a problem" (Tom, Interview #1, December 12, 2013). There are others who are simply seeing personal fitness as a means to an end: "I do enough exercise,"and "I do tennis, I go to the gym 2-3 times a week and I lift weights at home sometimes, I would do more hard core exercise outside of school and I already had enough physical activity every day" (Cammy, Interview #9 December 17, 2013). Finally, there were a small number of students who consider any activity at all to be a relevant replacement for PE. One student considered walking a sufficient replacement, "We go to Vancouver and do a lot of walking there too, around the malls" (Matthew, Interview #2, December 16, 2013).

Clearly, there is a disconnect, where physical activity (PA) is being considered on the same level as PE. Even if we were comfortable accepting that PA was a reasonable replacement for PE, there are some concerning qualifications for what may or may not constitute a reasonable level of PA. While some pursuits are better than others in the fact that they require learning to occur or rigorous physical demands, in our opinion, there is no substitute for the skills and lessons learned in a PE class. Meyer, et al. (2013) explain the delineation between PA and PE: "Providing regular participation in PA is therefore only one goal of PE, but may be the only opportunity to attain a minimum of PA for a considerable percentage of the inactive population" (p. 600). We acknowledge that PA is an important part of a PE course, however, there are several other important outcomes that are missed if PA is the only portion that is being used as a replacement. The British Columbia Ministry of Education, Skills and Training Physical Education 11 and 12 Integrated Resource Package (1997) clearly outlines the expectations for elective PE:

> Physical Education 11 and 12 provides opportunities for students to experience a variety of recreational pursuits, career interests, and activities that promote lifelong, healthy living. Students focus their learning in areas of personal interest and participate in activities that promote social interaction, community responsibility, and skill development. (p. 1)

By justifying their lack of enrollment in PE through an attachment to any sort of physical activity, students are not only missing out on many important learning opportunities, we are concerned that they are setting a precedent that PA is something that can take the place of PE. As this thinking becomes more prevalent, there is a chance that physical educators could simply be replaced by recreation activity coordinators. While no physical educator wants to realize this possibility, there exists a significant problem when further considering this possibility.

Perhaps a look into what types of activities are most enjoyed by students will allow physical educators to build enjoyable programs that are so popular, students won't dare stay away.

THEME SIX: STUDENT ENJOYMENT

Despite not enrolling in physical education, most/all students interviewed had the same positive comments with regards to the students' past enjoyment of physical education. One student commented, "It was fun. It is a chance to play a whole bunch of sports" (Devon, Interview #3, December 16, 2013). The students who did not enjoy their past experience in physical education were the students with the lower marks in their PE 10 class. The higher achieving students in PE 10 were the students who commented on physical education being fun, and they would have elected to take the course if there were no conflicts or they did not have such a heavy academic load.

Our literature review revealed that students choose not to elect physical education as a result of their past experience. Research completed by Higgins, Gaul, Gibbons and Van Gyn (2003) found that students who chose not to enroll in PE 11 did so because of their past experience, not because of their expectations of what the course would be like. Sinclair and Luke (1991) sourced other authors (Earl & Stennett, 1987; Figley, 1985; Rice, 1988) who have also concluded that determinants such as attitude play a crucial role in whether students continue with physical education. Positive attitudes towards physical education and fitness can lend itself to higher enrollment in elective PE, but we found that it is not the main determinant. One participant stated that, "I think it was very much one of the funnest times I've had, I got to compete in sports with my fellow classmates, which is something I enjoyed doing" (Mark, Interview #6, December 16, 2013). After reading this comment from this particular student, one would think that there is a clear correlation that a more enjoyable physical education program in the earlier grades would lead to higher enrollment in higher grades. However, this student who enjoyed his past experience in PE did not elect to continue because of a scheduling conflict, not because he did not enjoy the subject. Whereas a second student offered that she "wasn't a fan of PE in the past. I wasn't excited to go to gym so when we didn't have to take it I choose not to" (Sally, Interview #11, January 27, 2014). It is interesting to note that this same student received the lowest mark in PE of all our research participants where the previous student received a much higher grade. In our twelve interviews, there is a correlation between lack of enjoyment in past PE experience and lower marks in PE 10 as opposed to higher marks in PE 10 and enjoyment of past PE experience. Ennis (2013) states that, "Unfortunately, low skilled and reluctant students rarely increase their skills, enjoyment, or motivation to participate in a physically active lifestyle in recreational environments" (p. 153). Additionally, Kirk (2012) comments that "by the time most children reach secondary schools their perceived competence and motivation and hence their likely engagement in physical activity has already been formed and there is little that physical educators can do to change these dispositions" (p. 128). Additionally, Bevans, Fitzpatrick, Sanchez and Forrest (2010) comment, "perceived competence in PE was found to positively predict physical activity levels, both directly and through its relation with PE engagement" (p. 412).

Conclusion

It is clear that there are several barriers standing in the way of students selecting PE as a viable option for their elective needs. We have identified six specific areas that capture the essence of the difficulty students face in selecting a senior PE elective: academic achievement, scheduling, curriculum, student voice and choice, other relevant physical activities, and student enjoyment.

Our participants were able to share insight into their struggles, not only with finding space to fit PE into their daily schedules, but also with the motivating factors that lead to them to select an academic course or look elsewhere to find other ways to meet their physical activity needs. Through the information provided to us by the participants, we have a better idea why there is such a significant decline in the numbers associated with PE 11 and 12 at each research site. While it is difficult to know if these themes are consistent in other areas of our province, we can hypothesize that considering them when setting up balanced academic programs would be a practice that could benefit those charged with this increasingly important task.

References

Bevans, K., Fitzpatrick, L., Sanchez, B., & Forrest, C. (2010). Individual and instructional determinants of student engagement in physical education. *Journal of Teaching in Physical Education, 29*, 399-416.

British Columbia Ministry of Education, Skills and Training (1997). *Physical education 11 and 12.* [Integrated Resource Package]. Retrieved April 17, 2014 from https://www.bced.gov.bc.ca/irp/subject.php?lang=en&subject=Physical_Education

Bryan, C. L., & Solmon, M. A. (2012). Student motivation in physical education and engagement in physical activity. *Journal of Sport Behaviour, 35*(3).

Coe D. P., Pivarnik J. M., Womack C. J., Reeves M. J., Malina R. M. (2012). Health-related fitness and academic achievement in middle school students. *Journal of Sports Medicine and Physical Fitness, 52*(6), 654-60.

Deacon, B. W. (2001). *Physical Education curriculum review report.* Ministry of Education, Curriculum Branch. Ministry of Education.

Deci, E. L., & Ryan, R. M. (1985). *Intrinsic motivation and self-determination in human behavior.* New York: Plenum.

Ennis, C. D. (2013). Implications of exergaming for the physical education curriculum in the 21st century. *Journal of Sport and Health Science, 2*, 152–157.

Higgins, J.W., Gaul, C., Gibbons, S., & Van Gyn, G. (2003). Factors influencing physical activity levels among Canadian youth. *Canadian Journal of Public Health, 94*(1), 45-51.

Kirk, D. (2012). Physical education futures: Can we reform physical education in the early 21st century? *Ejrieps, 27*, 120-131.

Mandigo, J. & Holt, N. (2002). Putting theory into practice: Enhancing motivation through optimal strategies. *Physical and Health Education Journal, 68*(2), 41.

Meyer, U., Roth, R., Zahner, L., Gerber, M., Puder, J., Hebestreit, H., & Kriemler, S. (2013). Contribution of physical education to overall physical activity. *Scandinavian Journal of Medicine & Science in Sports, 23*(5), 600-606.

Ratey, J., & Hagerman, E. (2008) *Spark: The revolutionary new science of exercise and the brain.* New York: Little, Brown and Company.

Rinehart, R. (1998). Fictional methods in ethnography: believability, specks of glass, and Chekhov. *Qualitative Inquiry, 4*(2), 200-224.

Ryan, T. & Poirier, Y. (2012). Secondary physical education avoidance and gender: Problems and antidotes. *International Journal of Instruction, 5*(2),173-194.

Sallis, J. F. (2000). Age-related decline in physical activity: a synthesis of human and animal studies. *Medicine and Science in Sports and Exercise, 32*(9), 598-600.

Sinclair, G. D., & Luke, M. D. (1991). Gender differences in adolescent's attitudes toward school Physical Education. *Journal of Teaching in Physical Education,* 11(1), 31-46.

Trudeau, F. & Shephard, R. (2008). Physical education, school physical activity, school sports and academic performance. *The International Journal of Behavioral Nutrition and Physical Activity,* 5(1), 10-22.

CHAPTER SIX

Where have all the Girls Gone?
Female Choice in Senior Elective PE

BY ANGELA BIGIOLLI

Introduction

According to the Canadian Health Measures Survey data from 2007-2009, only 15 percent of Canadian adults get the recommended levels of 150 minutes of moderate-to-vigorous activity (MVPA) per week and only 7 percent of Canadian children get the recommended 60 minutes of MVPA per day (Colley et al., 2011). It is concerning that today's population does not fully understand the ramifications of leading an unhealthy, non-active lifestyle (Tremblay et al., 2012). The World Health Organization states, "Physical inactivity is the fourth leading risk factor for global mortality. Increasing levels of physical inactivity are seen worldwide. Globally, 1 in 3 adults are not active enough" (World Health Organization, 2014).

Government agencies in many countries are warning of an obesity crisis amongst school-aged children (Nowicka & Floodmark, 2008). The main factor is believed to be the failure to achieve the recommended levels of moderate-to-vigorous activity (MVPA) per day. Moreover, according to the Women's Sport and Fitness Foundation (WSFF) report (2011), research shows an equal level of activity between girls and boys in the early years with an ever increasing gender gap in the final years of elementary and high school. The WHO states that only 5 percent of girls aged 11-15 participate in the recommended levels of physical activity (World Health Organization, 2009).

In all Canadian schools there is a mandate for physical education (PE) programs to help students develop the skill, knowledge and attitudes necessary to be physically active throughout their lives (Gibbons, 2009: PHE Canada). In British Columbia, PE is listed as a required subject for all students from kindergarten up to and including Grade 10 in order to graduate. Research states that fewer than 10 percent of females choose to enroll in PE once it becomes an elective course after grade 10 in British Columbia (Gibbons, 2009). Many females become disenchanted with their PE experiences from kindergarten to Grade 10 and then turn their backs on additional courses in their senior year. In WSFF's policy report, over half of secondary girls say they "are put off sport and physical activity because of their experiences of school sport and PE" (2011). According to Gibbons and Humbert (2006), "there is some promising research that supports the notion that if the needs and interests of young women are incorporated into PE programs, they willingly participate" (p. 5). The coeducational senior PE elective that is prevalent in high schools at the present time does not meet the needs of these young women and is often criticized for the "failure to provide a gender equitable environment" (Fraser-Thomas & Beaudoin, 2004, p. 46).

PURPOSE OF STUDY

As I observed female students opting out of a senior co-ed PE classes, a new course was developed in order to increase participation and enjoyment in Senior PE. Since the implementation of this new program, which attempts to address the diverse interests and abilities of our senior female student population, there was 18 percent growth in female enrolment in senior PE, increasing our total enrolment of girls in all senior PE courses to 30 percent. The intent of this study is to understand female students' feelings, and respond to the question: What are the factors that influence female students' enrolment or non-enrolment in an elective senior girls PE class?

Methodology

Qualitative research integrates the methods and techniques of observing, documenting, analyzing and interpreting characteristics, patterns, attributes and meanings of human phenomena under study (Macdonald, 2012). The main purpose of qualitative research is to describe and understand rather than to predict and control. In this study, narrative inquiry is used to ask questions about female participants' experiences in PE, and to acknowledge where the participants have come from and why they are feeling the way they are about PE. Clandinin and Murphy (2007) state that care has to be made to listen empathetically, to not pass judgment and to suspend disbelief while listening to a participant's stories (p. 647). Narrative inquiry allows the researcher to focus on the human knowledge of students and an opportunity for them to tell their stories.

SETTING AND PARTICIPANTS

This study took place in a co-educational public secondary school in the Vancouver School District. The location of the school is considered inner city with a diverse population from a variety of socio-economic and cultural backgrounds. The student-population of the school is approximately 1700 students and consists of students from Grades 8 – 12. The PE classes at this particular school are segregated in Grades 8-10 and co-educational in Grades 11 and 12.

Prior to 2013, the only PE options that were available in the school were a fitness training class or a co-ed senior class that was predominately sport-based. In the 2013/2014 school year, an additional PE course was offered to help entice females in the senior grades to continue with physical activity within their school schedule. This course was offered to all girls in Grades 11 or 12 who were interested in continuing on with PE in a single-gendered class. When the course was first introduced during course selection in January of

2013, there were 66 requests for the new PE 11/12 girls course and 25 requests for the traditional co-ed PE 11/12 course. In order to maximize the placement of females in PE, the administration at the school decided to run two classes using the model of the newly developed PE course. In September of 2013, a total of 50 students were enrolled in the Girls PE 11/12 course. Due to course conflicts, this number was lower than the initial sign up of 66 females.

Overall, twenty-one participants volunteered to participate in this study. Six were in the girls PE 11/12 classes, eight were in the co-ed PE classes, and seven Grade 11/12 girls that were invited to participate in the study who had opted to not enroll in PE in that year.

DATA COLLECTION

Data collection for this study was conducted through three instruments/procedures. These were researcher observation and field notes, take home questionnaire/survey, and one-on-one interviews. Each of these data collection methods played an integral part of accessing participant information and allowed for data triangulation.

COURSE DESCRIPTION

This course description allowed the students to accurately acquire a sense of what the course would cover. The course description was as follows:

> The emphasis of this course is to provide an environment where girls will develop life-long healthy living habits. This course is meant to give girls the opportunity to participate in a wide variety of physical and leisure activities offered in an enjoyable atmosphere. The curriculum for the course may include a variety of activities such as: Yoga, Spinning, Pilates, Weight training, Fitness classes, Aqua fit, Power walking, Jogging, Swimming, Self Defence, Hip hop, Rock Climbing, Skating, Roller blading, Sailing, Wind surfing, Kayaking and Nutrition. An off-campus activity fee will be collected to pay for activities that will take place in sport establishments throughout the lower mainland.

The PE department felt it was imperative that the information was received by the PE 10 girls' classes prior to course selections that were taking place at the end of January 2013. This organized meeting allowed any questions about the course to be answered by the teacher that was teaching it the following year.

ETHICAL CONSIDERATIONS

Once the study began, my teacher colleague invited students from the PE 11/12 Girls' classes, the girls in the co-ed PE classes as well as any senior girl who was not enrolled in PE to participate in the study. She described the study to the girls and handed out assent and parental consent and explained that these forms were to be returned to the main office within two weeks.

Once the participants were determined, questionnaires were handed out to the fifteen girls that had returned their assent and parental consent forms. The researcher felt that allowing the girls to take home questionnaires for a week, instead of completing the questionnaires in class would allow participants time to answer the questions fully. Most of the responses that were returned were well thought out and included explanations that supported the feelings and experiences of the individual participants.

My colleague interviewed all six participants to avoid any sense of coercion since I was the teacher for some of the female students. The one-on-one interviews allowed the researcher to access ideas, thoughts and memories in the words of the individuals rather than in the words of the researcher.

DATA ANALYSIS

To understand the reasons why females chose to enrol or not enrol in a senior girls elective PE class, data was compared from the all field notes, questionnaires and transcribed interviews. The information was then categorized and coded into similar themes. The intent was to find common themes from all three data generation methods in order to report the findings.

Results

After a thorough review of the field notes, student questionnaires, written responses and one-on-one interview transcripts, there were a number of themes that emerged. Careful analysis of this data allowed for the following summary of results to be documented. This summary has been separated into two categories:

1) *Reasons for Grade 11 and 12 female students to enroll in a PE 11/12 girls course,* and

2) *Reasons for Grade 11 and 12 female students to not enroll in a PE 11/12 girls course.*

Both of these two categories encompass a number of themes that arose when the data was closely examined.

Reasons Grade 11 & 12 female students chose to enroll in a PE 11/12 girls course:

As I progressed through the research process and read through all the data over the past two years, the same responses kept appearing throughout. The following table categorizes the themes that emerged from the data.

COURSE CONTENT WAS NEW AND DIFFERENT

When this course was first taken through the new course process in late fall of 2012, statements were made that this new course would encourage more Grade 11 and 12 female students to take PE. A PE staff member stated that, "Finally, we are offering a course with activities like yoga, Zumba and weight training that girls will sign up for. They have been asking about this for years," (Field notes, November 21, 2012 PE department meeting). At the staff committee meeting on December 12, 2012 counselors gave the thumbs up to this new course with one counselor saying, "This new course will be an easy one to sell to the girls instead of the traditional Senior Co-ed PE course" (Field notes, December 12, Staff committee meeting). In January 2013, prior to course selection, PE 10 girls' classes were presented this new course. It was explained that the PE department had recognized a void in the course offerings at the senior level and that for the upcoming year PE would offer a PE 11/12 course for girls. The girls had lots of questions about the course and

Table 1

***Themes from Written Responses and Interview Transcripts:
Female choice to enroll in a PE 11/12 Girls Course.***

Course Content	• Fitness - Yoga and Zumba,
	• No expertise needed - minor games (Handball, wallball, war, etc.),
	• Options
	• Field Trips
Environment	• Fun, Less aggressive
	• Teacher compatible
	• Segregated
Fit and active	• Wanted to exercise
	• Health and fitness
	• Fitness guidance
	• No time

the conversations were very positive after the presentation. By the end, there were Grade 10 girls excited about enrolling in a new class with exactly the activities that they wanted to participate in.

In data from the surveys and the interviews, a number of students that had enrolled in this new class stated that they took this course because it wasn't all about team sports. According to Franca (Grade 12) in her interview, "It was a course with activities that I liked to participate in. Activities like gymnastics, dance and yoga, things that I can do well in. I am not very good at soccer and other team sports, so I didn't do very well in PE 8-10" (Franca, personal interview, April 7, 2014). The extensive participation in team sports at the younger grade levels seemed to give a negative association to PE from many different participants. The females were excited to play minor games like handball, wall ball and other activities that they didn't necessarily need expertise in.

In addition to these outlined activities, students were intrigued by this new course because this new course allowed the participants to voice their opinions in the activities and field trips that were going to happen during the year. The activity curriculum and field trips for 2013/2014 could be entirely different from future years as it was dependent on what the students wanted.

> Girls 11 and 12 was really smart, because like the first thing we did was, like, she asked us what we wanted to do in this class. I mean we can't do everything that everyone wants to do but, I mean I felt like I got a lot of choice this year. It was good. And that is why I mostly took the class, because I felt like that it was the sort of class where I could one do the stuff that I liked plus, have, like, more of an opinion and input in what to do. (Franca, personal interview, April 7, 2014)

A SAFE LEARNING ENVIRONMENT

The subsequent theme that the participants spoke or wrote about was that the learning environment had to be one that students would feel safe to learn and take risks in.

> It was important that the environment was one that you felt safe in to try new activities and field trips. There is nothing worse than trying something for the first time and making a fool of yourself, I hate being laughed at. (Susan, personal interview, April 2, 2014)

Students wanted to have fun and not worry about fitness and skill testing like they did in the junior PE classes. Susan (Grade 11) stated that during fitness testing, "There was so much pressure to, like, do good and you're always trying to get that 10, especially in the shuttle run" (Susan, personal interview, April 2, 2014). The students suffered from enough test anxiety in their academic classes and they wanted PE to be a place where success was attainable for everyone, not just the most athletic in the class.

Teacher compatibility was also important to a student's safe learning environment. Students felt that if they knew the teacher and liked the teacher they would enjoy PE a lot more.

> I felt more comfortable when her teachers were understanding. I knew that this teacher of the PE 11/12 Girls class was very understanding of her students. I had her before and she always talked about open lines of communication. She stressed that if you didn't feel very good or were having a rough day, to let her know and she would adjust the activity for you. (Fiona, written responses, February 28, 2014)

Having a female instructor was a deciding factor as well. In PE 8-10, the female classes were all taught by female teachers. At the senior level only one out of the six senior classes were taught by a female, so for some students there was a fear that they would end up with a male PE teacher if they enrolled in a co-ed senior class. However, enrolling in the PE 11/12 girls class guaranteed they would have a female teacher, likely one that the students had previously taken a class from.

This new PE class allowed females to continue their physical activity in a segregated, less aggressive environment. Many of the students that enrolled in PE 11/12 Girls wanted to stay in a segregated PE class. The participants didn't like the aggressiveness of the male students or the domination of males in activities.

> The boys were so focused on winning that they don't really pass to the girls or give them an option to try it out. I am okay at most activities but I get really bored playing with the boys when all I am is a spectator. Often times when we eventually get a chance and make a mistake, the boys laugh at us. (Susan, personal interview, April 2, 2014)

FIT AND ACTIVE

When analyzing the data participants stated that they did indeed want to be active. Contrary to popular belief, female high school students wanted to exercise and stay fit. Females wanted to learn how to stay fit and active in their high school years so that when they were adults there was more likelihood that they would continue physical activity. Females in Grades 11 and 12 felt that this class would keep them fit and introduce them to activities other than traditional team sports that they could continue participating in after finishing high school.

In addition to their education in health and fitness, females also saw this class as a time that they had to exercise. Most seniors in high school are so busy with school, work and studying that "a scheduled time for physical activity [is] a must in order for them not to develop into a blob" (Franca, personal interview, April 7, 2014). Participants felt that there was no time available in their day unless physical activity was scheduled in onto their timetable.

Reasons Grade 11 & 12 female students did not enroll in a PE 11/12 Girls course:

In addition to data that explains why female students chose to enroll in a PE 11/12 girls course, there is also data which explains why females chose not to enroll in the course. In this section there were two groups of girls that chose not to enroll in the PE 11/12 Girls course: *1) Females enrolled in co-ed PE 2) Females not enrolled in any PE.* In the table below, the data is once again grouped into four themes. Some of the themes are repetitive, but for differing reasons in each of the groups.

1.) FEMALES ENROLLED IN COED PE

Table 2
Themes from written responses and interview transcripts: Female choice not to enroll in a PE 11/12 Girls Course but enrolled in coed PE.

ENROLLED IN COED PE INSTEAD OF SENIOR GIRLS PE

Course Content	• More sports in coed PE
	• Not challenging
	• Boring
Environment	• Better competition with the boys
	• Faster paced
	• My friends were taking coed PE
Fit and active	• Wanted to sweat
	• Get in shape
Timetable issues	• Oversubscribed
	• Academics is a priority

COURSE CONTENT

The data that was extracted from the field notes, written responses and interview transcripts pointed to the course content as a major indicator as to why females chose not to enroll in the PE 11/12 Girls course. When the course was originally presented to the PE 10 classes, the most athletic girls in the class who did well in team sports and other activities were not interested in doing yoga and dance (Field notes, January 2013). This was validated in Elizabeth's (Grade 11) interview when she stated that:

> I had looked at the curriculum plan or the schedule on our wall in the gym and it had more things that I enjoy to do in senior PE than in girls PE. I didn't want to get stuck doing yoga every day. (Elizabeth, April 3, 2014)

ENVIRONMENT

The most prominent reason that females in co-ed PE did not choose to enroll in the PE 11/12 girls course was because they did not feel that it was going to be challenging enough. According to Elizabeth (Grade 11), she wanted to sweat in PE, so she chose co-ed PE. She felt like that "there's not necessarily more or better competition, it just feels like because there are boys in the class, I'll feel challenged" (Elizabeth, personal interview, April 3, 2014). Written responses made mention that by having males in the co-ed PE class, the activities would be more challenging. In Fiona's (Grade 12) interview she said that, "girls in PE 8 thru 10 didn't really try hard which made PE boring" (Fiona, personal interview, April 3, 2014).

Part of the reason that girls chose co-ed PE was because their friends were enrolling. Even though there was a chance that they wouldn't be in the same class with their friends, they were comfortable knowing that the majority of the girls in co-ed PE were there for the same reasons they chose the same PE.

FIT AND ACTIVE

In the collected data, the girls who chose to take mixed-gendered PE wanted to be in an active atmosphere, and they believed that co-ed would be more active than in PE 11/12 Girls. These fitness activities would allow them to stay fit without the added cost of outside fitness groups or clubs.

TIMETABLE CONSTRAINTS

One of the females who signed up for co-ed PE only took it because the PE 11/12 Girls would not fit into her timetable. There were certain academic courses that she had to complete for graduation and university, and she only had one block that she could take an elective in and that block only had co-ed PE. She knew that she wanted to take PE in order to give herself a break from homework and sitting through academic courses and she would take any PE course if PE 11/12 Girls was not available.

2) FEMALES NOT ENROLLED IN ANY PE

Table 3

Themes from written responses and interview transcripts: Females not enrolled in any PE courses.

NOT ENROLLED IN ANY PE

Course Content	• Didn't like the activities
	• Hate running
	• HATE PE
Social	• My friends were not taking PE
	• Didn't know anyone taking PE
Not Advertised	• Didn't know that this course was being offered.
	• My counsellor did not tell me about this new course
Timetable issues	• Oversubscribed
	• Academics is a priority
	• My parents wanted me to focus on my academics

COURSE CONTENT

By the time that this group data was analyzed there was a reoccurring theme. It was explained that once again course content was a determinant of whether females enrolled in any type of PE course. When analyzing the survey responses, participants used harsh stances like, "I hate PE" or "I hate running" to explain why they did not enroll in the PE 11/12 Girls course.

> Past PE classes did not really offer any type of activity that I could find success in. We always had skill testing and I didn't do very well. If only PE offered activities that we could just play in instead of learning skills all the time. I can throw a ball or a Frisbee but to stand there and keep throwing and catching to practice the skill without even playing the game, how fun is that? (Jenny, personal interview, April 7, 2014)

When the eight participants that chose to not enroll in any senior PE elective responded on their questionnaire, all replied that they did not enjoy PE because of the long units of traditional sports in their PE classes. They claimed that it was boring, that they weren't very good at the sports, and that the athletic girls always dominated the majority of the games being played.

SOCIAL FACTORS

The social aspect of PE proved to be a major factor in whether females chose to enroll in PE or not. In all accounts, the main reason that none of the females enrolled in the PE 11/12 Girls course or any other PE course was because their friends were not signed up for them or that they didn't know anyone taking the course. Friends play a major role in the lives of these young adults and as one participant wrote, "If I am going to do something wrong in class, I need my friend there to help me laugh it off or tell me that I didn't look that bad" (Fiona, personal interview, April 3, 2014).

NOT ADVERTISED

Some of the participants that did not sign up for this new course claimed that they did not know about the course. In the planning process, the intention was for counselors to introduce all new courses to the appropriate grades so they could make informed choices when it came to course selection. Apparently this was not the case as the Grade 11's going into Grade 12 were not informed of this new course that was being offered for the 2013/2014 school year. As one Grade 11 stated, "I didn't even know about the course because I would've taken it. I tried switching my electives but by the time I found out it was packed" (Jenny, personal interview, April 7, 2014).

TIMETABLE CONSTRAINTS

The final theme that appeared in the data was that the course would not fit into the participants' schedules. The course was only offered in two blocks and if those blocks didn't work for a participant's schedule, PE was the first thing dropped from their selection. One participant wrote that their academics were top priority so they could get into university and PE didn't even count as a university credit (Franca, personal interview, April 7, 2014).

LESSONS LEARNED

The culmination of the study showcased various opportunities for teachers to incorporate into their planning and teaching of female students. The following proposals outline what measures can be followed in order to increase numbers in elective PE 11/12 courses.

PROPOSAL #1: STUDENT VOICE IN CURRICULAR PLANNING.

Throughout the data, females reported that they did not like certain activities that they were forced to participate in throughout PE 8, 9 and 10. There was no escaping teacher directed units that were not fun for all of the students. Memories of past experiences with too much of one activity and not enough of other activities caused students to be bored. When the new elective PE course was presented and students were asked their opinions on what they wanted to achieve, play or learn this year, they became excited about the class. Students were engaged in the planning process and constructed a course that was balanced and student led. Ntoumanis and Biddle (1999) found that the best way to motivate students to take PE was by allowing students to have a 'voice' in curricular planning.

PROPOSAL #2: VARIETY OF COURSE CONTENT

PE classes tend to weigh heavily on team sports and competition. Having a balanced class in all areas of curriculum (team sports, individual sport, gymnastics, dance, outdoor education, aquatics, active living, fitness) as well as activities in community facilities would allow for the needs of all students to be met. As the PE 11/12 Girls class was created, it was required that the activities offered were balanced. Since the previous PE classes in grades 8, 9 and 10 consisted of mostly team sports and competition it was important to create a class of balanced activities that the females would appreciate.

PROPOSAL #3: INCREASED PLAYING TIME

Students don't like participating in isolation drills in order to learn a skill. Instead, they want to be active, playing and having fun. Remembering when they were young, laughter and smiles were brought by playing; not standing around learning a skill. A skill and drill emphasis is a substantial part of why most students, not just females, are reluctant to take PE in elective years. Teachers have to continually evaluate their methods of teaching and try new styles that could better motivate your students to learn and participate in activity.

PROPOSAL #4: GIVE ELECTIVE PE OPTIONS

All students are different. The creation of this PE 11/12 Girls class met the needs of females that were not feeling like co-ed PE is something that they wanted to participate in. This new class gave the females options to enroll in a class with activities that they enjoyed participating in. Replacing co-ed PE with PE 11/12 Girls is not recommended, but developing more courses that would help entice more males and females into PE in the elective years is desirable. There is talk about introducing a PE 11/12 Dance Elective to lure females into enrolling in PE in the future, but that would depend on the demand for that type of course. It is a PE department's responsibility to their student body to evaluate and re-evaluate course offerings from year to year. Times change, students change, it is our job as professionals to keep up with the demands to keep students in Elective PE.

Conclusions

The results of this study provided information on the factors that influence female enrollment in a PE 11/12 Girls course. The implementation of a PE 11/12 Girls course into a school that had previously offered only co-ed PE 11/12 was a step in the right direction. The female students of this school were waiting for a PE course that would give them a chance to be physically active in an environment that they would enjoy.

Not all females were open to enrolling in this class, but by the time of implementation of the course, more opportunities were available for all female students to enroll in PE as an elective. This new course helped to increase the number of females active in a senior elective PE course, and it was encouraging to find that females really wanted to be active in a way that met their needs.

Although this study was aimed at analyzing the female enrollment in a PE 11/12 course it also provided suggestions on what could be changed at the lower PE grades in order to promote a positive learning experience in females in PE 8 through 10. The results of this study helped the PE department analyze how PE is delivered in the school. If students, female or male, were not happy with their PE experience during their junior years, what needed to be altered in order to achieve the "FUN" factor that students expressed in the study?

Females will enroll in courses and participate in activity if it meets their needs. By supplying a variety of options for physical activity, more females may choose to participate. An ongoing evaluation of this course at the end of a school year would allow participants the voice in expressing the positives and negatives of the course. The teacher, in turn, could re-evaluate what she is trying to achieve and alter the course for the upcoming year.

It is in the best interests of future students to continue research in the area of female participation in activity. Investigation into female adults and their experiences in PE and physical activity through their school years would give insight in the decline of female participation. If their experiences are what is holding them back from being physically active in their later years, then the PE programs that we offer need to be addressed.

References

Bullying Awareness Week. (2012). Myths and fact about bullying. [online] Retrieved from http://www.bullyingawarenessweek.org/ [Accessed: 20 November 2012]

Canadian Universities and Colleges Higher Education and Employment in Canada. A guide to Canadian universities, community colleges, career colleges and jobs in Canada. [online] Retrieved from http://www.canadian-universities.net [Accessed: 01 March 2014].

Colley, R. C., Garriguet D., Janssen I., Craig C.L., Clarke J. & Trembly. (2011) Physical activity of Canadian Adults: Accelerometer results from the 2007 to 2009 Canadian Health Measures Survey. Statistics Canada: Health Reports, 22(1), 7-23.

Ennis, C.D. (1999). Creating a culturally relevant curriculum for disengaged girls. *Sport Education, and Society,* 4, 31-49.

Felton, G., Saunders, R., Ward, D., Dishman, R., Dowda, M., & Pate, R. (2005). Promoting physical activity in girls: A case study of one school's success. *Journal of School Health,*75(2), 57-62.

Fraser-Thomas, J., & Beaudoin, C. (2004). Girls' appreciation of new physical education curriculum classes. *Avante.* 10(2), 45-56.

Fisette, J.L. (2013). 'Are you listening?': Adolescent girls voice how they negotiate self-identified barriers to their success and survival in physical education. *Physical Education and Sport Pedagogy,* 18(2) 184-203.

Gibbons, S.L. (2009). Meaningful participation of girls in senior physical education courses. *Canadian Journal of Education,* 32(2), 222-244.

Gibbons, S.L., Gaul, C. & Blacklock, F. (2004) Built it and they will come: Designing of physical education program for high school women. *Physical and Health Education Journal,* 69(4), 17-23.

Gibbons, S.L. & Humbert, L. (2008). What are middle-school girls looking for in physical education. *Canadian Journal of Education,* 31(1), 167-186.

Gibbons, S., Wharf Higgins, J., Gaul C., & Van Gyn, G. (1999). Listening to female students in high school physical education. *Avante,* 5(2), 1-20.

Humbert, L. (1995). On the sidelines: The experiences of young women in physical education classes. *Avante,*1(2), 58-77.

Ntoumanis, N., & Biddle, S. H. J. H.(1999). A review of motivational climate in physical activity. *Journal of Sports Science,* 26, 197-214.

Ryan, Thomas & Poirier, Yves. (2012). Secondary Physical Education avoidance and gender: Problems and antidotes. *International Journal of Instruction,* 5(2) 173-194.

CHAPTER SEVEN

Helping Increase Girls' Physical Self-Efficacy through TGfU and the GPAI

BY BRENT JACKSON

Introduction

RECOGNIZING THE PROBLEM

Early in my teaching career at an all-girls school, I recognized the difficulty in teaching Grade 4 students how to effectively play soccer. As a result, I invented a game called Quarter Soccer (QS). The fundamental idea behind QS was to force students to play in a limited space, thereby helping them learn about spacing and positioning. A few years later, after a lesson in which I spent a great deal of time communicating (hollering) instructions on how to play, I sat at my desk, a frustrated teacher. I knew that the outcomes were not working for the girls, and I knew that I had to change the process. What I did not know was where to make changes, nor did I realize just how far back in the process I needed to go. This research project was an attempt to investigate the processes of engaging female students and improving their physical self-efficacy through the Game Performance Assessment Instrument (GPAI).

As an adult I realized how fortunate I was to have adults, teachers and coaches that in one way or another focused on the process. As I moved into my teaching and coaching career, I began to understand the positive effects of working towards process goals, rather than outcome goals. For the past 17 years I have worked in an all-girls school, and my history helped me appreciate how traditional teaching and coaching models can negatively impact females. For me, a natural progression was to begin investigating the process, and to perhaps uncover some piece of information or some glimmer of evidence that teachers can use to improve the Physical Education experience for girls. As my study of Physical Education curriculum models began to unfold, I started peeling back the layers of the Physical Education process from my perspective as a teacher, and from the perspective of my students. As I reversed my focus on the outcome of lost students, and worked through the processes, what I uncovered was disheartening. In general, traditional, behavioralist-type teaching models did not seem to invigorate positive attitudes towards Physical Education for many female students. Concerns about these teaching methods swirl around the social, cultural and masculine hegemonies that are perpetuated through those models of teaching Physical Education. The results of which leave female students with low motivation because they do not feel competent, and their competency is not strong because, in fact, their physical self-efficacy is low. How can a student spend this much time, this many years, in Physical Education and exit the curriculum with low physical self-efficacy, and without the motivation to participate in optional physical activities? Can Physical Education teachers affect positive change in physical self-efficacy through our teaching models and assessment tools?

THE RESEARCH QUESTION

As my research in to Physical Education progressed an "aha!" moment came shortly after being introduced to the Games Performance Assessment Instrument (GPAI). "The GPAI is a multidimensional system designed to measure game performance behaviors that demonstrate tactical understanding, as well as the player's ability to solve tactical problems by selecting and applying appropriate skills (Oslin, Mitchell, & Griffin, 1998, p. 231). Once I began thinking of GPAI as a compliment to TGfU methodology, I found that combining the two was potential innovation:

What were the effects of using the Game Performance Assessment Instrument during instruction and assessment of game play on Grade 7 girls' physical self-efficacy?

To answer the research question, I used quantitative research to gather data. By including a non-equivalent groups design, a control group, and repeated measures, the aim was to yield an objective result that can be generalized to larger populations.

THE INFLUENCE OF THE TEACHER ON STUDENTS' EXPERIENCES

In 1991, Luke and Sinclair identified and examined the potential determinants of male and female adolescents' attitudes toward school Physical Education. The authors conclude that the most negative influences on student's attitudes are 'curriculum' (39.2%) and 'teacher' (32.2%). As the teacher is the director of the curriculum, it is easy to imagine the two determinants working hand-in-hand to bring down the ship for any one student. Similarly, their study showed 'curriculum' (52.7%) dominating the list of positive determinants. However, 'the teacher' (6.1%) was only the fourth strongest positive determinant. Perhaps for these students the teacher has done a great job of controlling the variables, acting as the 'guide on the side,' and less the 'sage on the stage,' and as such fostered an atmosphere where students invest in the class, which led to high levels of positive engagement (Storey & Butler, 2012).

Current educators may not need reminding of the power of classroom autonomy, but the recent findings suggest that "participatory approaches to research and curriculum-making can serve to promote students' meaningful engagement in the critique and the reimagining of their Physical Education and physical activity experiences" (Enright & O'Sullivan, 2010, p. 203). The outcome of Luke and Sinclair's 1991 study has shown that regardless of the students' perceived experience, the major determinants are "well within the control zone of the teachers" (p. 45).

GENDER CONCERN

Citing the National Federation of State High School Associations, Kaestner and Xu (2010) noted that since the creation of Title IX in 1972, female participation in both Physical Education and school athletics has risen dramatically in the United States. Despite this fact, research shows that as children age their levels of physical activity decline, and that girls in particular have shown a greater rate of attrition (Malina, 2001). This, in addition to the fact that girls have shown a history of disengagement with Physical Education (Enright & O'Sullivan, 2010), is very troublesome.

Within the Canadian school system, since all students take part in Physical Education, we are able to connect most female children and adolescents to Physical Education, and yet we still continue to see a decline in both participation and engagement. The problem lies not with opportunity, but how we mishandle the opportunities. As discussed earlier, a lack of support from the teacher or curriculum can lead to a large proportion of adolescent females disengaging from Physical Education and physical activity (Cairney et al., 2012; Luke & Sinclair, 1991). It is unrealistic for teachers to expect most female students to feel successful in a sport-based Physical Education program as "most sports that currently hold status in society were created by adult men for men and are played using men's rules, equipment, and definitions of success" (Ennis, 1999, p. 46). Being aware of the unique needs of their students, including gender, is a must for teachers. Girls desire involvement and to feel as though they are contributing to classroom activities (Beveridge & Scruggs, 2000; Cairney et al., 2012), so we must build courses that help females connect to and engage with Physical Education. When constructing an atmosphere that is conducive to female success, one must first understand and relate with the nuances of self-efficacy, competency and motivation.

SELF-EFFICACY, COMPETENCY AND MOTIVATION

If you watch a Physical Education class, it does not take long to see if the curriculum is full of activities that are confidence cutters; a prevalent practice in most sport-technique based, traditional teaching models (Singleton, 2009). It is my experience that most students will make an effort if they feel safe and supported. Therefore I built the theoretical framework of this study around Albert Bandura's work on self-efficacy through his Social Learning Theory (SLT), and competency as seen in Susan Harter's Perceived Competency Motivational Theory (PCMT).

Albert Bandura defines self-efficacy as "people's beliefs about their capabilities to produce designated levels of performance that exercise influence over events that affect their lives" (1994, p. 71). For example, students will have high self-efficacy if they believe in their understanding of volleyball strategies and how to effectively employ those strategies during game play. In this light, when developing a Physical Education curriculum, it is extremely important for teachers to understand the basic principle behind Bandura's Self-Efficacy Theory: Individuals are more likely to engage in activities for which they have high self-efficacy and less likely to engage in those they do not. In explaining SLT, Bandura identified four major contributors to one's expectations of efficacy.

Experienced mastery:

"Successes raise mastery expectations; repeated failures lower them, particularly if the mishap occurs early in the course of events" (Bandura, 1978, p. 143)

Vicarious experience:

"Seeing others perform threatening activities without adverse consequences can generate expectations in observers that they too will improve if they intensify and persist in their efforts" (Bandura, 1978, p. 145).

Verbal persuasion:

"People are led, through suggestion, into believing they can cope successfully with what has overwhelmed them in the past" (Bandura, 1978, p. 145).

Emotional arousal:

"Stressful and taxing situations generally elicit emotional arousal that, depending on the circumstances, might have informative value concerning personal competency" (Bandura, 1978, p. 146).

It is difficult to argue with Bandura's (1978) assertion that through performance accomplishments, experience is the largest contributor to efficacy expectations, and I believe it is safe to say that traditional Physical Education teaching models rely heavily on verbal persuasion to feed a student's self-efficacy expectations. However, I see a great opportunity to increase students' physical self-efficacy through the vicarious experience. As a key contributor to self-efficacy expectations, there is incredible value in modeling, especially if the model is a classmate that the student can identify with, and the student engages in evaluating that classmate.

Susan Harter's Perceived Competency Motivation Theory (1978, 1981) suggests that people, especially children, are motivated by the perception of mastery in various areas and the perceived mastery will promote self-efficacy and motivate them to continue efforts to increase skill or competency. Students who feel they are good at Physical Education will persist when they meet a challenge. Those who have low self-efficacy in Physical Education class will hide, disengage, and (at worst) find a way out of the class. If many female students are removing themselves from activity, we must look at the process and find the root of our failure. Motivation to pursue improvement comes from competency, which in turn comes from a high (physical) self-efficacy. At the root of the developing life-long, active-living people is physical self-efficacy. After all, who wants to do something they are not good at?

TEACHING GAMES FOR UNDERSTANDING: ENGAGEMENT POTENTIAL

In 1982, Bunker and Thorpe noted that playing games itself has a great potential to motivate students and enhance their engagement with activities, and so brought in to the world a student-centered model of teaching Physical Education that is contemporarily known as TGfU. TGfU is a "learner-centred model that fosters the development of physical literacy through game-centred activities designed to enhance students' game performance, cognitive responses and skill development in a positive and highly motivational setting" (Mandigo, Butler, & Hopper, 2007, p. 14). Building on the fact that children love to play games, research has shown that using a student-centred approach to games has the potential to enhance player enjoyment, intrinsic motivation, and sustained involvement in an activity (Bunker & Thorpe, 1986; Butler, 2005; Mandigo & Holt, 2006).

TRADITIONAL APPROACH: PHYSICAL EDUCATION AS GYMNASTICS AND SPORTS-TECHNIQUES

Supported by teacher-centred, transmission teaching models, gymnastics or sports-techniques is the traditional view of what Physical Education is about (Tinning, 2012). Unfortunately, the approach of many teachers and coaches to Physical Education and sports remains tied to traditional models. One needs to look no further than Hockey Canada (HC) to see the entrenched models of development. In 2000, HC published their Player Development Pyramid as part of their Open Ice Summit. HC's pyramid (see Figure 1), then and now, places technical skills at the foundation and strategies at the apex (Hockey Canada, 2014). "This is reflective of the traditional philosophy of teaching games, which assumes individuals must have proficiency in motor skills prior to game play" (Fried & Maxwell, 2009, p. 161). This is the epitome of a traditional classroom where techniques perpetuate because many teachers simply regurgitate plans and drills modeled by their mentor (Butler, 2005; Haneishi, Griffin, Seigal, & Shelton, 2009). This response is hardly surprising "since appropriate responses are likely matters of knowing differently, not merely knowing more" (Davis et al., 2008, p. 8).

ASSESSMENT AND TEACHING GAMES FOR UNDERSTANDING

Assessment, like teaching models, is open to teacher autonomy, and offers a variety of forms. Within sport, and by extension Physical Education, some believe that the goal "is to properly identify athlete's abilities to function efficiently in predetermined situation" (Fried & Maxwell, 2009, p. 161). At some levels, in some situations, this may be true. However, in a typical Physical Education class, girls need involvement to feel as though they are contributing (Beveridge & Scruggs, 2000; Cairney et al., 2012). Why not combine assessment with Beveridge and Scruggs' (2000) TLC (Teacher, Learning environment, and Curriculum) model? Perhaps using the GPAI to enhance assessment as learning within a girls' Physical Education class will see efficacy grow?

"Though rules and strategies for playing games have changed over the years, methods used to teach and assess games have changed very little" (Oslin, Mitchell, & Griffin, 1998, p. 231). We assess skills on a summative basis, providing little feedback. By and large, a great deal of Physical Education assessment is "of learning". If teachers are trying to build physical literacy in our students, where is assessment "for learning" and "as learning"?

Figure 1. **Hockey Canada player development pyramid (2014).**

Interestingly, the GPAI can be used for assessment: of learning – by the teacher; for learning – feedback to a student; as learning – by the student using the tool. In Hopper's "Four Rs for Tactical Awareness" (2003), he writes "The GPAI works well to reinforce and diagnose tactical play that creates a foundation for skill practice" (p. 20). If there is a better way to teach, and teaching models such as TGfU are central players, then the GPAI should lead to more meaningful assessment and learning!

THE GAME PERFORMANCE ASSESSMENT INSTRUMENT

The GPAI is a tool developed for teachers and researchers to assess their students' progress in tactical understanding (Oslin, Mitchell, & Griffin, 1998). While observing a subject, the tool allows the user to code up to seven athletic components that paint a picture of the students' or athletes' tactical abilities. The seven components as developed by Oslin et al. (1998) can be seen in Figure 2.

For the purpose of this study, in which students would be observing each other, I chose to simplify the GPAI and use only three components. The point of my study was not to measure the actual tactical game abilities of the students, but rather to give them a stronger presence during instruction and assessment of Physical Education.

Figure 2. **Seven components of the Game Performance Assessment Instrument (Oslin, Mitchell, & Griffin, 1998, p. 233).**

1. BASE	Appropriate return of performer to a "home" or "recovery" position between skill attempts
2. ADJUST	Movement of performer, either offensively, or defensively as required by the flow of the game
3. DECISIONS MADE	Making appropriate choices about what to do with the ball (or projectile) during the game
4. SKILL EXECUTION	Efficient performance of selected skills
5. SUPPORT	Off-the-ball movement to a position to receive a pass (or throw)
6. COVER	Defensive support for player making a play on-the-ball, or moving to the ball (or projectile)
7. GUARD/MARK	Defending an opponent who may or may not have the ball (or projectile)

The developers support this by advising that "[s]implification of the GPAI is especially useful when students are involved in peer evaluation" (Oslin et al., 1998, p. 233). Additionally, the use of the tally method kept the GPAI manageable for the seventh-grade students that participated in this study.

Unfortunately, few studies make the test subjects use the GPAI, as the tool is mostly used in a researcher to subject method. Hopper (2003) concluded that the GPAI can be modified without compromising its effectiveness, and as stated earlier, it works well to reinforce and diagnose tactical play that creates a foundation for skill practice. Ireland and Urquhart (2012) used the GPAI as an observational learning tool to help students engage in class when not actually playing in game, and they concluded that having students observe each other proved an effective learning tool. These results are very encouraging as it paves a clear path for teachers to move away from assessment of learning and the traditional skill and knowledge tests that are weak indicators of student learning experiences (Black & Wiliam, 1998). Instead, involving students in assessment 'for learning' and 'as learning' is the kind of energetic shot in the arm that desperately needs to take hold in Physical Education curriculum, and allows innovative tools to "produce significant learning gains when compared with the existing norms of classroom practice" (Black & Wiliam, 1998, p. 25).

NO CANNONBALLS ALLOWED

Despite its failings, Physical Education is not going to fall off the face of the earth, because comparative dynamics says that living and learning forms have erratic profiles since they are coupled to other forms, grander systems (Davis et al., 2008). Physical Education is not only coupled to students and teachers, but many other forms as well, including curriculum, schools, and Provincial governments. We must recognize this as a hallmark of complex phenomena, and remember that Physical Education is not "one size fits all. If you get it, fine, if not, tough luck!" (Canada, 2013). Rather, it is complex, layered, and— as described in *Engaging Minds* (2008) — like a fractal image; "a recursive process – that is, [a] series of elaborations in which the starting place of each stage is the output of the previous stage" (p. 26).

Methods

DESIGN

The purpose of this study was to investigate the effects of using the GPAI on Grade 7 girls' physical self-efficacy during game play. Due to the narrow scope of the research question, I used quantitative research to gather data for this study. By including a non-equivalent groups design, a control group, and repeated measures, the aim was to yield an objective result that can be generalized to larger populations. Although I had previously taught the students from School B, I needed to disconnect myself from the teaching portion of this study and remove the threat of construct validity in the form of experimenter expectations. Therefore the three teachers who volunteered to participate proctored as research assistants.

The non-equivalent groups design allowed me to use intact groups believed to be similar for the treatment and control groups, as random assignments were not attainable. Using this design fairly compares the treatment group with the control group, but I recognize that one can never be sure the groups are comparable. The two research groups for this study are based on similar environments/settings:

SCHOOL A – CONTROL GROUP (TGFU ONLY):

- ~ 60 Grade 7 girls
- Independent all-girls' day school
- PreK – 12
- Situated in an affluent neighborhood
- Well established school, 75+ years old
- Classes taught by teachers with 29 and 34 years experience.

SCHOOL B – TREATMENT GROUP (TGFU AND THE GPAI):

- ~ 40 Grade 7 girls
- Independent all-girls' day school
- PreK – 12
- Situated in an affluent neighborhood
- Well established school, 75+ years old
- Classes taught by a teacher with 27 years experience

The control group is a group of subjects closely resembling the treatment group in many demographic variables but not receiving a factor under study. In this study the classes at both schools were lead through the same TGfU based volleyball and basketball lessons, and thus placed under the same conditions. However, the GPAI treatment condition was not introduced to School A. This allowed me to introduce the GPAI treatment condition to School B and test the affects of the GPAI on girls' physical self-efficacy over time.

Repeated measures are collected in a longitudinal study in which change over time is assessed. I used a repeated measures design to evaluate the students at School A and School B with the TGfU condition of the research, and the GPAI treatment condition. Repeated measures of the PSEQ were used to *(a) determine a baseline of girls' physical self-efficacy; (b) assess the effects of the Teaching Games for Understanding (TGfU) teaching model on girls' physical self-efficacy; (c) assess the effects of using the GPAI on girls' physical self-efficacy.*

PARTICIPANTS

In this study the participants were seventy Grade 7 girls and three teachers from two independent single-gender schools. School A provided 33 student participants and two teacher participants. School B provided 37 student participants and one teacher participant. In School A, the student participants came from three PE classes of 20 students, where the volleyball unit was taught by Teacher 1 (29 years experience), and the basketball unit was taught by Teacher 2 (34 years experience). In School B the student participants came from two PE classes of 20 students, where Teacher 3 (27 years experience) taught the volleyball and basketball units.

All of the students approached by the researcher had the opportunity to participate in this study, and it was made clear to the students that their participation or lack of participation in the study had no significance on their academic standing in PE. Those students who elected not to participate in the study were able to fully participate in the lessons, and they were given alternative games to play while their classmates completed the questionnaire. The number of participants used in this study was based on the number of students who elected to participate.

DATA COLLECTION

Data collection occurred through the completion of the PSEQ three times over the course of four to six months. The questionnaire was first completed early in the school year, prior to any major themes being taught. These data were considered the Baseline results. The second completion of the questionnaire was at the conclusion of the volleyball unit (Post VB), and the third time the questionnaire was completed was at the end of the basketball unit (Post BB).

PHYSICAL SELF-EFFICACY QUESTIONNAIRE

The Physical Self-Efficacy Questionnaire (PSEQ) is a two-part questionnaire designed to identify the participants' level of physical self-efficacy. Part One of the PSEQ is the Perceived Physical Ability Subscale (PPAS), and it was designed by Ryckman, Robbins, Thornton and Cantrell (1982) as part of their Physical Self-Efficacy Scale. Part Two of the PSEQ was the Athletic Competence Subscale (ACS) developed by Harter (1982) as part of the Perceived Competency Scale for Children. As the PSEQ was constructed from two independent questionnaires the questions from Part One and Part Two were structurally different (see Figure 3). Therefore, it was not possible to statistically compare the results of Part One with the results of Part Two, and data gathered from Part One and Part Two were analyzed separately.

Figure 3. **Sample questions from the PSEQ.**

Part 1
Perceived Physical Ability Subscale (PPAS)
Please circle a number on the scale.
1 = strongly disagree, 6 = strongly agree

1. I have excellent reflexes.

1   2   3   4   5   6

2. I am not agile and graceful.

1   2   3   4   5   6

Part 2

Athletic Competence Subscale (ACS)

Please put an X in the box that represents your best answer.
Mark ONLY ONE BOX for each question.

Question #	Really true for me	Sort of true for me				Sort of true for me	Really true for me
1.	☐	☐	Some kids do very well at all kinds of sports	**BUT**	Other kids don't feel that they are very good when it comes to sports.	☐	☐
2.	☐	☐	Some kids wish they could be a lot better at sports	**BUT**	Other kids feel they are good enough at sports.	☐	☐

Results

For this study, I used a two-way mixed designed ANOVA to analyze the main effects of the study over time (three repeated measures); the context of the study (school), and the interaction effects between time and school on the PPAS and the ACS. I examined the main effect of time on the PPAS and the ACS. In addition, I examined the main effect of school on the PPAS and the ACS, and the interaction effect between time and school (see Table 3). The two-way mixed design showed a significant interaction effect between time and school on the PPAS therefore I can say that using the GPAI during instruction and assessment had a positive impact on Grade 7 girls' physical self-efficacy during game play.

Table 1.

Descriptive table for the PSEQ - Perceived Physical Ability Subscale.

Means and standard deviations of time effects for the Perceived Physical Ability Subscale, Part One of the PSEQ.

		Baseline		Post VB		Post BB	
	N	M	SD	M	SD	M	SD
School A	29	44.72	8.26	43.79	8.31	47.24	8.07
School B	35	40.91	7.46	42.86	7.35	44.20	7.89

Table 2.

Descriptive table for the PSEQ - Athletic Competency Subscale.

Means and standard deviations of time effects for the Athletic Competency Subscale, Part Two of the PSEQ.

		Baseline		Post VB		Post BB	
	N	M	SD	M	SD	M	SD
School A	29	16.93	3.55	17.21	3.38	17.86	3.39
School B	35	16.91	3.36	17.40	3.74	18.37	3.67

Table 3.

Analysis of Variance for PSEQ - Perceived Physical Ability Subscale.

Source	Df	F	p.
Between subjects			
School	1	1.953	.167
Error	126		
Within subjects			
Time	2	14.987	.001
Time*School	2	4.120	.021
Error	252		
Significant at p.<0.05 level.			

The two-way mixed design ANOVA showed that:

(1) the change over time was significant (F (2, 252) = 14.987, p < .01),

(2) there was not a significant effect of school (F (1, 126) = 1.953, p > .05),

(3) and there was significant interaction effect between time and school (F (2,252) = 4.120, p < .05).

DISCUSSION

My research analyzed two different conditions in Physical Education and how they might affect Grade 7 girls' physical self-efficacy. To check the findings I relied heavily on the questionnaire data; however, the study also used feedback from teacher participants who each provided a short summary of their experience. The data collected from the teacher participants was organized by school, so that it could offer further insight of the student and teacher experience at School A (TGfU) and School B (TGfU and the GPAI). Teacher One and Teacher Two were from School A, and Teacher Three was from School B. From the assessment I was able to draw out significant points and areas for growth. In addition, because of the significant improvement in physical self-efficacy over time at both School A and B, I also speculated about the potential impact of using a TGfU teaching model on seventh-grade girls' physical self-efficacy.

KEY FINDINGS FROM THE DATA ANALYSIS

To my knowledge, I have provided in this report the first and only experimental evidence showing that incorporating the GPAI within TGfU lesson plans directly results in increased physical self-efficacy in Grade 7 girls during games. Although the research focused on a narrow group, it my hope that these findings will propel future research to broaden the scope of the investigation and look further in to the positive and long-term outcomes of improving students' physical self-efficacy. The analysis of data demonstrated a significant positive change in student physical self-efficacy (see Figures 4 and 5).

The descriptive statistics provided in Table 1 and Table 2 show an overall growth in physical self-efficacy at both schools. Of note was the change in School A from Baseline to Post VB to Post BB in Part One of the PSEQ (see Figure 4). Here the data shows a drop in physical self-efficacy from Baseline to Post VB, and then significant growth from Post VB to Post BB. School A had Teacher One lead the volleyball unit and Teacher Two lead the basketball unit; however, at this point it is very difficult to find the cause of this pattern of results. I can only speculate and ask more questions. For example, is this result related to the school's expectations for volleyball proficiency or could it be related to the teacher's expectations? In contrast, School B (GPAI) had Teacher Three conduct all volleyball and basketball lessons, and the data yielded significant growth in students' physical self-efficacy in both Part One and Part Two of the PSEQ (see Figures 4 and 5). This finding further solidifies the connection between the GPAI and increasing physical self-efficacy.

Figure 4. **Impact of time, Perceived Physical Ability Subscale (Part One).**

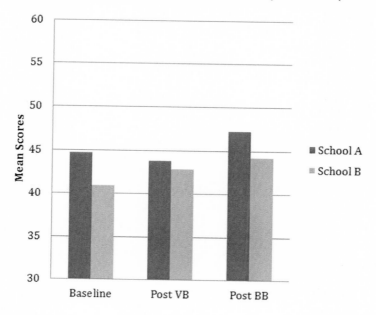

Figure 5. **Impact of time, Athletic Competency Subscale (Part Two).**

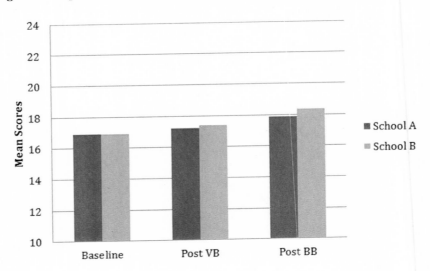

ASSESSING THE EFFECTS OF THE GPAI ON GIRLS' PHYSICAL SELF-EFFICACY

According to Harter (1978), perceived mastery in various areas motivates children, and that perceived mastery will promote self-efficacy and motivate them to continue efforts to increase skill or competency. "After participating in the warm ups, the girls were confident and eager to accept the challenges of the next components of the lesson" (Teacher One, personal communication, May 2014). Looking at the big picture of physical literacy, this strikes right at the goals of the "British Columbia Ministry of Education Integrated Resource Package" (2006). However, these outcomes are not achievable if we don't examine the process that creates the opportunities for mastery. What do teachers require for the 'perception of mastery' in volleyball or basketball? What is it we want students to master? Is it an ability to perform high-level skills and tactics in a challenging, open-ended environment? Is that possible? After all, proficiency demands hundreds of hours practicing . The reality is that most Physical Education classes do not have enough time, yet for years teachers have hammered away on sports-technique based Physical Education expecting at some point children will master the adult version of a game.

In this study, the GPAI gave the participants in School B an opportunity to engage in learning and develop their knowledge through assessment as learning capacity. The statistical evidence of this study supports using TGfU and the GPAI as factors in developing physical self-efficacy. In addition, notes provided by a teacher participating in the study suggest that the GPAI is more powerful than even the data analysis suggests. The teacher participant at School B made the following comments in response to the questions:

1. *Did you notice, feel, or engage in the idea of students' physical self-efficacy while teaching these units?*

> The main observation here is the fact that with an increased level of student's self-efficacy there is a great improvement in one's participation and commitment to the objectives of the class. (Teacher Three, personal communication, May 2014)

2. *Please share anything that you noticed or felt was significant during your time participating in this study.*

> I found the GPAI to be a powerful tool, and I think that the more complex the concept, the more effective that it would be. (Teacher Three, personal communication, May 2014)

Contextually these comments lend further credit to the GPAI as an instrument that can bring students together promoting assessment as learning, and assessment for learning in a peer-to-peer relationship. To which Bandura's (1978) Social Learning Theory states that people can learn new information and behaviors by watching other people. Each time a student, regardless of physical abilities, provided feedback to a classmate she engaged in knowing, learning and teaching of a concept (Davis et al., 2008). What do your students do when they are sitting on the sidelines? I am not surprised to see the significant growth of physical self-efficacy in School B as "success builds on success, because each accomplishment can strengthen a child's motivation" (Ross, 2006, p. 68).

Conclusion

In order to advance, the worldwide Physical Education community must continuously ask questions, such as investigating and subsequently supporting constructionist based student centred teaching models such as TGfU (Butler, Storey, & Robson, 2012; Mandigo et al., 2007; Singleton, 2009). Still, some have sought to understand issues surrounding declining female physical activity (Cairney et al., 2012; Kaestner & Xu, 2010), and items such as the role of gender, the teacher and the curriculum are continuously investigated in an attempt to uncover where we are as a learning community. Searching for the answers is a complex and constantly unfolding process. For instance, Luke and Sinclair (1991) sought to discover gender differences in adolescents' attitudes towards Physical Education only to discover that the curriculum was both the biggest positive determinant and the biggest negative determinant. Their study, like so many, tapped at the heart of a major issue in Physical Education, as it aimed to discover where the process was breaking down. To some the answer has become pretty clear. We are losing student interest, and female students in particular, to outdated teaching models, curriculums and assessments that do not work for today's students (Beveridge & Scruggs, 2000; Cairney et al., 2012; Constantinou, Manson, & Silverman, 2009).

Butler (2006) validated TGfU as an effective way to develop motor skills and develop the whole child . The idea of including the GPAI as a condition in a TGfU based lesson came about after being introduced to the assessment tool in a curriculum studies course. To me, incorporating the GPAI into a student-centered lesson plan made a great deal of sense. It could give the students an opportunity to engage in authentic assessment of their own performance instead of receiving a summative report limited to skills. Receiving feedback from a game you just played, and then applying at your next opportunity underlines assessment for learning. In conjunction, the GPAI also provides a potentially powerful ability to provide learners with an assessment as learning. By assessing their peers, students are no longer sitting on the sidelines talking about lunch; instead, they focus on providing classmates with authentic feedback, and constructing their understanding of the game. The question immediately arose: Can the GPAI also impact physical self-efficacy?

Although I did not recognize it at the time, it was growth mindedness that drew me to the idea of changing my approach towards teaching elementary girls, and the results of this research are a significant point in my journey as a teacher. I had, at times, felt frustrated by the models of teaching and assessment once considered best practice. I duplicated those models because they were the standard of teaching and learning that was prevalent throughout my time in elementary and secondary school. Additionally, during my time in secondary school I was a successful male athlete included in the inner circle of Physical Education. I was given encouragement and support by the Physical Education staff, which I felt I could relate with best. Therefore I neatly fit the mold as a cultural conduit of male stereotypes in Physical Education presented by Brown and Evans (2004). Although I have very much enjoyed my teaching career, hindsight has helped illuminate the gaps in my preparation for teaching in an all-girls school. I took Dweck's (2006) concept of a growth mindset and embraced the challenge of switching models. Frustrated as I may have been, I knew there was a better way to teach Physical Education, and this research supports the notion that, indeed, there is a better way to teach Physical Education to girls.

POSSIBLE FUTURE RESEARCH DIRECTIONS

The major finding from my research is that using the GPAI as part of instruction and assessment has a positive effect on Grade 7 girls' physical self-efficacy. As a teacher currently embedded in an all-girls environment, I highly recommend TGfU, the GPAI or other student-centred teaching and assessment models. The use of a decentralized model is uncomfortable for some, yet the rewards are potentially immense for all involved. It is my hope as a researcher that my study may ignite some future research, in which direction I cannot predict. However, there are some areas I would recommend as a starting point.

Firstly, my use of a quasi-experimental research design and the subsequent non-equivalent group design resulted in a narrow scope of research participants. The schools in my study were independent schools, and the subjects largely came from affluent neighborhoods. It would seem a natural extension to take this research and conduct it over multiple schools from various socio-economic neighborhoods and involving both genders. Further investigating with a random sample, especially one that includes boys, would give more insight into the GPAI as a developmental tool for physical self-efficacy. Of course, one could also replicate this study in an all boys' environment. Either way, the potential is there to dig further down in to the world of motivation in Physical Education.

Secondly, I see my study as a small window into the world of student-centred assessment tools. That window could be thrown open, as there are many assessment tools that could be investigated for potential effects on students' self-efficacy or motivation in Physical Education. The idea of moving Physical Education away from inauthentic assessment of learning into the more dynamic and complex assessment as and assessment for learning presents some exciting possibilities.

Looking ahead to the future of Physical Education, I can only envision a profession that includes student-centered models such as TGfU, and the potential of the GPAI as a student-to-student assessment tool has only been scratched. At this time, further research will help educators and future educators fully understand the motivations of students and just how the GPAI and TGfU can help develop physical self-efficacy.

References

Bandura, A. (1978). Self-efficacy: Toward a unifying theory of behavioral change. *Advances in Behaviour Research and Therapy*, 1, 139–161. Retrieved from http://www.sciencedirect.com/science/article/pii/0146640278900097

Bandura, A. (2006). Toward a Psychology of Human Agency. *Perspectives on Psychological Science*, 1(2), 164–180. doi:10.1111/j.1745-6916.2006.00011.x

Bandura, A. (2010). Self-Efficacy. In W. E. Weiner, Irving B.; Craighead (Ed.), *The Corsini Encyclopedia of Psychology* (4th ed., pp. 1534–1536). John Wiley & Sons.

Beveridge, S., & Scruggs, P. (2000). TLC for better PE: Girls and elementary physical education. *Journal of Physical Education, Recreation & Dance*, 71(8), 22–27.

British Columbia Ministry of Education. (2006). Physical Education Integrated Resource Package. Retrieved from http://www.bced.gov.bc.ca/irp/course.php?lang=en&subject=Physical_Education&course=Physical_Education_K_to_7&year=2006

Brown, D., & Evans, J. (2004). Reproducing gender? Intergenerational links and the male Physical Education teacher as a cultural conduit in teaching physical education. *Journal of Teaching in Physcial Education*, (23), 48–70.

Butler, J. I. (2006). Curriculum constructions of ability: enhancing learning through Teaching Games for Understanding (TGfU) as a curriculum model. *Sport, Education and Society*, 11(3), 243–258. doi:10.1080/13573320600813408

Butler, J. I., Storey, B., & Robson, C. (2012). Emergent learning focused teachers and their ecological complexity worldview. *Sport, Education and Society*, (April 2012), 1–21. doi:10.1080/13573322.2012.680435

Cairney, J., Kwan, M. Y., Velduizen, S., Hay, J., Bray, S. R., & Faught, B. E. (2012). Gender, perceived competence and the enjoyment of physical education in children: a longitudinal examination. *The International Journal of Behavioral Nutrition and Physical Activity*, 9(26), 1–8. doi:10.1186/1479-5868-9-26

Constantinou, P., Manson, M., & Silverman, S. (2009). Female Students' Perceptions about Gender-Role Stereotypes and Their Influence on Attitude toward Physical Education. *Physical Educator*, 66(2), 85–96. Retrieved from http://www.eric.ed.gov/ERICWebPortal/recordDetail?accno=EJ862181

Davis, B. (2009). EDCP501 [lecture notes]. Retrieved from https://connect.ubc.ca

Davis, B., Sumara, D., & Luce-Kapler, R. (2008). *Engaging Minds*. New York, N.Y.: Routledge.

Dishman, R. K., Motl, R. W., Saunders, R., Felton, G., Ward, D. S., Dowda, M., & Pate, R. R. (2004). Self-efficacy partially mediates the effect of a school-based physical-activity intervention among adolescent girls. *Preventive Medicine*, 38(5), 628–36. doi:10.1016/j.ypmed.2003.12.007

Dweck, C. (2006). Mindset: *The new psychology of success.* New York: Random House LLC.

Ennis, C. D. (1999). Creating a culturally relevant curriculum for disengaged Girls. *Sport, Education and Society,* 4(1), 31–49. doi:10.1080/1357332990040103

Ericsson, KA. (1990). The scientific study of expert levels of performance: general implications for optimal learning and creativity. *High Ability Studies,* 9, 75-100.

Griffin, L., Butler, J., Lombardo, B., & Nastasi, R. (2003). An introduction to teaching games for understanding. T*eaching Games for Understanding in Physical Education and Sport,* 1–9.

Griffin, L., & Patton, K. (2005). Two Decades of Teaching Games for Understanding: Looking at the Past, Present, and Future. In L. Griffin & J. Butler (Eds.), *Teaching Games for Understanding: theory, research, and practice.* (pp. 1–17). Champaign, IL: Human Kinetics.

Harter, S. (1978). Effectance motivation reconsidered: toward a developmental model. *Human Development,* (1), 34–64.

Harter, S. (1982). The Perceived Competence Scale for Children. *Child Development,* 53(1), 87–97.

Harter, S. (2012). Self-Perception profile for children: Manual and questionnaires.

Kaestner, R., & Xu, X. (2010). Title IX, girls' sports participation, and adult female physical activity and weight. *Evaluation Review,* 34(1), 52–78. doi:10.1177/0193841X09353539

Luke, M., & Sinclair, G. (1991). Gender differences in adolescents' attitudes toward school physical education. *Journal of Teaching in Physical Education,* (11), 31–46.

Mandigo, J., Butler, J., & Hopper, T. (2007). What is teaching games for understanding? A Canadian perspective. *Physical & Health Education Journal,* 73(2), 14–20.

McAuley, E., & Gill, D. (1983). Reliability and validity of the physical self-efficacy scale in a competitive sport setting. J*ournal of Sport & Exercise Psychology,* (5), 410–418.

Oslin, J., Mitchell, S., & Griffin, L. (1998). The game performance assessment instrument (GPAI): development and preliminary validation. *Journal of Teaching in Physical Education,* 17, 231–243.

Pate, R. R., Ward, D. S., Saunders, R. P., Felton, G., Dishman, R. K., & Dowda, M. (2005). Promotion of physical activity among high-school girls: a randomized controlled trial. *American Journal of Public Health,* 95(9), 1582–7. doi:10.2105/AJPH.2004.045807

Ross, P. E. (2006). The expert mind. *Scientific American,* 295(2), 64–71.

Ryckman, R. M., Robbins, M. A., Thornton, B., & Cantrell, P. (1982). Development and validation of a physical self-efficacy scale. *Journal of Personality and Social Psychology*, 42(5), 891–900. doi:10.1037//0022-3514.42.5.891

Schwartz, B. (2005). Barry Schwartz: The Paradox of Choice. [Video file]. Retrieved from http://www.ted.com/talks/barry_schwartz_on_the_paradox_of_choice.html

Singleton, E. (2009). From Command to Constructivism: Canadian Secondary School Physical Education Curriculum and Teaching Games for Understanding. *Curriculum Inquiry*, 39(2), 321–342. doi:10.1111/j.1467-873X.2009.00445.x

Van Dongen-Melman, J. E. W. M., Koot, H. M., & Verhulst, F. C. (1993). Cross-cultural validation of Harter's Self-Perception Profile for Children in a Dutch sample. *Educational and Psychological Measurement*, 53(3), 739–753. doi:10.1177/0013164493053003018

Van Gyn, G. H., Higgins, J. W., Gaul, C. A., & Gibbons, S. (2000). Reversing the trend: girls' participation in physical education. *Canadian Association for Health, Physical Education, Recreation and Dance*, 66(1), 26–32.

CHAPTER EIGHT

Reflections on Player Learning: A Self-Study of Coaching Praxis

BY SIMON DYKSTRA

Introduction

This project seeks to advance my coaching beyond a traditional praxis of "skill acquisition [and] towards developing an athlete's entire self" (Hyland, 1990, as cited in Denison, 2012, p. 355). It began with an inquiry into how a shift in praxis towards constructivist underpinnings would improve player learning. Specifically, I undertook a self-study to reflect upon the learning experiences of my basketball team during their upcoming season.

RESEARCH QUESTIONS

How can methods of inquiry such as self-study and autoethnography enable me to locate my coaching narrative and assess my perceived constructivist shift?

What experiences have shaped and are embodied in my coaching philosophy?

How might more recent constructivist views on coaching and player learning enrich both player growth and team improvement?

2. Literature Review

2.1 TRADITIONAL COACHING SCIENCE

Traditional coaching research and the associated certification programs such as Canada's NCCP have historically offered claims to truth based on fields of physiology, psychology and biomechanics as the basis for analysis and factual knowledge (Gilbert & Trudel, 2004). Indeed, quantitative research toward a better understanding of coaching effectiveness appears to be rare (Gilbert & Trudel, 2004). This may be due in part to coaching literature being narrow in scope and unable to account for a complexity that exists in coaching (Côté, 2006). While handbooks and certification courses based on coaching science may prepare novices for entry into a coaching role the "complexity of coaching" (Côté, 2006, p. 220) often lies hidden from quantitative methods.

2.2 SELF-STUDY AND AUTOETHNOGRAPHY

Many researchers have embarked on self-study methodologies to innovate and improve their educational practice (Schön, 1983, 1987, 1991). By employing reflective approaches, coaches also may be empowered to greater self-awareness (Cassidy, Jones, & Potrac, 2004). Included in this self-study was the desire to understand how I view player learning and how I have coached in a very traditional, autocratic way. While it is important to consider that all coaches carry a world-view or narrative into their sport roles, these are based in all our unique experiences in and outside of sport. Indeed, an individual's life experience has a significant effect upon their ability to coach and teach others (Winchester, Culver, & Camiré, 2011).

It may be true to say that coaches are always learning, improving or becoming (Jarvis, 2006). However, there may be organizational or paradigmatic structures that may or may not help us in the way we grow (Denison, 2010). In institutionalized settings, there are often real obstacles or difficulties inherent for coaches to consider when they implement new ideas or approaches. Indeed in many cases the existence of a type of anti-intellectualism prevents coaches from challenging taken-for-granted practices (Denison, 2010). In developing the space and intention for reflection, it may be also be less likely to occur in institutionalized contexts that are overly techno-rational, traditional and hierarchical (Denison, 2010). When a coach wants to evolve or shift their praxis they may first need the realization or feeling that coaching beliefs, intents and actions are not in harmony (Butler, 2005):

> The essential ingredient for change is a core belief in innovation rather than previous practice or experience. This taps into the passion and idealism that drove us to join the profession in the first place, to want to become the best that we can be as educators, and dare to hope for the same for our students. (2005, p. 40)

When coaches want to transform coaching praxis, Cassidy, Jones and Potrac (2004) highlight a willingness to go past the competitive results to employ reflection as the integral process to improvement.

> …a coach may become more aware of the values and beliefs that shape their practices which may result in better and more inclusive coaching, leading to enhanced athlete learning and therefore performance… reflecting on one's practice is not an easy or quick exercise and that there are many traditions, rituals, and so- called norms associated with the sport culture that act as constraints on one's willingness to experiment with becoming a reflective coach. (2004, p. 31)

2.3 A SOCIAL CONSTRUCTIVIST LENS

Lave and Wenger (1991) first described how situated ways of knowing occur across the various formal and informal contexts of our lives. All knowledge is taught, reinforced and regulated within a particular community of practice and within a context or activity. In this study, the knowing ways of a school basketball team and program are complex, but can be positioned for analysis of the activity:

> ...the process of changing knowledgeable skill is subsumed in processes of changing identity in and through membership in a community of practitioners; and mastery is an organizational, relational characteristic of communities of practice. (p. 64)

Anna Sfard (1998) researched roles situated in a mathematics learning community. Her writing uses the participationist metaphor to show learning is less about the individual mind and what goes into it and more about the interactions that take place with others in an activity. In a team environment, it is by "becoming a member, that has the ability to communicate in the language of this community and act according to its particular norms" (Sfard, 1998, p. 6).

While the understanding the collective nature of a learning community is integral to transforming a teaching and coaching praxis, it is meaningful to remember that all our players have had unique sports experiences. In his description of embodiment Jarvis (2009) outlines growth as a:

> [C]ombination of processes throughout a lifetime whereby the whole person – body (genetic, physical and biological) and mind (knowledge, skills, attitudes, values, emotions, beliefs and senses) – experiences social situations, the perceived content of which is then transformed cognitively, emotively or practically (or through any combination) and integrated into the individual person's biography resulting in a continually changing (or more experienced) person. (Jarvis, 2009, p. 25)

Coaches and teachers play such important parts in player growth and understanding within their coaching approach and community of practice. They bring together a very complex network and create shared understandings within a community of practice. The Soviet psychologist Lev Vygotsky (1978) proposed that individuals learn in very human, social ways and within collective, shared understandings. Included in this notion is that coaches are like *more capable others*, who support individual player growth, understanding and discovery. The more capable other connects others beyond previously understood worlds, through processes such as scaffolding, modeling, and mentoring. Similarly, Anna Sfard (2008) explains the role of an interlocutor in formal math learning:

> In the case of meta-level learning, when the routine to be learned involves new meta-rules or new

mathematical objects, its reinvention by the learner is highly unlikely. In this case, the learning would typically occur through scaffolded individualization that is through interaction with mathematics who are already insider in the target discourse. (2008, p. 259)

... [t]he participationist vision of human development implies that any substantial change in individual discourse, one that involves a modification in meta-rules or introduction of whole new mathematical object, must be mediated by experienced interlocutor. (2008, p. 254)

A school based sports coach often plays the role of interlocutor (Sfard, 2008) or more capable other (Vygotsky, 1978). Their leadership nudges their players and teams along a continuum of becoming; helping them to emerge into new, embodied capabilities. It is also important that coaches create lessons that challenge players to grow, or extend their maximum proximal development (Vygotsky, 1978). A coach can begin to mesh the collective intelligence of a team through an approach to competition, through training activities and through cognitive challenges which synthesize player adaptation and improved ways of knowing. Vygotsky underpins the player-centred approach to coaching as a more caring, human act. Coaching becomes a relationship of 'collaboration with others, some of whom are relative experts on the task in hand (and some of whom may be relative novices)' as well 'as a result of the "taking in" of the culture by which the child [read learner] is surrounded (Cassidy, Jones, & Potrac, 2004, p. 73).

2.3 TEACHING GAMES FOR UNDERSTANDING (TGFU) AND GAME SENSE

Bunker and Thorpe (1982) conceptualized an approach to help improve the teaching of games and sport in physical education. The "understanding" of it is that ultimately it is the players who must make sense of the game. They must be the agents who synthesize new experiences with what they previously have come to understand. In particular, TGfU improves the teaching of games because it promotes important transferable skills to players (Butler, 2006). This includes the empowerment that players gain when they realize they have figured it out for themselves; synthesizing and applying prior knowledge to new situations (Butler, 2006).

Many traditional approaches still perpetuate the myth that sport improvement is based largely on skill development (Light, 2013) and not player growth which is much more complex. Many coaches also may hold traditional assumptions about learning (Light, 2008) that remain based on the direct, behavioral approaches deeply embedded in Western culture (Davis, Sumara, &

Luce-Kapler, 2000). These assume player learning to be an explicit, linear and measurable process of internalized knowledge. They also purport "predetermined fundamental motor skills as being a prerequisite for playing games and sport" (Light, 2008, p. 22). A constructivist coach must go beyond the motor skills to consider many contextual variables, including: age, experience, gender, and goals of the learner. They also need to harmonize complex institutional, parental and administrative influences in their praxis (Rovegno & Dolly, 2006).

While many important cognitive outcomes may be associated with constructivist approaches to coaching sport, it is also important to note that there may be many improved affective outcomes for models such as TGfU, which have been shown to improve links between individual athletes and a positive community of practice, which may also improve intrinsic motivation (Pope, 2005).

3. Methodology

3.1 SELF-STUDY AND AUTOETHNOGRAPHY

This autoethnography sought to locate my coaching narrative and mediate some of the key past events of my coach identity. It endeavored to locate transformative data that could provoke "other possibilities in both the way that I 'know' (epistemology), and the way that I 'see' (ontology); rather than to continue to legitimate what is already known" (Bruce, 2013, p. 807). A clearer understanding of our formative experiences, our past reflections and all manner of narrative artifacts can position educators towards self-improvement of praxis (Hamilton & Pinnegar, 1998).

Researching the data of a life in basketball coaching included autobiographical, historical, cultural, and political events with thoughtful reflection on "texts read, experiences had, people known and ideas considered" (Hamilton & Pinnegar, 1998, p. 236). Starting in September 2013, I collected as much of my coaching past that I could find, including videos, certificates, manuals, plans, daily notes, diagrams, clinic materials, team pictures, clippings and other evidence of a coaching narrative. During the process, I regularly recorded observations when the opportunity for reflective thoughts emerged. Key reflective and formal conversations and interactions with players were audio recorded in practice and game settings. All research was collected during September to March.

3.2 PARTICIPANT INFORMANTS

Twelve team members were asked for their permission to participate in reflective journals. Nine players, aged 14-15 agreed to submit journal writ-

Table 1.

Player Participants - Journal Writing Design.

Source	Participants	Entries	Date	Writing Time	Journal Triggers & Prompts
Journal Response 1	Junior Players	9	Nov 14	15 minutes prior to practice	Reflect upon past experiences playing "pick-up" basketball. What do they enjoy about unorganized/organized basketball? (Appendix A)
Journal Response 2 (in season)	Junior Players	9	Dec 18	15 minutes handed out at end of practice	Reflect upon perceived individual strengths. What areas have they chosen to improve upon in our team setting? (Appendix B)
Journal Response 3 (in season)	Junior Players	9	Jan 21	15 minutes prior to practice	Reflect on their growth. what do they want to know more about? What ways do they want the team should improve? (Appendix c)
Journal Response 4 (post season)	Junior Players	6	Feb 20	15 minutes prior to practice	What areas would they like to keep improving? What ways they have grown as individuals, as a team? Including on court and off court relationships in the team context? (Appendix D)

ings on four predetermined dates. The season commenced in November with an exhibition schedule, including three tournaments throughout November to February, which culminated at the Vancouver Junior Boys Championships. Journals responses were written in private in the gym before practice. Players were told that their submissions were anonymous, to avoid the influence of a power relationship as much as possible. Participants submitted their writing through a third party teacher who both collected and assigned identification codes. Participants were assured that they could engage in reflection without having their authorship known.

3.5 DATA CODING

After collecting participant data, I coded themes using the McGill University program Qualyzer (http://qualyzer.bitbucket.org/). These general themes emerged from player reflections and my coaching recordings in action. After creating a list of codes to describe each response, they were thematically unified, reviewed and summarized within the following discussion and findings.

4. Validation & Credibility

As a qualitative self-study, it is the reader who will ultimately judge the validity of its findings. The sense of verisimilitude may be felt by readers who identify with the findings, discussion and experience of engaging with these words. From the onset, it was not my intent to uncover generalizable principles or rational truths. Instead, these findings are shared for their own merit as depictions or representations of a very contextual, situated research experience. I hope they might add to the growing body of local coaching stories. Perhaps some of these reflections may in some small way help others to improve their approach to school based coaching.

5. Findings: The 2013-2014 Junior Basketball Team

In the first journal, players were asked to show prior understandings and basketball experiences in both formal and informal settings. I troubled their notion of my role with the prompt: "What do you like about playing without a coach?"

A1: *When... unorganized, I feel a lot freer in terms of going 1 on 1*

C4: *Playing unorganized...is nowhere near as fun as playing on a team...the game just looks very messy...when I play unorganized basketball ...*

A9:   *... uncomfortable when... unorganized ...I like it better when there is a coach to organize.*

B2:   *Playing a pickup game... if there's a ball hog it sometimes frustrates me...*

B1:   *...team basketball is...my choice over unorganized, pick-up games.*

A2:   *... No refs...means bad calls judged on the offensive players word. The teams may be unfair...*

After reading their words, I gained a better sense of each player and who they were. I also learned more about the risk they took to try out for our school team. They relayed important information back to me about why they chose to play basketball. To what degree did they want to belong to a team? Through my whole career as a player, I never was asked to reflect upon why I joined the team. It's an important connection to make for all the players. I enjoyed connecting my past experience growing up to the outlook my players held. I always question whenever another coach says bluntly, "kids have changed!"

SECOND JOURNAL

In the second journal players were prompted to identify intentional growth. I wanted to know more about why they chose these areas to improve. This journal had a rewarding outcome- the players started to imagine better how they wanted to grow reflect upon their own improvement, and continually assess their success. I enjoyed their self-evaluations.

A1:   *I chose to become a better shooter and passer...to improve on basics...to become a leader... I feel really tense and nervous... I want...confidence to be able to play relaxed.*

C4:   *... to become a better shooter...a better passer to limit turnovers...a better rebounder... play better defense...relaxed... having fun*

C6:   *I want to become more confident...if I become more confident I can help our team much more.*

B4:   *... I am often scared...coach will get mad at me and sub me off...if I relax ...I will be able to hit more shots*

I noticed a lack of confidence by experienced players. It startled me to read that some of my players who appeared very self-assured wrote that they were scared. The understanding emerged that our self-talk was a huge part of growth. The Growth Mindset (Dweck, 2006) has approached the language we can use as coaches to help players regain confidence. If students believe their potential is not fixed in their DNA; they are more apt to take risks and learn from failure. This journal reinforced my belief that player potential is largely influenced by a mindset towards effort, challenge, and the rewards of feedback. A coach can help improve player growth and development, but they need to first show players it is they who need to "persist in the face of setbacks, see effort as the path to mastery, learn from criticism and find inspiration and lessons in the success of others" (Sproule et al., 2011, p. 690).

THIRD JOURNAL

The third journal continued to assess perceived improvement and growth in collaboration with the collective performance of the players. Every coach needs to mesh individual experience and roles with team performance. Some key entries are included below:

B2:   *...more confident on court ...improved my basketball IQ*

C1:   *...more rounded than in October... became less afraid... realized that the defenders give me a lot of space to shoot... I can now drive, shoot and pass.*

B1:   *...confidence has grown......my team has more trust in me...*

B4:   *... running game has gotten better... finishing skills have gotten better...*

A4:   *I feel I've grown as a player...I've been able to accept my role as a player*

B2:   *Improved... chemistry.. skills, everything....we actually are confident that we might win...we're a whole new team.*

C1:   *...much more competitive...*

B1:   *...we've begun to put more trust in one another...we have a better chance of winning cities.*

C4:   *...everyone on the team has made a commitment to being a better player...we kept getting better and I hope it continues this way.*

A1:   *... over time we really are familiar with what everybody does.*

B2:   *... trusting others*

A1:   *... We grow as a team from each player's individual successes.*

I am mixed about giving players strict roles and positions at an early age, before they mature physically. Throughout our season, I tried to continually harmonize team improvement with individual player growth. The journal process also became important to check with players about their own expectations in their emerging, improving roles on the team.

The constraint approach can help design training situations that help all players improve. This helps mediate player and team growth in certain tactical areas. For example, certain geographic modifications to the playing boundaries or number of allowed passes or dribbles, or even the number of players may improve understanding in a small-sided game. If players are to be optimally challenged, they might be given better opportunities to grow through a constraints approach. One of my favorite constraints is limiting of dribbles to improve spacing and cutting to space. It also leads to improvement in pivoting and shielding of the ball. Another key constraint was asking players to defend in different ways, either by centering on the pivot foot or certain gap distances relating to the ball and the player's quickness. There is much to learn in designing adaptive situations for players to learn from. The principles of TGfU have helped immensely in this area.

FOURTH JOURNAL

During our last journal session, players were asked to provide a summative assessment of their experiences during the season. Some of their key findings are included:

B4: *On the court: we played as a team, we improved our game in every aspect*

Off the court: we didn't let each other down...

C6: *On: playing as a team, winning games*

Off: Building chemistry... hanging out together

A4: *On: defensively*

Off: communicating, being accountable

C6: *...something to learn from. I didn't like...losing to teams we could easily beat*

A1: *...we grew as a team on/off the court ...we fought hard and beat them showing trust... a huge turning point which is why it is my favorite memory*

A4: *...will definitely remember all of the work that we put in into becoming a good team*

As the season progressed, I noticed journals becoming more detailed, and as I began to code and group their journal reflections, I wondered if players had indeed become more trusting of the process and each other. Perhaps they were simply more comfortable with reflective writing. I am reminded by the notions of complexity and emergence found in the writings of Davis, Luce-Kepler and Sumara (2000) who suggest a constructivist approach to coaching should be less about me telling players what they don't know, and more about helping them notice what they haven't noticed before. One aspect which came through this journal was the sense of a collective. Although we were not a championship team, we progressed closer to our potential and we learned more about whom we were as a collective. This would hopefully help the community moving through their successive roles in our basketball program.

6. Conclusions

Throughout this inquiry I reflected upon an intended shift towards constructivist perspectives on athlete learning,

> ...coaching is a complex activity...you're not always going to get out of it what you put in...you do have to...get involved in order to guide the process....indirectly with interrupting bad habits, creating flow... player input... ultimately the learning system...this very complex activity thrives and regenerates and replicate itself on so many different level... this is what I call the tinkering phase. How much of tinkering is a natural function of a [good] coach and how much of it is an embodied artifact of their own [being] coached and their own learning? (2013-09-26)

My first experiences in basketball were in an intense, competitive environment of a large public secondary school. The head coach was a dominant figure in the school. In many ways repeating the traditional approach to instruction and feedback seems natural, after all it was those first coaches in high school and university who taught me the enduring principles that they knew would lead to success on the court. While I try to improve, innovate and better understand the young people I coach, the unfortunate reliance on challenging players in negative ways is a default behavior difficult to resist. Deep inside I want to speed up the learning process—to get immediate traction with drills and tactical lessons. My desire also is to have the team reflect how I want to be judged by others, to look well organized. This puts pressure on me to tell players what to do, rather than create situations where they must figure it out and learn how to play themselves. It's still a very complex art, being a teacher and a competitive coach. Indeed many other coaches find it too difficult to break from institutional socialization (Casey & Fletcher, 2012). In competitive sports it is very difficult to change one's praxis from traditional methods. Jones and Potrac (2004) summarize this dilemma for many coaches,

> ... tried and trusted methods gleaned from experience have tended to override both the integration of academic knowledge into coaching practice, and the innovation that reflection upon such applied knowledge can produce ... many coaches, wary of stepping outside a comfort zone of given drills and discourse, tend to coach the way they were coached. (p. 3)

Another important area for my coaching growth is to improve the relationships among the team and develop well-rounded people. While I think adapting and evolving my practice towards a constructivist, player centred approach is not easy, it has made my coaching more enjoyable, personable and humble. Coaching school-aged learners is so much more than the product of results. The words of Gearity and Denison (2012, p. 355) help me relocate how important an educator coach is in our communities and our public schools:

> Becoming an educator coach would serve to prepare athletes to engage in democracy, and strive for inclusive and diverse ways of living. A vision for the educator-coach going forward is to help create new norms aligning sport with these broad educational foundations. (2012, p. 355)

Measuring a coach's effectiveness by their amount of wins parallels the unfortunate reliance by many who call for standardized test scores to indicate teacher effectiveness in the classroom. While effective coaching often appears to be successful, it cannot be measured by wins. The stories of other local coaches and teachers who are trying to improve, innovate and adapt may help us change the current landscape in sports and education. In coaching for positive change, Côté (2006) calls for coaches to open dialogues with other coaches, to share practical knowledge about improving our situated contexts. While lasting change is often difficult (Butler, 2005), sometimes it is the only way we as coaches can line up our coaching with our beliefs, intents and actions. In approaching a constructivist stance, my role as a coach has become more complex, but it is broader in scope and definitely more positive. It has become more enjoyable to focus on growth and improvement rather than wins and losses. Although competition gives feedback that all teams need to improve game play, school games, team sports and physical education are all important part of a holistic learning experience. A school coach is in the unique position to move beyond the tactics on the court to innovative a learning environment that promotes the development of the whole player. As Davis (2005) writes,

> Teaching cannot be about zeroing in on predetermined conclusions. It can't be about the replication and perpetuation of the existing possible. Rather, teaching seems to be more about expanding the space of the possible and creating conditions for the emergence of the as-yet unimagined. (p. 87)

Through the lens of player-centered coaching, this educator coach has found it possible to keep more open minded towards more recent educational perspectives on player learning.

References

Brown, J. S., Collins, A., & Duguid, P. (1989). Situated cognition and the culture of learning. *Educational Researcher.* doi:10.3102/0013189X018001032

Bruce, J. (2011). Dancing on the edge: A self-study exploring postcritical possibilities in physical education. *Sport, Education and Society,* 18(6), 807–824. doi:10.1080/13573322.2011.613457

Bullough, R. V., & Pinnegar, S. (2001). Guidelines for Quality in Autobiographical Forms of Self-Study Research. *Educational Researcher.* doi:10.3102/0013189X030003013

Bunker, D., & Thorpe, R. (1982). A model for the teaching of games in secondary schools. *Bulletin of Physical Education.* 18, 5–8. Retrieved from http://articles.sirc.ca/search.cfm?id=112955

Butler, J. (2005). TGfU pet-agogy: Old dogs, new tricks and puppy school. *Physical Education and Sport Pedagogy,* 10(3), 225-240.

Butler, J. I. (2006). Curriculum constructions of ability: Enhancing learning through Teaching Games for Understanding (TGfU) as a curriculum model. *Sport Education and Society,* 11(3), 243–258. doi:10.1080/13573320600813408

Callary, B., Werthner, P., & Trudel, P. (2012). How meaningful episodic experiences influence the process of becoming an experienced coach. *Qualitative Research in Sport, Exercise and Health.* doi:10.1080/2159676X.2012.712985

Casey, A., & Fletcher, T. (2012). Trading places: From physical education teachers to teacher educators. *Journal of Teaching in Physcial Education,*

31, 362–380. Retrieved from http://www.eric.ed.gov/ERICWebPortal/recordDetail?accno=EJ997934

Cassidy, T., & Jones, R., & Potrac, P. (2004). *Understanding sports coaching: The social, cultural and pedagogical foundations of coaching practice.* London: Routledge.

Clandinin, J., & Connelly, M. (2004). Knowledge, narrative and self-study. In J. J. Loughran, M. Hamilton, V. LaBoskey, & T. Russell (Eds.), *International Handbook of Self-Study of Teaching and Teacher Education Practices* 15(12) 575–600. Springer Netherlands. doi:10.1007/978-1-4020-6545-3_15

Courneya, C.A., Pratt, D.D., Collins, J.B. (2008). Through what perspective do we judge the teaching of peers? *Journal of Teaching and Teacher Education,* 24(1), 69-79.

Côté, J. (2006). The development of coaching knowledge. *International Journal of Sports Science and Coaching*, 1(3), 217-222.

Davis, B., Sumara, D. J., & Luce-Kapler, R. (2000). *Engaging minds: Learning and teaching in a complex world.* Mahwah, NJ: L. Erlbaum Associates.

Davis, B. (2005). Teacher as consciousness of the collective. *Complicity: An International Journal of Complexity and Education,* 2(1), 85-88.

Davis, B., & Sumara, D. (2007). Complexity science and education: Reconceptualizing the teacher's role in learning. *Interchange*, 37(1), 53-67.

Davis, B. (2008). Complexity and education: vital simultaneities. *Educational Philosophy and Theory,* 40(1), 46-61.

Denison, J. (2010). Planning, practice and performance: The discursive formation of coaches' knowledge. *Sport, Education and Society*, 15(4), 461–478.

Dweck, C.S. (2006). *Mindset: The new psychology of success.* New York: Random House.

Gearity, B., & Denison, J. (2012). Educator-coach as stranger. *Cultural Studies and Critical Methodologies,* 12(4), 352-356.

Gilbert, W. D., & Trudel, P. (2004). Role of the coach: How model youth team sport coaches frame their roles. *The Sport Psychologist,* 18(1), 21–43.

Gilbert, W. D., & Trudel, P. (2004). Analysis of coaching science research published from 1970-2001. *Research Quarterly for Exercise and Sport,* 75, 388–399. doi:10.1080/02701367.2004.10609172

Hamilton, M. L., & Pinnegar, S. (1998). Conclusion: the value and the promise of self-study. In M. L. Hamilton (Ed.), *Reconceptualizing teaching practice: self-study in teacher education* (pp. 235–246). London: Falmer Press.

Jarvis-Selinger S, Pratt D.D., Collins JB. (2010). Journeys toward becoming a teacher: Charting the course of professional Development. *Teacher Education Quarterly*; 37(2), 69-96.

Jarvis, P., (2006). *Towards a comprehensive theory of human learning: lifelong learning and the learning society.* New York, NY: Routledge.

Jarvis, P., (2006). *The theory and practice of teaching.* Taylor & Francis. Retrieved 15 March 2014, from <http://www.myilibrary.com?ID=53901>

Jarvis, P., (2007). *Globalisation, lifelong learning and the learning society, sociological perspectives: Lifelong learning and the learning society.* New York, NY: Routledge.

Jarvis, P., (2009). *Learning to be a person in society.* London: Routledge.

Jarvis-Selinger, S., Collins, J.B., and Pratt, D.D. (2007). Do academic origins influence perspectives on teaching? *Teacher Education Quarterly,* 34(3), 67-81

Jones, Robyn; Cassidy, Tania. (2004). *Understanding sports coaching: the social, cultural and pedagogical foundations of coaching practice.* Taylor & Francis. Retrieved 30 May 2014, from <http://www.myilibrary.com?ID=5161>

Jones, R.L. (2007). Coaching redefined: an everyday pedagogical endeavor. *Sport, Education and Society,* 12(2), 159–73.

Jones, R. L. (2009). The sports coach as educator: Reconceptualising sports coaching. *International Journal of Sports Science and Coaching,* doi:10.1260/174795406779367701

Jones, R. L. (2009). Coaching as caring (the smiling gallery): Accessing hidden knowledge. *Physical Education & Sport Pedagogy,* 14(4), 377–390. doi:10.1080/17408980801976551

Kirk, D., Macdonald, D., & O'Sullivan, M. (2006). *Handbook of physical education.* London: SAGE. doi: http://dx.doi.org.ezproxy.library.ubc.ca/10.4135/9781848608009

Lave, J., & Wenger, E. (1991). Situated learning: Legitimate peripheral participation. *Learning in doing,* 95, 138. doi:10.2307/2804509

Lave, J. (1991). Situating learning in communities of practice. In L. B. Resnick, J. M. Levine, & S. D. Teasley (Eds.), *Perspectives on socially shared cognition.* Washington D.C.: American Psychological Association.

Light, R., & Fawns, R. (2003). Knowing the Game: Integrating Speech and Action in Games Teaching Through TGfU. Quest. doi:10.1080/00336297.2003.10491797

Light, R. (2008). Complex learning theory- its epistemology and its assumptions about learning: implications for physical education. *Journal of Teaching in Physical Education,* 27(1), 21-37.

Light, R. L. (2013). *Game Sense: pedagogy for performance, participation and enjoyment.* London: Routledge.

Pinnegar, S. & Hamilton, M. L., (2009). *Self-study of practice as a genre of qualitative research: theory, methodology, and practice.* New York: Springer Netherlands. doi:10.1007/978-1-4020-9512-2

Rovegno, I & Dolly, J.P.(2006). Constructivist perspectives on learning. In D. Kirk,

D. Macdonald, & M.O'Sullivan (Eds.), *The handbook of physical education.* London: Sage Publications.

Schön, D. A. (1987). *Educating the reflective practitioner.* San Francisco: Jossey-Bass Publishers.

Schön, D. A. (1983). *The reflective practitioner:* How professionals think in action. New York: Basic Books.

Schön, Donald A. (1991) *The reflective turn.* New York: Teachers College Press.

Sfard, A. (1998). Two metaphors for learning mathematics: Acquisition metaphor and participation metaphor. *Educational Researcher,* 27(2), 4–13. doi:10.3102/0013189X027002004

Sfard, A. (2008). *Thinking as communicating: Human development, the growth of discourses, and mathematizing.* New York: Cambridge University Press.

Sproule, J., Ollis, S., Gray, S., Thorburn, M., Allison, P., & Horton, P. (2011). Promoting perseverance and challenge in physical education: the missing ingredient for improved games teaching. *Sport, Education and Society.* doi:10.1080/13573322.2011.601149

Vygotsky, Lev S. (1978). *Mind in Society: The development of higher psychological processes.* Cambridge, MA: Harvard University Press.

Winchester, G., Culver, D., & Camiré, M. (2011). The learning profiles of high school teacher-coaches. *Canadian Journal of Education,* 34(4), 216–233.

CHAPTER NINE

Narrative Inquiry of Online PE: What is the Experience of Online PE Students?

BY SUSAN KIMURA

Introduction

Traditional physical education (PE) is by most accounts a commonly shared experience born out of similar course content in British Columbia (BC) high schools. However, with the innovation of online courses, this may not be the case for all students. Current research indicates there are potentially many benefits to offering PE online such as timetabling, advancing through mandatory courses and offering more variety of courses (Ransdell, Rice, Snelson, & Decola, 2008). However, literature by Mohnsen (2012) and Mosier (2012) indicates the urgent need for more research at the K-12 level, especially in areas concerning student learning in an online environment. At the moment, it seems the education system is developing more and more online programs. But, in order to further develop its educational potential, it would seem that it is also important to gather students' perspectives to provide critical analyses of such courses. While many studies focused on post-secondary education, there is a need for research at the K-12 level. In Bennett's 2012 study of Canadian education, Bennett writes that "[BC] continues to lead in the provision of K-12 online learning for students. With a total student population of 649,952 in 2010-11, BC ranked first in online registration with 88,000 unique students enrolled in one or more online courses" (p. 17).

RESEARCH QUESTION

This research investigated the phenomenon of online PE by studying the question, "What is the experience of online PE students?"

BACKGROUND

In the province of BC, according to the BC Ministry of Education, every student in every grade up until grade 10 receives PE (British Columbia Ministry of Education Integrated Resource Package (BCIRP), 2008). A growing area of research on the topic of online education is expanding especially in areas of higher education; however, there is very limited inquiry for K-12 online education and, in particular, for investigation of online physical education (OLPE). To offer discussion on a topic that continues to expand in our school system, this study is not arguing the implementation or the quality of OLPE; rather, this research considers the human element against the backdrop of the technological world as it explores the personal narratives of OLPE students.

HISTORY AND BC FOCUS

According to Bennett (2012), "BC has the most extensive online presence, in terms of numbers and percentage of student participation … [and] it also has the most extensive regulatory regime" (p. 4). Because there is government support, BC's online education is growing (p. 6).

Buschner (2006) states that "no data exists for learning via OLPE" (p. 4), and asks "what evidence is available to validate this approach to learning for secondary students?" (p. 4). In addition, Murphy and Rodrigues-Manzanares (2009) looked at motivation and PE, and acknowledge that "high-school distance education (DE) has not yet received extensive attention compared to DE at the post-secondary level" (p. 2). Mosier (2012) also states that "due to the paucity of research in virtual physical education (VPE), one can only speculate as to why students are choosing VPE" (p. 6). Mohnsen's (2012) research is valuable to the OLPE community because it explores the proper implementation of online PE lessons. In it she lists ten advantages of online learning. "Teachers can make content changes quickly and easily" and "teachers can personalize teaching for each student" (p. 43) are two advantages for the teacher while the rest are benefits for the student. An interesting advantage of OLPE from Mohnsen's research, which was missing from most of the other literature, was the flexibility of OLPE for students. While Yaman (2009) refers to the same benefit as "flexible scheduling" (p. 66), it is Mohnsen's word choice "sleep in" that offers a biological perspective, and suggests that teens operate on a slightly different time clock than adults.

As an emerging and developing course platform, OLPE has several criticisms of concern despite many positive reviews. Starting with Buschner (2006) who balanced his findings with a straightforward list of five disadvantages of OLPE: 1) The perceived threat of PE teaching positions; 2) The message that sitting in front of a computer motivates and sustains moderate to vigorous levels of physical activity in the light of an obesity crisis; 3) Students may be avoiding interactions and PE because it is difficult, thus also avoiding learning responsibility, personal and social behaviour, teamwork, and decision-making in an online environment; 4) Some OLPE courses have failed the test of comprehensive physical education according to the National Association for Sport and Physical Education as opposed to physical activity; and finally, 5) No data exist for learning via OLPE.

Ransdell et al. (2008) suggested that taking OLPE "is equivalent to rewarding sedentary behaviour and that it does not allow for the usual 'checks and balances' afforded with traditional health-related fitness courses" (p. 46). Hence, one of the major criticisms surrounding OLPE is that of honesty and academic integrity to ensure daily physical activity. Daum and Buschner's (2012) research looked at design of OLPE with the US national standards and notes that an emphasis on fitness curriculum and the cognitive domain; however, they found that OLPE courses did not meet the national guidelines of 225 minutes of PE/week and in fact there were OLPE courses that did not require physical activity (p. 95).

THEORETICAL FRAMEWORK

Lev Vygotsky, a major theorist of social constructivism, believed that understanding is created through levels of unknowing and knowing (1962). The tenets of constructivism are: 1) a complex and relevant learning environment; 2) social negotiation; 3) multiple perspective and multiple modes of learning; 4) ownership in learning; and 5) self-awareness and knowledge construction (Almala, 2005, p. 10) and describe the learner in an environment where there is guidance from another to help create meaning in activities that hold relevance.

Almala (2005) supports OLPE by stating that "the constructivist learning paradigm emphasizes that there is no single or objective reality 'out there,' which the instructor must transmit to the learner. Rather, reality is constructed by the learner during the course of the learning process" (p. 10). Powell and Kalina (2009) wrote, "Ideas are built and constructed from experience to craft personal meaning" (p. 241). The social constructivist theory asks if self-discovery, leading to self-motivation and independence, is realized by the online learner. Thus when guided by an instructor, constructivism is applicable to online learning as it is designed to promote active learning among community members through threads, bulletin boards, email and more as it embodies a decentralized style of teaching. Bennett and Green (2001) agreed that "constructivist theory can be applied to online learning environments...[as it] is not necessarily carried out in isolation" (p. 3). By seeing OLPE through the lens of constructivism there is an online community that is anticipating stories of learner collaboration and construction of knowledge that goes beyond checking off "PE" on a to-do list.

Methodology

Narrative Inquiry (NI) was chosen as a compatible methodology in researching the experiences of students who enrolled in an OLPE. Narrative inquiry uses lived experience to help tell the tale of those who opted out of mainstream PE during their high school years, and in particular, those students with an OLPE experience. The NI methodology involved using the lens of social constructivism to better understand how OLPE students created their own reality of what physical education looked like in their world. According to Chase (2011), the distinguishing element of NI is analyzing voices within each narrative rather than focusing solely on themes found across interviews. Journals and activity logs of PE experiences were used as data. Thomas (2012) stated that NI is considered knowledge that is measured not against traditional criteria but in our understanding of the human condition (p. 212). In the manner of social constructivism, NI promotes the idea that there is not a single truth, but multiple and varied realities; as such, NI seems a fitting choice for this study. Ontologically, NI is based on evaluating personal experience; recognizing that each experience is a unique manifestation of self, revealing one of many truths and leading to a greater understanding of the social world.

PARTICIPANTS

The participants were former OLPE students from school districts in the greater Vancouver area. The participants were Caucasian siblings, born and raised in the lower mainland. Patricia (pseudonym) graduated high school in 2013 and Rory (pseudonym) is in Grade 11. Both attended the same high school and enrolled in the same online course. Data were collected through course outlines, online assignments and interviews that were voice recorded and transcribed for analysis. Sample interview questions are found as Appendix A (p. 197). The first interview explained the purpose and interest in this topic, and set the stage for trust so that the environment felt safe and comfortable. This was followed up with guided and semi-guided interviews and a final interview to ensure that all collaborators were satisfied with the outcome of the interviews. Initially open coding was used to group the participants' answers. Axial coding was used to employ a deeper analysis of the interviews where thematic relationships of competition, communication and choice emerged.

To validate these themes as an accurate interpretation of their experiences and not simply based on the researcher's motives, I returned to the participants with the transcriptions and discoveries. This was particularly important in this study because "as researchers exploring human experiences, we often live with the 'fear of offending' our participants, particularly at the analysis and subsequent representation stage; this is a situation that is especially 'problematic when dealing with small sample sizes in narrative research'" (Thomas, 2012, p. 213). Knowing this and my inability to remove myself from this study, I acknowledge the fact that I am entrenched, imbedded and implicated in what is reported. It is noted that this study does not assume sweeping generalities nor does it speak the truth about all OLPE courses;it does, however, make a valuable deposit toward future research on this topic.

CONTEXT

The OLPE course requirements of these particular participants involved a daily exercise log where they would journal what type of exercise they did, record their heart rate, and reflect on how they felt overall. They were given an opportunity to choose their fitness goals, self-design their own workouts and monitor their own progress. These students also needed to develop a personal nutrition plan. Written paragraph responses to thematic threads or articles about physical activity were also part of the programme. In-person fitness tests at the beginning, middle and end of the course were required whereby the participants would make an appointment with their online teacher for a standardized fitness test based on flexibility, strength and conditioning.

Findings

Upon analyzing the data, themes emerged from Patricia and Rory's experiences. The findings were organized around the reasons for taking OLPE, the message PE sends to students, and the alternative options offered by OLPE. Patricia's reasons for taking OLPE differ from Rory's reasons, but both experiences highlight the importance of family support and a sense of empowerment when it came to choosing the direction of their education. As Bedard and Knox-Pipes (2006) support, "the desire for online learning often stems from the sense of control the student gains…the student in an online world is a free agent able to make choices and direct his or her learning in order to gain the most" (p. 17).

COMPETITION: THE REASON FOR TAKING ONLINE – PE: PATRICIA'S STORY

Patricia is a young girl who graduated from high school in 2013. She is a self-described non-athlete who has no coordination, and in her early teens went through what she said were her awkward years. It was a time when she felt unsure of herself and perhaps a little uncomfortable in her own skin; as most do in their adolescent years. There is a sense that there is residual discomfort surrounding that time in her life as she makes shoo-ing motions with her hands, not making eye contact, literally trying to wave away those past feelings when she talks.

Patricia felt the competitiveness of PE acutely starting around grade five. For Patricia, PE was a fun class in elementary school, "[b]ecause it was then just like, oh yay, everybody wins if you do your best (laughs and pretends to cheer)".

She then found that, after Grade 5, PE became a hierarchical world where the lowest denominators were those whose lack of ability were on display in front of the whole class as everyone else who had finished the task could wait and watch. And that is when PE began to lose its appeal. According to Patricia, PE classes began taking on a competitive nature with the focus of most classes on team activities such as basketball, volleyball, dodge ball and soccer. She did not like the spotlight, and found that her lack of ability in the skills needed to perform adequately drew negative attention, which directed the spotlight on her and caused her to retreat from PE: "I just didn't want to you know, like, go to class anymore because I just couldn't do it [PE] anymore, everything started moving too fast and I needed a slower pace" (Interview, May, 2014). Looking deeper into her story, there was a sense that the competitive nature of her PE classes undermined her ability to play games at the speed that was required. In Ntoumanis' 2001 study on motivation in PE he writes: "those who perceive that they lack physical competence usually find the PE experience meaningless…and engage in it only because it is the rule or because of fear of punishment" (p. 236). For Patricia, the games held no meaning for her, and she did not recognize any significance of them in her life, stating, "I'm never going to get together with a bunch of people to like, play soccer. I don't even know that many friends who would want to play" (Interview, May, 2014).

COURSE CONFLICT: THE REASONS FOR TAKING ONLINE PE – RORY'S STORY

Rory is Patricia's younger brother. At 5'7", he is a bit taller than his sister and has a slim build. By Rory's confession, he found PE to be neutral territory. He neither liked PE particularly well, nor did he dislike it; but,he too chose to do PE online. Rory explained that, for him, PE was a hoop to jump through until grade 10 because it was mandatory, so he took the course in school until Grade 9. After finding out that his sister took OLPE, he decided to take the same path; however, his reasons were different from his sister's: Rory told me that his interest is in English language and literature. He wanted to start focusing on his major early, so he needed to make room in his timetable. Dropping PE was the easiest way to free up one block for another academic course. Rory is not alone in this approach: Bedard and Knox-Pipes support the idea that "learning online appeals to a wide variety of students who need to complete requirements for graduation, [and] pursue special interests…it also requires greater self-discipline but it can give the student more freedom to 'attend' class at times that are more convenient" (2006, p. 17).

The theme of competitiveness was less prominent in Rory's story than that of Patricia's; he also stated that he enjoyed swimming and running when he was younger, and that these sports plus weight lifting were his choice activities for his online course. "I enjoyed doing these activities (swimming and running) because they don't have to be overly competitive" (Fitness log, May, 2014).

The competitive nature that most sports incite is one of the driving forces behind great athletes, yet it somehow disservices a portion of young people who feel that the bar is set faster, higher, stronger (Didon, 1881). By removing themselves from that competitive environment, these OLPE students chose to be in charge of their education and responsible for their outcome. For Rory, PE was a course to cross off from the list of mandatory classes in order to be able to take the subjects he was most interested in pursuing. As a result he took OLPE. When asked about his experience with traditional PE and his reasons for enrolling in OLPE, he responded:

> Yeah, it really didn't matter to me. I guess I kinda liked it. But it wasn't what I was interested in. I'm more interested in English. Like English literature, that kinda stuff ... Well, I really wanted to start taking more English courses and I didn't have any more space in my timetable because we have to take HCE [Health and Career Education]. And since I knew that I could take PE online, I just did. And what was really good was I got to start in the summer to get it over with quicker ... Yeah, it kinda was but it wasn't that bad 'cause I could do it [PE] when I didn't have a lot of homework or on the weekends. (Interview, May, 2014)

Rory's decision to take PE online was for no other reason than to get it out of the way. From this, we might naturally conclude that enrolment in traditional PE may be negatively affected if more students knew about OLPE, regardless of their partiality to traditional PE classes.

COMMUNICATION: PATRICIA'S STORY

The negative emotions that Patricia felt about PE also came from her relationship with her PE teachers, especially in high school. All of Patricia's PE teachers were male even though there were a couple of female PE teachers on staff; however, this did not seem to be an issue. The greater problem was that she thought for certain that her PE teachers hated her because she was not good in PE, again referring to competence in skill. Yet this time, her dislike of PE grew out of how it was communicated to her: She noticed the lack of time and guidance spent on her compared to the attention that other more athletic students received.

> I just HATED PE. I think, no, I KNOW that all the PE teachers hated me. Oooh especially Mr.~. oops... sorry. I didn't mean to say his name, it's just that... oooh (she curls both hands into a fist and shakes them side to side). They couldn't care if I was there or not. Probably better that I wasn't so that it would make their life easier. I just sucked at PE. (Interview, May, 2014)

What was communicated in Patricia's case was that she did not belong. Likewise, Ashton-Warner (1968), in her book Teacher, believed in the power of relationship in education when she wrote, "it is not so much the content of what one says as the way in which one says it. However important the thing you say, what's the good of it if not heard or, being heard, not felt" (p. 17). She simply wanted to get it over and done with and in the interview it seemed as if even the online version of PE was difficult. Patricia enrolled in OLPE without ever having taken an online course before. Academically, she was an average C+ to B student. In traditional PE classes, she averaged a C+-letter grade, but in her online course she nearly failed and received a final letter grade of C-. What kept her from actually failing the course was in part due to her father's help and an even greater motivating fear of returning to her PE teachers at school for permission to re-enrol in the course. There was no discussion as to whether or not she was able to re-take it online. The dread that she felt was concerning to me, as it was hard to think about other students who may have similar feelings associated with taking PE.

Here are two paths of communication that materialized from Patricia's narrative: first, the fear of communication; and second, the lack of communication. The first instance of communication was a face-to-face relational dynamic stemming from an emerging pedagogy that posits the interaction between teachers and students as critical to learning. The book, No Education Without Relation (Bingham & Sidorkin, 2010) presents essays on the importance of healthy communication in order to create a climate of safety when teaching and learning. In particular, Biesta's essay titled, "'Mind the gap!' Communication and the educational relation" (2010) argues that in addition to a transfer of information, communication is the social space between teacher and learner where meaning is created (p. 16). This may have been a crucial missing element with Patricia and her PE teachers as mentioned earlier in the lack of time and effort spent on feedback.

The second communication dynamic stems from the discipline online courses require to stay interested and active in a virtual space. The online situation seems best suited for the motivated student who enjoys the subject matter and vigorously pursues online engagement with the course material, chat-room discussions and the instructor. In this case, there were no online discussions or threads to contribute to, so it was easy for Patricia to disengage from OLPE. Because Patricia found PE generally difficult and confessed in interviews that—without the direct contact of a teacher and a physical space to attend, coupled with her embodied history of PE–she lacked the desire to work hard at the course and found herself almost failing it.

COMMUNICATION: RORY'S STORY

Rory's communication story is less dramatic since his attitude and relationship with his PE past was fairly neutral. His advantage came in seeing how OLPE played out in his sister's life and it was a learning moment for him as he embarked on the world of online learning. Rory also had another asset, which was the confidence he had in his written communication skills because he was an A-student in English. Therefore, since many assignments in his OLPE course were based on written submissions, he found them easy enough to do. In addition, he had a bit more incentive to complete the course quickly since he took OLPE on top of a full course load, which left little time to squander unlike his sister who took a "spare block" in her timetable thinking that she would use it to work on her PE course. Unfortunately Patricia did not manage her time as wisely as she had hoped.

THE ACTUAL EXPERIENCE AND CHOICE

The experiences of the participants seem just as varied as those who take traditional PE. OLPE seems to be designed to offer curriculum that suit student enrolment profiles and learning environment in order to meet the Ministry's PE mandates. The participants each speak of their unique experiences in terms of assignments, activities and assessments, similarities and differences.

CHOICE: PATRICIA'S EXPERIENCE

Patricia's relayed her OLPE experience:

> Yeah it was definitely worth it. I'm glad I did it. It was kinda hard sometimes but there was no way I was going to go back to school PE, so yeah … Way more work. I thought it would be great because I would be on my own, I didn't think it would be that much more work than in-school PE … We had to do SO much writing, it wasn't even funny…if I had known there was going to be that much writing I might've changed my mind. (Interview, May, 2014)

Another reason why Patricia found OLPE difficult was the amount of journaling she had to do.

In her daily exercise log she was asked to consider not only the activity choice for the day but also register an emotional check on how she felt that day and when she was doing the exercise. These short but daily writing pieces were not easy to maintain and Patricia found herself falling behind on journaling assignments. She indicated that, "[w]riting about daily activity and answering questions" was something she would never want to do again. There were other assignments that were of interest, such as outlining a healthy eating plan and organizing a weekly exercise routine along with a progression. At times, this made traditional PE seem easier when she simply had to go to class and participate; however, it still was not enough to convince her that it was a better situation and indicated, "[t]he amount of work and finding the time to do the physical activity" were her biggest challenges.

Patricia's choice of physical activities included yoga, running on the treadmill, free weights and mixed martial arts. She had to submit heart rates when she exercised and although she sheepishly said that she was tempted to cheat, she did not know enough about how high or low her heart rate should be at any given time so she did not cheat. The activities she chose were individual activities that could be done on her own time without drawing attention to herself. She could stop when she wanted to and move at a different pace. Being able to choose her activity was empowering. Having said that, when asked about obstacles in taking OLPE she added that a lack of motivation and procrastination (Interview, May, 2014) were factors. She noted that OLPE was more enjoyable than traditional PE but that she still hated it (Interview, May, 2014). In the end, having a personal choice in activities was still significant in that she was invested in the exercises, which made her feel accomplished. Finally, Patricia had input on what she was interested in. Gibbons (2009) notes that "a disconnection occurs between what many girls value in PE and what they experience...some young women do not associate their physical activity preferences with those included in their PE courses...[and choose] to leave PE as soon as the opportunity [is] available" (p. 224).

CHOICE: RORY'S EXPERIENCE

Rory registered with the same online school as his sister, which took approximately six to seven months to complete. His assignments were similar. Rory's first assignment had to be completed prior to starting the course. It consisted of preliminary lessons that asked about his current fitness level, his past involvement in activities, target heart rate charts and guides, planning a weekly exercise routine, and parental supervision with comments from his father. In this pre-planning work, Rory expressed that he was interested in being physically fit, but recognized that he was not investing as much time into it as he could. Rory found that the writing in OLPE took the most amount of time. The following is his view of what he would not want to do again:

> Logging specific results about daily exercises like heart rates and self-motivation stuff, and especially reflections. Sometimes I just couldn't be reflective on what I was doing. I did like making our own exercise programmes though, but it was hard at first because I'd like, never done one you know. (Interview, May, 2014)

When Rory spoke of his OLPE experience he was calm and rational. There were no rolling eyes, waving arms, or clenched hands, which seemed to indicate that he was more satisfied than his sister with both traditional PE and on-line PE. Rory story supports that he approached the course differently based on Patricia's experience, knowing "from the start that it would be harder so I went into OLPE with the expectation that I had to work harder" (Interview, May, 2014). He was quite pleased that his grades improved in PE without having to do regular PE activities and received a mark in the 90% range.

CHOICE: PATRICIA AND RORY'S PE FUTURES

It can be claimed that one of the overarching goals of PE worldwide is to promote healthy living and active lives for the purpose of promoting good public health. However, Armour and Harris (2013) argue that "there is little robust historical or contemporary evidence to suggest that PE in most countries has achieved anything significant in terms of encouraging lifelong engagement in physical activity or improving public health" (p. 202). As for Patricia and Rory's PE progression: They both dropped the class after grade 10 and admit that they have only loosely attended to a fitness plan, but feel confident and competent in the activities they chose for themselves in their online course. Patricia mentioned that she felt quite comfortable going to the gym by herself, because she knows how to operate the cardio equipment and how to monitor her own fitness levels. She also took steps to move her jogging outdoors and find a community 'fun run' to participate in.

> I still go to the gym sometimes. I'm also going to try, maybe like, the Sun Run next year. I know it's taken me, like, so long to get started but I think I can actually do it [the race] with music". [Yoga is] kinda boring though on your own. Maybe I should join a group or something like that because I did sign up for mixed martial arts when I did [online] PE ... I can check my heart rate and I do have a bit more awareness of physical fitness ... Better time management for sure I wasn't very motivated and not good at it [time management]. Oh, I also learned that I can handle situations independently more better. (Interview, May, 2014)

As for Rory, he tried to continue to go to the gym with his father, but found that his schooling takes much of his time. Nevertheless, he sees exercising and being fit as a personal pursuit, saying, "I still enjoy going for runs which I only began from doing OLPE" (Interview, May, 2014). While he did not make new discoveries about himself through OLPE, he did say that he was more active in OLPE than traditional PE because "it was all me" (Interview, May, 2014). When asked what he learned through OLPE, Rory acknowledged that he learned how to plan workouts and found it a more worthwhile experience than traditional PE, even though it was more intensive than traditional PE. The reason, he explained, was because, "I would be able to do it on my own pace" (Interview, May, 2014). Taking OLPE opened up opportunities for the participants to pursue activities that carried meaning and purpose for them, and prepared them to participate beyond the classroom.

Conclusion

The participants agreed that journaling was the most time consuming part of the online course, because it was a task that was done in addition to the actual physical activity. It was also agreed that there was a major difference between the two types of PE courses, as they typically did not write in PE classes; take quizzes or tests; reflect on how they felt; monitor heart rates; or design or record fitness levels. And since the writing took more time than expected, and was quite frequent, it may have lost its effectiveness in having the participants thoughtfully reflect on their learning goals. On the other hand, choice was seen as an important factor in making OLPE enjoyable as the participants were able to decide what type of exercise they were going to engage in, and this seemed to make it more meaningful as it carried into the future.

CLOSING THOUGHTS

The unknown is usually the catalyst of uncertainty in OLPE, but with these narratives as a start, it is hoped that others may see a bit of themselves in the participants' stories and find understanding. There is still much more to unearth surrounding OLPE, especially within the context of a Canadian, high school perspective. This research is simply a starting point; a conversation that will hopefully develop into a meaningful contribution to the possibilities of OLPE studies. From these findings, we may see that OLPE in the lower mainland is providing an alternative opportunity for those who opt out of traditional PE and that it gives students a choice. For Patricia and Rory, OLPE offered a safe place for students to land.

References

Almala, A. H. (2005). A constructivist conceptual framework for a quality e-learning environment. *Distance Learning*, 2(5), 9-12.

Armour, K., & Harris, J. (2013). Making the case for developing new pe-for-health pedagogies. *Quest*, 65(2), 201-219.

Ashton-Warner, S. (1963). *Teacher.* New York: Simon & Schuster.

Barbour, M. K. (2010). *State of the nation: K-12 online learning in Canada.* Vienna, Virginia: International Association for K-12 online learning. Retrieved from www.inacol.org

Barbour, M., Siko, J., Sumara, J., & Simuel-Everage, K. (2012). Narratives from the online frontier: A K-12 student's experience in an online learning environment. *The Qualitative Report,* 17(20), 1-19.

Bedard, S., & Knox-Pipes, B. (2006). Online distance learning: The K-12 student's perspective. *Distance Learning,* 3(4), 13-19.

Bennett, G., & Green, F. P. (2001). Student learning in the online environment: No significant difference? *Quest,* 53(1), 1-13.

Bennett, P. W. (2012). *The sky has limits: online learning in Canadian K-12 public education.* Toronto, Ontario: Society for Quality Education. Retrieved from http://site.ebrary.com/id/10544930?ppg=1

Bernard, R. M., Abrami, P. C., Lou, Y., Borokhovski, E., Wade, A., Wozney, L., . . . Huang, B. (2004). How does distance education compare with classroom instruction? A meta-analysis of the empirical literature. *Review of Educational Research,* 74(3), 379-439.

Bingham, C., & Sidorkin, A. M. (Eds.). (2010). *No education without relation.* New York: Lang, Peter.

British Columbia Ministry of Education. (2008). *The British Columbia physical education 8 to 10 Integrated Resource Package.* Retrieved from whihttps://www.bced.gov.bc.ca/irp/pdfs/physical_education/2008pe810.pdf

Buschner, C. (2006). Online physical education. *Journal of Physical Education, Recreation & Dance,* 77(2), 3-8.

Clandinin, D. J. (2006). Narrative Inquiry: A Methodology for Studying Lived Experience. *Research Studies in Music Education,* 27(44), 44-54.

Clandinin, D. J., Pushor, D., & Orr, A. M. (2007). Navigating sites for narrative inquiry. *Journal of Teacher Education,* 58(21), 21-35. doi:10.1177/0022487106296218

Clandinin, J. D., & Connelly, F. M. (1990). Stories of Experience and Narrative Inquiry. *Educational Researcher,* 19(5), 2-14. Retrieved from http://www.jstor.org/stable/1176100

Daum, D. N., & Buschner, C. (2012). The status of high school online physical education in the United States. *Journal of Teaching in Physical Education,* 31, 86-100.

Davis, B. (2010). *UBC Connect.* Retrieved from http://www.elearning.ubc.ca/connect

Davis, B., Sumara, D. J., & Luce-Kapler, R. (2008). *Engaging Minds: Changing Teaching in Complex Times.* New York: Routledge.

Didon, Henri. (1881). Retrieved from http://registration.olympic.org/en/faq/detail/

id/29

Gibbons, S. L. (2009). Meaningful Participation of girls in senior physical education courses. *Canadian Journal of Education*, 32(2), 222-244.

Hannum, W. H., Irvin, M. J., Banks, J. B., & Farmer, T. W. (2009). Distance education use in rural schools. *Journal of Research in Rural Education*, 24(3), 1-15.

Horn, M. B. (2010). K-12 online education is increasingly hybrid learning. *Distance Learning*, 7(2), 18-20.

Huber, J., Caine, V., Huber, M., & Steeves, P. (2013). Narrative inquiry as pedagogy in education: The extraodinary potential of living, telling, retelling, and reliving stories of experience. *Review of Research in Education, 37*, 212-242. doi:10.3102/0091732X12458885

Mohnsen, B. (2012). Implementing online physical education. *Journal of Physical Education Recreation & Dance, 83*(2), 42-47.

Mosier, B. (2012). Virtual physical education: A call for action. *Journal of Physical Education, Recreation & Dance*, 83(3), 6-10.

Murphy, E., & Rodriguez-Manzanares, M. A. (2009). Teachers' perspective on motivation in high school distance education. *Journal of Distance Education,* 23(3), 1-24.

Ntoumanis, N. (2001). A self-determination approach to the understanding of motivation in physical education. *British Journal of Educational Psychology, 71,* 225-242.

Powell, K. C., & Kalina, C. J. (2009). Cognitive and social constructivism: Developing tools for an effective classroom. *Education*, 130(2), 241-250.

Ransdell, L. B., Rice, K., Snelson, C., & Decola, J. (2008). Online health-related fitness courses: A wolf in sheep's clothing or a solution to some common problems? *Journal of Physical Education, Recreation & Dance*, 79(1), 45-52.

Rhea, D. J. (2011). Virtual physical education in the K-12 setting. *Journal of Physical Education, Recreation & Dance, 82*(1), 5-6.

Rice, K. L. (2006). A comprehensive look at distance education in the K-12 context. *Journal of Research on Technology in Education*, 38(4), 425-448.

Schaefer, L. (2013). Narrative inquiry for physical education pedagogy. *International Journal of Pedagogies & Learning, 8*(1), 18-26. Retrieved from http://search.proquest.com.ezproxy.library.ubc.ca/docview/1470864816?accountid=14656

Sparkes, A. (2002). Different tales and judgement calls. In A. Sparkes, & A. Sparkes (Ed.), *Telling tales in sport and physical activity: A qualitative journey* (pp. 191-225). Champaign, IL: Human Kinetics.

Thomas, S. (2012). Narrative inquiry: embracing the possibilities. *Qualitative Research Journal*, 12(2), 206-221. doi:1-.1108/14439881211248356

U.S. Department of Education Office of planning, Evaluation, and Policy Development Policy and Program Studies Service. (2010). *Evaluation of evidence-based practices in online learning: A meta-analysis and review of online learning studies.* Washington, D.C. Retrieved from www.ed.gov/about/offices/list/opepd/ppss/reports.html.

White, E. (2004). Virtual high school: does it make the grade? *Literary Clavalcade,* 16-18.

Yaman, M. (2009). Perceptions of students on the application of distance education in physical education lessons. *The Turkish Online Journal of Education Technology,* 8(1), 65-74.

Vygotsky, L. S. (1962). *Thought and Language.* Cambridge MA: MIT Press.

CHAPTER TEN

Reconceptualizing and Reframing Pedagogy, Curriculum and Research through Complexity Thinking

BY ALAN OVENS, TIM HOPPER & JOY BUTLER

Introduction

Complexity is an idea whose time has come (Byrne, 2005, p. 98).

This chapter is based on the premise that physical education phenomena are inherently complex and explores the possible relevancies that complexity thinking may have for the field of physical education. In one sense, complexity has always confronted those working in physical education. The issue is not that educational phenomena are complex, but about the appropriateness of the frameworks we use to make sense of the 'messiness' that is inherent in complex educational settings. As the title of this chapter indicates, complexity offers the opportunity to question how we conceptualize and frame the issues central to curriculum, pedagogy and research in physical education. We invite our readers to use the lens of complexity thinking to reconceptualize ideas and issues to form potential emergent theories in our field. The idea of frame draws attention to the interpretative process involved in constructing meaning or making sense of the world. Frames are tacit perceptual mechanisms that transform the unfamiliar into meaningful and normative categories (Lawson, 1984) that are, in turn, central to the construction of shared meanings typifying particular discursive fields (Bernstein, 2000). Our objective in supporting the possibility of reframing the field is not one linked to a representational epistemology of changing perspective to gain a more accurate understanding of reality. Rather, the meaning of the term 'reframe' that we hope to invoke is linked to a quest of finding more complex and creative ways of interacting with our reality, with which we can then use to interact in yet more complex and creative ways (Osberg, Biesta, & Cilliers, 2008). From a complexity perspective, reframing implies there are no final solutions, only new ways to interact that lead to new emergent possibilities. This sort of project is anything but straightforward, particularly given the lack clarity around the concept and the relative 'newness' that complexity has in the physical education literature. But it is one in which we collectively hope to 'expand the space of the possible' (Davis & Sumara, 1997).

At the outset it is important to address two potential misconceptions that may arise for readers when presented with the claims that complexity offers something new to physical education scholarship. Firstly, it is important to state that complexity does not constitute a single body of thought or unified theory, either in the natural or social sciences. Despite the use of terms such as 'complexity science' and 'complexity theory', there is no consensus around matters of research approach or agreed body of knowledge (Alhadeff-Jones, 2008; Richardson & Cilliers, 2001). As noted by Mason (2008), ideas about complexity derive from disciplinary fields as diverse as physics, biology, economics, sociology, and law. What complexivists do have in common is a broad agreement on what constitutes a complex phenomenon or entity. Consequently, rather than defining it by its modes of inquiry, complexity is "… more appropriately characterized in terms of its objects of study" (Davis & Sumara, 2006, p. 5). Most commonly, the objects of study are modeled as a 'system' of interacting entities, in which the 'system' is perpetually constructing its own future as continuity and transformation (Stacey, 2001). The critical aspect is not to focus on the system, but on the process of interaction between the elements that enables the emergent properties and forms that are the focus of our inquiry (Byrne, 2005). The potential of complexity for physical education, then is not as some explanatory system or metadiscourse that provides a more complete or superior set of explanations, but rather in the way it presents as a source domain rich with possible analogies for understanding human action, knowledge, identity and learning (Stacey, 2001).

Secondly, it is important to dispel the notion that complexity represents either a regression to some form of naïve scientism or the importing of models and methods from the natural sciences that are inappropriate for educational inquiry. To the contrary, the perspective complexity represents is consistent with the evolution of post-enlightenment thought and emerges from the collective efforts of those philosophers and scientists working within both the natural and social sciences who attempt to challenge a mechanistic, reductionist view of the world (Gare, 2000, p. 335). For example, postmodernism and complexity share a similar sense of the implausibility of grand narratives and the impossibility of independent objective observation (Kuhn, 2008). Complexity thinking pays attention to diverse disciplinary sensibilities while acknowledging the multidimensionality, non-linearity, interconnectedness and unpredictability encountered in human activity. It arises among rather than over other discourses and is oriented by the realization that the act of comparing diverse and seemingly unconnected phenomena is both profoundly human and, at times, tremendously fecund (Davis & Sumara, 2006, p. 8).

The aim of this chapter is to provide an overview of complexity and reflect on its possible value to physical education. It begins by providing an overview of what we mean by complexity thinking and it focuses on some of the themes that have been most used in education. This provides an introduction to complexity for the non-specialist audience from which the following presentations may build. The paper then addresses the question of what complexity thinking may contribute to physical education scholarship by considering the discursive tensions in areas central to the field such as research, curriculum, learning, teaching and embodiment.

WHAT IS COMPLEXITY?

The task of trying to understand complexity is itself, complex. Definitions, by their very nature, seek certainty and stability of meaning and the irony is that these are the very qualities that complexity seek to challenge. Complexity is also not a field of study easily defined by its constituent concepts or contributing disciplines. Alhadeff- Jones (2008) suggests that disorder has often shaped the evolution of research focused on complexity, giving rise to different generational forms and the heterogeneity of meaning and multiplicity of definitions and trends that currently exit. In their attempt to make sense of the field, Richardson and Cilliers (2001) define three different themes or communities: hard complexity science, which aims to uncover and understand the nature of reality; soft complexity science, which makes use of complexity as a metaphorical tool to understand and interpret the world; and complexity thinking, which adopts a philosophical approach to considering the implications of assuming a complex world. In a similar manner, Byrne (2005) explores some of the philosophical variations in the way complexity is used and distinguishes between simplistic complexity, which has a focus on the general set of rules from which emergent complexity flows, and complex complexity which has a focus on the contingent and contextual nature of complex forms. Such classifications, while somewhat artificial, point to the way the varied discourses, histories and concepts that represent complexity are highly nuanced, intertwined and potentially inconsistent.

Our own preference lies with the idea of complexity thinking and the way it foregrounds this form of inquiry as an attitude which is potentially generative of, and pays attention to, diverse sensibilities without making claims to, or being trapped by, universals or absolutes. It is a view that argues that while complexity may not provide us with the conceptual tools to solve our complex problems, it "shows us (in a rigourous way) why these problems are so difficult" (Cilliers, 2005, p. 257). Complexity thinking, as Davis and Sumara (2006) point out, prompts a kind of "level jumping between and among different layers of organization enabling attention to be oriented towards —other dynamic, co-implicated and integrated levels, including neurological, the experiential, the contextual/material, the symbolic, the cultural, and the ecological" (p. 26). In other words, complexity thinking is transphenomenal (requires awareness of phenomena at different levels of organisation), transdisciplinary (requires border crossing between theoretical frames) and interdiscursive (requires an awareness of how discourses intersect, overlap and interlace) (Davis, 2008; Davis & Phelps, 2005).

While acknowledging the field of complexity is difficult to define, even to the point of questioning if it is a field, a starting point is to have a shared set of meanings of concepts and ideas that are frequently referred to. The following discussion provides an overview of some of the key themes that have the most frequent uptake in the education literature, namely complex systems, emergence, and adaptation.

COMPLEX SYSTEMS

A general starting point is that complexity generally exists in situations in which a large number of agents are connected and interacting with each other in dynamic ways (Mason, 2008). An agent is understood as something that takes part in an interaction of a system and is itself subsequently changed: a person, a society, a molecule, a plant, a nerve cell, a PE student, a teacher, etc. The behavior of these systems is said to be complex because the relationships between multiple elements give rise to emergent qualities that cannot be reduced to the sum of their constituent parts or to a central agent responsible for overall control of the system (Byrne, 2005; Cilliers, 1998). As a property of the system, complexity is situated between order and disorder. That is, complex systems are neither predictable nor regular in the way they act. However, neither are they random nor chaotic. Complex systems tend to display features of both dimensions, sometimes displaying highly patterned and ordered features while simultaneously being surprising and unpredictable (Morrison, 2008).

Complexity is not always a feature of systems with many interconnected elements. Simple and complicated systems are also composed of multiple components, but can be characterized as closed systems capable of decomposing to their individual parts and whose workings follow predictable and precise rules (Cilliers, 2000). In other words, complicated systems may have many component parts, but each component relates to the others in fixed and clearly defined ways. Each component is inert and not dynamic or adaptive. The modern computer is an example of a highly complicated system that has many interdependent parts that can be taken apart and reassembled. The way it works can be confusing for a novice, but the expert technician can understand the range of parts required and the rules determining the way the parts relate. In this sense, simple and complicated systems are conceptualized as mechanical in the way they function, giving them the ability to behave in predictable ways. This means that something like a computer or car works the same way each time it starts.

By contrast, complex systems are self-organizing and adaptive forms constituted through a large number of non-linear, dynamic interactions. Complex systems, such as brains, classes of students, or economies, are characterized by patterns of relationships that exist within each system as a whole. When the system is taken apart, either physically or theoretically, it is this relational aspect that is destroyed and this subsequently prevents an understanding of the system's dynamics and properties (Byrne, 2005). In complex systems the individual components are self-organizing, adaptive agents in their own right, while interdependent with those with which they are connected. The individual components, while displaying a unity at one level, are themselves complex systems at a different scale (often referred to as the nestedness of self-similar systems). Davis and Sumara (2006) provide a useful summary of qualities that must be manifest for a system to exhibit complexity.

- Self-organized- complex systems/unities spontaneously arise as the actions of autonomous agents come to be interlinked and co-dependent;

- Bottom-up emergent- complex unities manifest properties that exceed the summed traits and capacities of individuals agents, but these transcendent qualities and abilities do not depend on central organizers or overarching governing structures;

- Short-range relationships- most of the information within a complex system is exchanged between close neighbors, meaning that the systems coherence depends mostly on agents immediate interdependencies, no on centralized control or top-down administration;

- Nested structure (or scale-free networks)- complex unities are often composed of and often comprise other unities that might be properly identified as complex- that is, as giving rise to new patterns and of activities and new rules of behavior;

- Ambiguously bounded – complex forms are open in the sense that they continuously exchange matter and energy with their surroundings (and so judgments about their edges may require certain arbitrary impositions and necessary ignorances);

- Organizationally closed- complex forms are close in the sense that they are inherently stable- that is, their behavioral patterns or internal organizations endure, even while they exchange energy and matter with their dynamic contexts (so judgments about their edges are usually based on perceptible and sufficiently stable coherences);

- Structure determined- a complex unity can change its own structure as it adapts to maintain its viability within dynamic contexts; in other words, complex systems embody their histories – they learn – and are thus better described in terms of Darwinian evolution than Newtonian mechanics;

- Far-from equilibrium- complex systems do not operate in balance; indeed, a stable equilibrium implies death for a complex system.

(Davis and Sumara, 2006, p. 5-6).

Complex systems form when the agents of the system are attracted to certain pattern of behaviour over time. For example, in a physical education setting, such attractors can be:

- singular where a class of students for example all focus on a similar solution to a movement task,

- periodic, where certain behaviours are repeated that influence the system such timed games in tournaments,

- within observable bounds, such as the rules and boundaries in a game of soccer, but within those bounds anything is possible; or

- random, where attractors happen but without connection or regard to other parts of the system such as a class of kindergarten children engaged in playground play where suddenly unconnected play becomes united by a common interest for many of the children.

Constraints on a system mediate attractors' power to control the system and, as noted by Ennis (1992), these constraints allow teachers to set up learning conditions in an attempt to shape a system of students' emergent learning.

EMERGENCE

One of the most important ideas central to complexity is the notion of emergence. Emergence can be defined as the appearance of a property or feature not previously observed as a functional characteristic of a system (Cilliers, 1998; Mason, 2008; Richardson & Cilliers, 2001). In other words, new and often unexpected properties, patterns and behaviours can emerge which cannot be predicted from an analysis of the individual system components or the way these components interact (Mason, 2008). In a very real sense, complex systems become more than the sum of their parts. Examples include the way consciousness emerges from networks of neurons in the brain, teamwork emerges from the activities of players, and meaning emerges from language. Such properties disappear if the parts of the system are disassembled and individually analyzed.

Emergence draws attention to three important ideas inherent to an ontology of complex systems. Firstly, the idea of 'supervenience' highlights how the emergent property is dependent on its constituent parts. The emergent property exists only as a function of component interactions occurring at a lower level. Secondly, the emergent properties are more than the sum of the parts and are not just the predictable aggregate of the way the parts interact. Thirdly, the emergent property is not 'epiphenomenal' in which the property exists as either an illusion or descriptive metaphor. Rather, the emergent property exhibits 'downward causation' in that it has causal effects on the components at the lower level. For example, the act of running causes the individual parts of the body to change positions and move (since the 'body system' must remain together in such an act). In this way, emergent properties impose boundary conditions or constraints that restrict the freedom of the component parts.

Emergence also highlights the interdependent relationship that exists between the elements or agents of a complex system and the environment that affords such a system. Once a system reaches a certain critical level of diversity and complexity a phase transition takes place, what Barab et al. (1999) calls an autocatalytic state (self-organize in a continuous activity drawing on available resources) to create a system that sustains itself as its constituent elements inter-act and in turn interconnect with the environment. Therefore, complexity thinking foregrounds a contextual ontology where phenomena such as learning, curriculum, teaching, are emergent in response to how contributing agents, as part of a collective, adapt and self-organize in relation to the constraints of a context.

ADAPTATION AND LEARNING

Adaptation is the ability of complex unities to continuously and actively re-orient their structures in order to maintain coherence in relation to their worlds. For example, new neural pathways are created as people learn new skills and teams develop strategies to enhance game play. It is the adaptability and self-organizing processes inherent in complex systems, based on the interest of survival in a changing environment, that create new and emergent possibilities for system-wide understanding and acting (Mason, 2008). Adaptation offers an insight into how complex systems learn and, as such, an analogy for how we can understand human learning.

Critically, the system must contain enough diversity in its make-up to allow it the ability to adapt to the demands of the environment, but there must also be enough redundancy (commonality) between agents of the system so that if any part of the system fails the other agents can compensate. In addition, the system needs redundancy to facilitate neighborly interactions as the agents of the system participation in the environment develop skills in co-mingling roles associated with the intents of the system. As the complex system inter-acts it forms a relationship with the environment so when the conditions are just right an autocatakinetic process starts where the system, drawing on available resources, develops a self-sustaining exchange with the environment. The conditions in the environment need to offer enabling constraints (affordances) that limit what the system can do, preventing it being overwhelmed, but at the same time offer an openness to possibilities to which complex system can take advantage. The system must have the capacity to retain the products of previous exchanges, but also the ability to discard elements that are no longer useful. The system forms around nested self-similar structures that emerge from inter-actions around simple rules that initiated the system's ability to dynamically unfold.

Complexity in physical education

The following section attempts to address the question of what complexity has to offer physical education. In one sense, this is a question about how complexity thinking can facilitate the development of post-enlightenment thought in ways that have the potential to generate new, creative and innovative ways of understanding educational phenomena, which themselves lead to new, creative, innovative forms of engagement. For many, complexity provides a rich source domain of analogies and language, which allows them to gain new perspectives on their own work. While we acknowledge this potential, we suggest that complexity also offers a particular philosophical orientation that enables physical educators to gain transphenomenal, transdisciplinary and interdiscursive insights. We demonstrate this in the following section by focusing on the key themes of research, curriculum, learning, teaching and embodiment. In relation to each theme, we summarize the key debates and perspectives represented in the physical education literature and consider how complexity may be taken up by physical educators to generate new insights and ways of working within this theme.

RESEARCH

Historically in physical education, there has been an active questioning of the appropriateness of those forms of inquiry aligned with the modernist project of uncovering universal truths based on a reductionist natural science approach (for example Hellison, 1988; Kirk, 1989; Schempp, 1987; Siedentop, 1987, 1989; Sparkes, 1989, 1991, 1993). More recently, recognizing the growing influence of gender and cultural studies, as well as the contribution from poststructuralism and postmodernism, there has been an increased awareness and discussion of the ways culture, language, subjectivity, politics, ideology, power and narrative, all permeate efforts to understand phenomena that elude traditional analytic methods (for example Bain, 1995; Faulkner & Finlay, 2002; Fernadez- Balboa, 1997; Kerry & Armour, 2000; Nilges, 2001; Sparkes, 1993, 1995, 2002; Wright, 2004). Complexity thinking offers a way to frame debates around research in ways that embrace post-modern sensibilities whilst offering a way to theorize educational phenomena that does not become fixed, anchored to a tradition or blind to the unanticipated (Davis & Sumara, 2006). Complexity thinking accepts postmodern insights about the relational nature of knowledge, truth and identity. However, complexivists argue that such questions are not just a matter of human, intersubjective negotiation- they are also a function of the mutually affective relationships among all phenomena. Complexity thus opens onto the more-than-human world.

CURRICULUM

Debates around curriculum frequently centre on how changing social beliefs about what is important for the education of young people relate to the work of physical education teachers. Traditional, rationalist notions of curriculum view the relationship between policy and practice as hierarchical and emphasize linearity, control, learner passivity and knowledge-transmission (Jess, Attencio and Thorburn, 2011). In such a view pedagogical practice becomes the practical articulation of policy and the agency of the teacher constructed as either conforming or resisting policy (Ovens, 2010). However, such views do not adequately account for the globalization of knowledge and culture, the complexities of power, the influence of networked social relationships and the 'messy' nature of teaching as situated, cultural work. Complexity thinking draws attention to curriculum as a fluid, interactive and unpredictable process emerging within nested, open, interdependent complex systems (Ovens, 2010). It characterizes curricula as nodes, hubs and links in decentralized networks of human knowing rather than as essential or basic knowledge in discrete disciplines (Barab et al., 1999; Davis & Sumara, 2006). It problematises the relationship between policy and practice as complex and constantly in a state of flux. It mobilizes the need for sensibilities that foreground the way key ideas are enabled and constrained by accountability structures interdependent with teachers work spaces. Seen in the light of the dynamic, self-organizing and adaptive nature of interdependent systems, traditional notions become not only unrealistic but even stifling or suppressing as ways of understanding the changing nature and relevance of physical education as a subject area and set of practices within the contemporary schooling contexts of late modernity (Kirk, 2010; Penney & Chandler, 2000).

LEARNING

Concerns with the orthodoxy of behaviourist and cognitivist notions of learning have been regularly voiced within the physical education literature. For example, Rovegno and Kirk (1995) suggested there was a need to generate new ways to think about the learning process within their early critique of socially critical work in physical education. They suggested there needed to be increased attention to how children learn, develop and experience physical education. Such calls are consistent with post- modern sensibilities that challenge dualist thinking and knowledge hierarchies that devalue the embodied forms of learning associated with physical education. Since their call there has been an increased awareness of how learning is conceptualized and supported within physical education settings, with an interest holistic, relational understandings of the learner engaged in activity in physical, social, cultural environments. However, as Light (2008) observes, while there has been an increased interest in constructivist theories of learning, little attention has been paid to the assumptions about learning and knowledge about learning inherent in such theories. He suggests the value in complexity thinking is its ability to focus attention on the key assumptions and discourses clustered under the banner of these new theories of learning.

TEACHING

Mirroring the constructivist shift in learning has been the increased interest in the teaching role and the ways teachers should structure the lesson setting. For those working in the sport biosciences, concerns around lesson structure are linked to understanding human movement as a non-linear dynamical system and the importance of manipulating lesson activities to facilitate the emergence of functional movement patterns and decision-making behaviours (Chow et al., 2007; Davids, Button, & Bennett, 2008). For those working in the education field, concerns with lesson structure are linked to constructivist and situated learning principles that promote the need for collaborative participation by students in learning communities capable of providing relevant, meaningful and conceptually 'rich' learning opportunities (Macdonald, 2004; Rovegno, 2006). Complexity thinking has been taken up by physical education scholars as a generative field for furthering such discussions, particularly by those working in the area of Teaching Games for Understanding (for example, Butler & Griffin, 2010; Hopper, Butler, & Storey, 2009). More recently, Jess, Attencio and Thorburn (2011) have outlined how complexity thinking underpinned the use of constructivist and ecological models to inform curriculum development in Scottish Physical Education. They point out that this approach is underpinned by a belief that there is no one correct way to teach. However, they also point out that this belief does not mean that 'anything goes', suggesting that instead this implies a need for the teacher to draw on a broad range of pedagogical strategies. By being sensitive to the way learners learn in different ways and at different rates, behaviourist approaches are not rejected, but sometimes employed "as part of developing a richer and more extensive repertoire of pedagogical strategies" (Jess et al., 2011, p. 195).

EMBODIMENT

The body is central to the work of physical education, particularly as it is the object that needs to be physically educated. The evolution of post-enlightenment thought has also increased uncertainty around the nature of the body. Naturalistic perspectives conceptualize the body as a natural biological entity, different in nature and subservient to the mind. The implication from this perspective is that learning is something only associated with the mind and involves a shift in mental state, from one of ignorance to one of knowledge (Beckett & Morris, 2001). Those coming from a poststructuralist position have provided a strong critique of this position, preferring instead to promote the idea that the body is constructed within the languages used to describe it as well as being shaped by the social practices and contexts in which it is situated (Giblett, 2008). According to this approach, the individual becomes embodied as discourses create particular subjectivities in relation to comportment, muscularity, shape and size (Azzarito & Solman, 2009). Phenomenologists provide yet another perspective and focus on the way the body provides the basis of participating in and perceiving of the world. For them, the body is a thinking, feeling, moving body, which is not just an entity existing in the world, but is intentionally oriented to constructing the world in which it exists (Hass, 2008).

Complexity thinking has the potential to explore the tensions between the three perspectives in a generative, creative way. As Shilling (2004) notes, there is a need to consider "how the body is not only a physical location on which society inscribes its effects, but a material source of social categories and relations and a sensual means by which people are attached to or dislocated from social forms" (p. xvii). Complexity thinking resists the essentialism inherent in each perspective, replacing it instead with a transphenomenal sensibility that recognizes that the 'fleshiness' of the body is simultaneously resourced with a range of cognitive, affective and movement capabilities that generate both sensual and symbolic meanings as an acculturation process of living in, and inhabiting, the world.

Concluding thoughts

As many social commentators have highlighted, we are living in 'new times' that are characterized by profound social and cultural change emerging from increasing globalized connectivity and the flow of information such social networks allow. The view presented in this paper is not that complexity thinking (or science, or theory) will provide access to more or better truths, but that it may be better suited to the demands of understanding and constructing educational practices within this rapidly changing, ever-more complicated times. Complexity thinking provides a conceptual framework that has the potential to offer fresh insights into themes central to physical education and extend the debates in new, generative ways. It addresses the concerns for a sociological perspective that views physical education phenomena as emerging from the networks of relationships, that interconnect locally, nationally and globally, in which physical educators are enmeshed (Green, 2002, 2006). It suggests a significant reworking of social ontology that "rejects scientific objectivity, relativist subjectivity and struturalist or post-structuralist inter-subjectivity…" suggesting instead "… holding all of these in dynamic, co-specifiying, conversational relationships while locating these in a grander, more-than-human context" (Davis and Sumara, 2006, p. 15). The use of complexity thinking in physical education is still young and evolving. It is not without its critics, which provides a healthy and necessary constraint on its optimistic claims. However, in 'new times' the capacity to think complexly presents itself as a necessity, in both an analytical sense and political sense, as a practical guide to future action.

With permission from Drs. Alan Ovens and Tim Hopper, May 5th, 2015.

References

Alhadeff-Jones, M. (2008). Three generations of complexity theories: Nuances and ambiguities. In M. Mason (Ed.), Complexity Theory and the Philosophy of Education (pp. 62-78). Chichester: Wiley- Blackwell.

Azzarito, L., & Solman, M. (2009). An investigation of students' embodied discourses in physical education: A gender project. Journal of Teaching in Physical Education, 28, 178-191.

Bain, L. (1995). Mindfulness and subjective knowledge. Quest, 47, 238-253.

Barab, S., Cherkes-Julkowski, M., Swenson, R., Garrett, S., Shaw, R., & Young, M. (1999). Principles of Self- Organization: Learning as Participation in Autocatakinetic Systems. 8(3), 349-390.

Beckett, D., & Morris, G. (2001). Ontological performance: Bodies, identities and learning. Studies in the Education of Adults, 33(1), 35-48.

Bernstein, B. (2000). Pedagogy, symbolic control and identity: Theory, research, critique (Revised ed.). Oxford: Rowman & Littlefield.

Butler, J., & Griffin, L. (2010). More Teaching Games for Understanding: Moving Globally. Champaign: Human Kinetics.

Byrne, D. (2005). Complexity, Configurations and Cases. Theory, Culture & Society, 22(5), 95-111.

Chow, J., Davids, K., Button, C., Shuttleworth, R., Renshaw, I., & Araujo, D. (2007). The role of nonlinear pedagogy in physical education. Review of Edcuational Research, 77(3), 251-278.

Cilliers, P. (1998). Complexity and Postmodernism: Understanding Complex Systems. London: Routledge. Cilliers, P. (2000). Rules and Complex Systems [Article]. Emergence, 2(3), 40-50.

Cilliers, P. (2005). Complexity, deconstruction and relativism. Theory, Culture & Society, 22(5), 255-267. Davids, K., Button, C., & Bennett, S. (2008). Dynamics of Skill Acquisition: A Constraints-Led Approach. Champaign, IL: Human Kinetics.

Davis, B. (2008). Complexity and education: Vital simultaneities. Educational Philosophy and Theory, 40(1), 46-61.

Davis, B., & Phelps, R. (2005). Exploring the Common Spaces of Education and Complexity: Transphenomenality, Transdisciplinarity, and Interdiscursivity. Complicity: An International Journal of Complexity and Education, 2(1), 1-4.

Davis, B., & Sumara, D. (1997). Cognition, complexity and teacher education. Harvard Educational Review, 67(1), 105-125.

Davis, B., & Sumara, D. (2006). Complexity and Education : Inquiries into Learning, Teaching, and Research. Mahwah, NJ: Lawrence Erlbaum Associates.

Faulkner, G., & Finlay, S. (2002). It's not what you say, it's the way you say it! Conversation Analysis: A discursive methodolgy for sport, exercise and physical education. Quest, 54, 49-66.

Fernadez-Balboa, J.-M. (Ed.). (1997). Critical Postmodernism in Human Movement, Physical Education, and Sport. Albany: SUNY Press.

Gare, A. (2000). Systems theory and complexity. Democracy and Nature, 6(327-339). Giblett, R. (2008). The Body of Nature and Culture. Basingstoke: Palgrave Macmillan.

Green, K. (2002). Physical Education Teachers in their Figurations: A Sociological Analysis of Everyday 'Philosophies'. Sport, Education and Society, 7(1), 65-83.

Green, K. (2006). Physical Education and Figurational Sociology: An Appreciation of the Work of Eric Dunning. Sport in Society: Cultures, Commerce, Media, Politics, 9(4), 650-664. Hass, L. (2008). Merleu-Ponty's Philosophy. Bloomington, IN: Indiana University Press.

Hellison, D. (1988). Our constructed reality: Some contributions of an alternative view. Journal of Teaching in Physical Education, 8, 123-130.

Hopper, T., Butler, J., & Storey, B. (2009). TGFU...Simply good pedagogy: Understanding a Complex Challenge Victoria: Physical and Health Education Canada.

Jess, M., Atencio, M., & Thorburn, M. (2011). Complexity theory: supporting curriculum and pedagogy developments in Scottish physical education. Sport, Education and Society, 16(2), 179-199.

Kerry, D., & Armour, K. (2000). Sport Sciences and the promise of phenomenolgy: Philosophy, method and insight. Journal of Teaching in Physical Education, 52, 1-17.

Kirk, D. (1989). The orthodoxy in RT-PE and the research/practice gap: A critique and alternative view. Journal of Teaching in Physical Education, 8, 123-130. Kirk, D. (2010). Physical Education Futures. London: Routledge.

Kuhn, L. (2008). Complexity and educational research: A critical reflection. In M. Mason (Ed.), Complexity Theory and the Philosophy of Education. Chichester: Wiley-Blackwell. Lawson. (1984). Problem setting for physical education and sport. Quest, 36(46-60).

Light, R. (2008). Complex learning theory- Its epistemology and its assumptions about learning: Implications for Physical Education. Journal of Teaching in Physical Education, 27, 21-37.

Macdonald, D. (2004). Rich tasks, rich learning? Working with integration from a physical education perspective. In J. Wright, D. Macdonald & L. Burrows (Eds.), Critical Inquiry and Problem-Solving in Physical Education (pp. 120-132). London: Routledge.

Mason, M. (2008). What Is Complexity Theory and What Are Its Implications for Educational Change? Educational Philosophy and Theory, 40(1), 35-47.

Morrison, K. (2008). Educational philosophy and the challenge of complexity theory. In M. Mason (Ed.),

Complexity Theory and the Philosophy of Education (pp. 16-45). Chichester: Wiley-Blackwell.

Nilges, L. (2001). The twice told tale of Alice's physical life in wonderland: Writing qualitative research in the 21st century. Quest, 53, 231-259.

Osberg, D., Biesta, G., & Cilliers, P. (2008). From Representation to Emergence: Complexity's challenge to the epistemology of schooling [Article]. Educational Philosophy & Theory, 40(1), 213-227. doi: 10.1111/j.1469-5812.2007.00407.x

Ovens, A. (2010). The New Zealand Curriculum: emergent insights and complex renderings. Asia-Pacific Journal of Health, Sport and Physical Education, 1(1), 27-32.

Penney, D., & Chandler, T. (2000). Physical Education: What Future(s)? Sport, Education and Society, 5(1), 71-87.

Richardson, K., & Cilliers, P. (2001). What Is Complexity Science? A View from Different Directions. Emergence, 3(1), 5-23.

Rovegno, I. (2006). Situated perspectives on learning. In D. Kirk, D. Macdonald & M. O'Sullivan (Eds.),The Handbook of Physical Education (pp. 262-274). London: Sage

Rovegno, I., & Kirk, D. (1995). Articulations and silences in socially critical work on physical education: Towards a broader agenda. QUEST, 47(4), 447-474.

Schempp, A. (1987). Research on teaching in physical education: Beyond the limits of natural science. Journal of Teaching in Physical Education, 6, 111-121.

Shilling, C. (2004). Educating bodies: Schooling and the constitution of society. In J. Evans, B. Davies & J. Wright (Eds.), Body Knowledge and Control: Studies in the Sociology of Physical Education and Health (pp. xv-xxii). London: Routledge.

Siedentop, D. (1987). Dialogue or exorcism? A rejoinder to Schempp. Journal of Teaching in Physical Education, 6(4), 373-376.

Siedentop, D. (1989). Do the lockers really smell? Research quarterly for exercise and sport, 60(1), 36-41.

Sparkes, A. (1989). Paradigmatic confusions and the evasion of critical issues in naturalistic research.Journal of Teaching in Physical Education, 8, 131-151.

Sparkes, A. (1991). Towards understanding, dialogue and polyvocality in the research community: Extending the boundaries of the paradigms debate. Journal of Teaching in Physical Education, 10(2), 103-133.

Sparkes, A. (1993). The paradigms debate: An extended review and celebration of difference. In A. Sparkes (Ed.), Research in Physical Education and sport: Exploring alternative visions. London: Falmer Press.

Sparkes, A. (1995). Writing people: Reflections on the dual crisis of representation and legitimation in qualitative inquiry. Quest, 47, 158-195.

Sparkes, A. (2002). Telling tales in sport and physical activity: A qualitative journey. Champaign, IL: Human Kinetics.

Stacey, R. (2001). Complex Responsive Processes in Organisations: Learning and Knowledge Creation. London: Routledge.

Wright, J. (2004). Post-structural methodologies: the body, schooling and health. In J. Evans, B. Davies & J.Wright (Eds.), Body Knowledge and Control: Studies in the Sociology of Physical Education and Health (pp. 19-31). London: Routledge.

Chapter 8

APPENDIX A

Questionnaire #1

Player Number Code: _____

Thank you for taking the time to complete this journal. When you are done, please submit to Mr. _____ our Athletic Director. Please do not show other players your journal responses until the year has concluded. It will be handed back to you after the season.

Preseason

1. Write how playing basketball makes you feel when it is unorganized (pick-up) with friends or people you know.

2. If you have played on a team before, think of experiences you enjoyed in the past. Write about them below. You may use the backside of this paper for organization or extra writing space

_____

_____

_____

_____

_____

_____

_____

_____

_____

_____

_____

_____

_____

Chapter 8

APPENDIX B

Questionnaire #2

Player Number Code: _____

Thank you for taking the time to complete this journal. When you are done, please submit to our Athletic Director. Please do not share your journal responses until the year has concluded.

In Season

How do you want to grow in the game of basketball this season?
1) Become a better shooter
2) Become a better passer
3) Become a better rebounder
4) Understand how to play defense
5) Understand how to become a leader
6) Learn how to relax more in games
7) Learn how to become more confident
8) Have more fun during the close games.
9) Other areas? Your choice _____.

Include the reasons why you chose the above areas to improve.

_____
_____
_____
_____
_____
_____
_____
_____

Chapter 8

APPENDIX C

Questionnaire #3

Player Number Code: _____

Thank you for taking the time to complete this journal. When you are done, please submit to our Athletic Director. Please do not share your journal responses until the year has concluded. It will be handed back to you after the season.

Midseason

Describe if your game has grown or changed since the first few practices we have had as a team. Explain why you think this has happened.

_____
_____
_____
_____
_____
_____
_____
_____
_____
_____
_____
_____
_____
_____
_____
_____
_____
_____

Chapter 8

APPENDIX D

Questionnaire #4

Player Number Code: _____

Thank you for taking the time to complete this journal. When you are done, please submit to our Athletic Director. Please do not show other players your journal responses until the year has concluded. It will be handed back to you after the season.

Journal response #4 – Post Season

In what ways could you say we had success on and off the court?

On	Off
On	Off

What areas of your play or skills would you most like to improve?
1.
2.

Looking back, what areas should we have worked on more as a team this year?
1.
2.

How was the overall experience this year? Include what you liked about the season and what you did not like, and what you will remember the most. (Use back for writing space)

Chapter 9

APPENDIX A

Sample interview questions

1. After having taken OLPE what would you never want to do again?
2. What are you still doing that you learned from OLPE?
3. Why did you decide to take OLPE? What were some key considerations?
4. Were there any similarities between the online version and other PE courses?
5. Were there any differences between the online version and other PE courses?
6. What were some of your expectations of OLPE prior to taking the course?
7. How did you find out about OLPE?
8. Did you feel that you did more work in an OLPE course?
9. Have your grades changed much when taking OLPE?
10. Would you recommend OLPE to others? Why?
11. If this is not your final year in school will you enroll in OLPE next year, school PE or drop PE altogether?
12. What supports do you feel you need while talking OLPE?
13. What has been the greatest challenge so far in OLPE? What has been the least challenging?
14. Have there been any obstacles in taking OLPE?
15. What grade did you start taking OLPE?
16. What time commitment is required of OLPE?
17. Can you say that you enjoyed PE through the OL experience?
18. Would you say that you learned more about yourself through OLPE?
19. What did you do, or how did you approach OLPE that contributed to your success?
20. Describe one group activity you participated in.
21. Were the evaluations that took place similar or different to school PE?
22. Would you be able to say that you were more or less active in OLPE than school PE?
23. If you could change or suggest one modification to the OLPE course what would it be? School PE?
24. What new thing did you discover about yourself through OLPE?
25. How was your time management in an OL environment?
26. Have you taken an OL course before taking OLPE?
27. What did you appreciate about OLPE

List of Figures & Tables

CHAPTER ONE

8   Figure 1. Sample Teaching Perspectives Profile.

9   Figure 2. Pyramid of Beliefs, Intentions and Actions.

11   Table 1. Founders' ideal TGfU teacher's Teaching Perspectives Profiles.

12   Figure 3. Founders ideal profiles and K-12 Norms.

16   Figure 4. Benchmarks for TGfU Beliefs

18   Figure 5. Benchmarks for Intentions (Butler, 2012)

19   Figure 6. Benchmarks for Actions (Butler, 2012)

22   Figure 7. Developmental Perspective in TGfU

23   Figure 8. Nurturing Perspective in TGfU

CHAPTER TWO

37   Figure 1. Major Research Themes.

38   Figure 2. Summary of Major Research Themes.

     Figure 3. Collaboration and Relationship Data Summary.

40   Figure 4. Leadership and Support Data Summary.

42   Figure 5. Curricular and Pedagogical Innovations (CPIs) Data Summary.

43   Figure 6. Cultural Change Data Summary.

45   Figure 7. Barriers to Enacting Change and Implementing CPIs.

50   Table 2. Stage indicators of CPI change.

CHAPTER THREE

59   Table 1. Overview of Student Participants.

CHAPTER FOUR

76   Table 1. Paired-samples t-test results for individual questions.

77   Table 2. Paired-sample t-test results for total average from all questions.

CHAPTER SIX

110   Table 1. Themes from written responses and interview transcripts: Female choice to enroll in a PE 11/12 girls course.

113   Table 2. Themes from written responses and interview transcripts: Female choice not to enroll in a PE 11/12 Girls Course but enrolled in coed PE.

115   Table 3. Themes from written responses and interview transcripts: Females not enrolled in any PE courses.

CHAPTER SEVEN

127   Figure 1. Hockey Canada player development pyramid (2014).

128   Figure 2. Seven components of the Game Performance Assessment Instrument (Oslin, Mitchell, & Griffin, 1998, p. 233).

132   Figure 3. Sample questions from the PSEQ.

133   Table 1. Descriptive table for the PSEQ - Perceived Physical Ability Subscale.

Table 2. Descriptive table for the PSEQ - Athletic Competency Subscale.

134   Table 3. Analysis of Variance for PSEQ - Perceived Physical Ability Subscale.

135   Figure 4. Impact of time, Perceived Physical Ability Subscale (Part One).

136   Figure 5. Impact of time, Athletic Competency Subscale (Part Two).

CHAPTER EIGHT

149   Table 1. Player Participants - Journal Writing Design.

About the Authors

Dr. Joy Butler (Editor, Associate Professor) is Physical Education Teacher Education (PETE) Coordinator and Graduate Coordinator in the Department of Curriculum and Pedagogy at the University of British Columbia.

Continued on page xix.

George Kanavos has been an educator for the better part of two decades. George is a counsellor and teacher who strongly believe in physical literacy and emotional intelligence to accompany all the other wonderful aspects of school life for students and everyone in the school community. Building healthy environments and healthy relationships is the cornerstone of education and George has striven for it. Building a balanced life while devoting himself to his family has grounded him to grow and emerge as a better educator and better person. Thank you to everyone in my journey.

Stephen McGinley is a newly appointed Adjunct Teacher Professor and the PE Teacher Education area coordinator at The University of British Columbia (UBC). He was most recently the PE Department Head and Assistant Athletic Director at Archbishop Carney Secondary in the Catholic Independent Schools of Vancouver Archdiocese in Port Coquitlam. Currently, Stephen teaches the elementary and secondary physical education methods and the inquiry I and inquiry II courses in the teacher education program at UBC. Stephen's passions lie in engaging all learners and creating and sustaining conditions for professional collaboration. He is a firm believer that when we open ourselves up to listen, share and collaborate, best practices emerge.

Charmaine Lum was born in New Westminster, BC and currently lives in Vancouver. She is in her fourth year of teaching with the Surrey School District and is very grateful to be able to teach Intermediate Physical Education and Grade 7. She was very fortunate to have dedicated teachers and coaches in her life and aspires to provide her students with the same, if not more, opportunities that she was given by these individuals. Charmaine coaches competitive club softball and is a proud participant of multiple hockey leagues for women in Vancouver.

Paisley Rankine is a secondary school teacher in the Surrey School District. She attained her BSc from the University of Victoria, completed her teacher education at Simon Fraser University and recently accomplished her MEd from the University of British Columbia. She is passionate about the teaching profession and truly enjoys working with her students. Playing sports and leading an active lifestyle has always been apart of Paisley's life, and this is evident in her work as a physical educator and her commitment to her athletes as a volunteer volleyball and track and field coach. Her greatest role is that of mother to her young son Hunter that she shares with her husband Steve.

David Dunkin graduated from the University of Alberta in 2000 with a Bachelor of Education and a Bachelor of Physical Education. In 2014, he graduated from the University of British Columbia with a Masters of Education in Physical Education. David spent the first 10 years of his teaching career in Alberta where he taught Physical Education at both junior high and high school. For the past 5 years, he has lived in Whistler and taught in the Sea to Sky Corridor. He is currently the Vice-Principal at Howe Sound Secondary School in Squamish.

Kara Wickstrom: Entering my fifteenth year of teaching at Southridge, I continue to be deeply engaged with life-long learning. I can't say graduate studies didn't come without challenges as a full-time teacher and mother of two young boys. Looking back on the past two and half years, I am proud of my accomplishments and feel that I am better equipped entering into this new era of knowing, thinking, and learning. I have learned that there is always more to learn about our disciplines and how to approach those areas of expertise in new ways. When I began teaching in 2000, I wanted to make a difference and impact the lives of my students. After recently gaining a refreshed and greater understanding of the changes in my field, I have discovered new innovative ideas to approach my teaching practice.

Angela Bigiolli is currently teaching Physical Education in the Vancouver School Board. She has over 18 years of teaching and coaching experience including organizing intramurals, city championships and provincial championships at her school. She holds her undergraduate degree in Human Kinetics and Education from the University of British Columbia, and has recently completed a Masters degree, also from UBC, in Physical Education: Teaching Games for Understanding. Angela would like to thank her family, husband Remo and her two daughters, Nadia and Julia for all their love and support.

Brent Jackson has worked for 15 years as a Physical Education teacher and the Athletic Coordinator at York House School in Vancouver. In 2014 he completed his M.Ed. (Curriculum and Pedagogy), to go along with two previous degrees: B.H.K. (1999), and B.Ed. (2000). The University of British Columbia granted all three degrees. Happily married, and the father of two, Brent loves combining family time and being active. A former varsity track and field athlete he now rests his laurels on his coffee cup, which claims he is the "best dad ever!"

Simon Dykstra is an educator coach in the Vancouver School District. After playing varsity basketball at SFU he continued to play and coach professionally in Europe. He has also enjoyed coaching basketball at the elementary, secondary and university level. He lives with his wife Kari and two children in East Vancouver. He is thankful to all his past coaches for the time and care they have devoted to help young people improve and grow through their school sport experiences. In particular, Simon would like to acknowledge the mentorship and support of Coach Stan Stewardson. Thanks Stan.

Susan Kimura currently works as a high school Physical Education and Japanese Language teacher at West Point Grey Academy in Vancouver, BC. She completed her undergraduate degree in Asian Studies, her Teacher Education in the secondary programme and her Masters of Education in Physical Education with the focus on Teaching Games for Understanding guided by Dr. Joy Butler. At school she is highly involved in the Cross Country programme and is a grade 9 advisor. Susan is an avid runner and enjoys participating in numerous races throughout the year.

Acknowledgments

Never doubt that a small group of thoughtful, committed citizens can change the world; indeed, it's the only thing that ever has.

Margaret Mead

Thanks to all the authors for their commitment to their work, for meeting timelines and for working meticulously and thoughtfully on their chapters along the way.

Thanks to all the authors' partners and families for their patience, support and tolerance for those long hours at the computer.

Thanks to the reviewers who helped edit and also made suggestions for improved chapters (listed on page x).

Thanks to faculty and staff in Professional Development Community Engagement (PDCE), who had administrative oversight of the cohort under the leadership of Associate Dean, Mark Edwards, and cohort administrators, Tracey Pappas and Yvette Kharoubeh.

Thanks to Jeanne Kentel for getting the ball rolling in my absence, for finding reviewers and for keeping the authors on track and to Joann Anokwuru for diligently organizing author permission forms, biographies, and photographs.

Particular thanks go to: Jessica Bania of Portland, Oregon for her highly professional work on the whole book, which included final edits, book layout, and front cover design.

are girls more successful in
same sex physical and health
education classes.